ROUTLEDGE LIBRARY
AGRIBUSINESS AND LAND USE

Volume 5

ESTATE CAPITAL

ESTATE CAPITAL

The Contribution of Landownership to Agricultural Finance

D. R. DENMAN

Routledge
Taylor & Francis Group

LONDON AND NEW YORK

First published in 1957 by George Allen & Unwin Ltd

This edition first published in 2024
by Routledge
4 Park Square, Milton Park, Abingdon, Oxon OX14 4RN

and by Routledge
605 Third Avenue, New York, NY 10158

Routledge is an imprint of the Taylor & Francis Group, an informa business

British Library Cataloguing in Publication Data
A catalogue record for this book is available from the British Library

ISBN: 978-1-032-48321-4 (Set)
ISBN: 978-1-032-48626-0 (Volume 5) (hbk)
ISBN: 978-1-032-48631-4 (Volume 5) (pbk)
ISBN: 978-1-003-38999-6 (Volume 5) (ebk)

DOI: 10.4324/9781003389996

Publisher's Note
The publisher has gone to great lengths to ensure the quality of this reprint but points out that some imperfections in the original copies may be apparent.

Disclaimer
The publisher has made every effort to trace copyright holders and would welcome correspondence from those they have been unable to trace.

Estate Capital

THE CONTRIBUTION OF LANDOWNERSHIP
TO AGRICULTURAL FINANCE

BY

D. R. DENMAN
M.A., PH.D.

University Lecturer in Estate Management
University of Cambridge

FOREWORD BY
THE DUKE OF NORTHUMBERLAND

Ruskin House
GEORGE ALLEN & UNWIN LTD
MUSEUM STREET LONDON

TO

R. M. D.

*Printed in Great Britain
in 10 point Times Roman at
The Aberdeen University Press*

FOREWORD

THE Department of Estate Management at Cambridge University, which among other responsibilities has the task of studying the economics of landownership, was established shortly after the war. Three booklets dealing with Estate Duty Anomalies, Reserve Fund and Maintenance Funds, and Estate Incomes, which commanded wide attention, were early products of these studies. Subsequently, generous and timely support was given for an extension of the work when it was announced in February 1954, that research in landownership conducted by the Department would be financed by United States Conditional Aid Funds, under a general scheme which had the declared intention of fostering "activities and studies into social and economic factors affecting the efficiency of the economy and in particular those which prevent the ready and rapid adoption of the most modern techniques".

Impartial and thorough investigation is required in order to call attention to the problems of rural landownership and in order to sustain a case for their solution. Many consider that landownership receives insufficient attention when steps are taken to ensure the stability of the agricultural industry. Whatever the size of the estate, the burden of landownership is a heavy one: taxation is penal; repairs allowances are insufficient; death duties are more harmful to agriculture than beneficial to the Exchequer. The crux of the problem rests upon the owner's ability to form and preserve sufficient estate capital. The offer of a one-third grant towards the cost of eligible work recently announced in the Farm Improvement Scheme is to be warmly welcomed, for while it does not solve the fundamental problem it is a recognition, not only of the difficulties in raising money, but also of the national need for investment in farm improvement.

Our United States friends will find our conception of landownership and agricultural tenancy in the main different from theirs. Our landowner either lets his land to a farm tenant in return for a cash rental or, alternatively, farms the land himself. The law expects him to provide and improve the buildings and services but liability for repairs and maintenance is shared with the tenant if the farm is let, and the latter's working capital in livestock, machinery and crops is his own. There are in the United Kingdom no landlord and tenant relationships similar to those favoured in the United States, where the owner may play a part in farming the land and take a proportion of the profits.

This report of a three years' study clearly indicates the grave problems which face a rural landowner in Britain today. The subject demands and is worthy of careful study. If some new phrases seem strange we should try to understand why they have been coined, for investigations into the economics of landownership are new and they therefore require new definitions of general ideas peculiar to themselves—of which " estate capital " is an example.

The author rightly acknowledges the help owners and their agents have given him and his colleagues. It may have been tiresome to have had one's estate among the sample of those surveyed, but well worth while in the result. Landowners are wise to assist in impartial studies of this kind, which are essential to a better understanding of the agricultural industry, and of the important part landownership plays. It will be gratifying both to the United States and to ourselves to know that research work in the Department is to develop. The author is to be congratulated on producing an extremely interesting and valuable report and I commend this book to all who are interested in understanding the problems of the rural landowner today and the importance of his contribution to British agriculture.

NORTHUMBERLAND

Alnwick Castle
Northumberland

INTRODUCTION

MUCH thought has been given to the formation of capital in agriculture and to the collateral problem of credit. Thinking is usually confined to investment in agricultural machinery, livestock, crops and stores and is seldom wide enough to include farm buildings and land improvement. Lack of insight rather than ignorance sets the limitation. Capital in farm buildings and land improvement is of paramount importance to agriculture but it differs from capital in machinery, stores, and stock, because whenever formed or provided it becomes part of the land. It cannot be dissociated from landownership. And landownership is not agriculture. Farm buildings and land improvement and, indeed, the very land itself are forms of capital fundamental to agriculture and yet not of it. To provide them is the burden and prerogative of landownership.

This book introduces the notion of estate capital. The term is coined to denote the contribution of landownership to the capital requirements of agriculture. It is not a speciality, germane only to a particular form of tenure or system of landownership. The term is universally pertinent. Wherever man settles he creates property in land and hence estate capital.

As treated here the subject relates only to landownership in contemporary Britain. Formation and provision of estate capital answering the needs of British agriculture are illustrated from the findings of four surveys covering 1½ million acres in Great Britain. The surveys were conducted by the Department of Estate Management of Cambridge University from 1952 to 1956. The work was costly and could not have been accomplished apart from the generosity of American Conditional Aid Funds. A modest beginning had been made in 1952, and the Conditional Aid Funds enabled an extensive work to be built upon that foundation.

Novel facts and figures are given in the text and Tables. Inadequacy and incompleteness were unavoidable as time was limited. Continuation of the work in years to come will add to the present evidence and redeem its disqualifications. Sufficient is provided to illustrate the salient features of estate capital, its relevance to agricultural finance and its essential nature as a form of capital standing over against agriculture and yet essential to the industry.

The first three chapters of the book describe the essential nature of estate capital and define those features of its character which the evidence from the surveys illustrates. The following chapters, with the exception of the last, present the evidence. The facts presented are those of the surveys and the reader should bear this in mind especially when reading the chapters on restraints and inducements, and should not mistake the observations made there for my own personal views. In the last chapter I have attempted to give my own views, based on the evidence of the surveys, of the problem of providing estate capital to agriculture.

Conditional Aid Funds financed the work. But nothing could have been accomplished had it not been for the unstinted goodwill and co-operation of numerous landowners, land agents, and tenant farmers, and the ready backing given to the enquiry by the Country Landowners' Association and the professional institutions whose members are professionally associated with land affairs. If anything worthy has been achieved much credit is due to this ready co-operation.

I personally am exceedingly indebted to many colleagues in the Department of Estate Management, whose names follow the description of the surveys in the Appendix and who assisted in the collection of field data, the collation of evidence and the computative work. My thanks are particularly due to my friend and colleague Mr. Neil Elliott, M.A., who, before his appointment to the Portland Estates, was responsible for much of the organisation of the surveys, especially the surveys of the larger estates. I am also indebted to Mr. J. F. Q. Switzer, M.A. and Mr. R. G. A. Lofthouse, F.R.I.C.S. who have read the proofs of the text, and to my secretary, Miss Paula Jenkins, whose painstaking work has made order from the chaos of my manuscript.

D. R. DENMAN

CONTENTS

TABLES

TABLES

CHAPTER ONE

The Estate Cradle

Proprietorship underlies economic activity

THE economic world is divided into land, labour and capital. The classical economists first made the division. It was logical for them to do so, for previously they had peopled the world of production with landowners, workers and capitalists.[1] Had they been content with the world of people and not created an abstract one, the subsequent train of economic thought might have dwelt more intensely upon what is peculiar to persons in economic activity, in especial the institution of proprietorship.

Land and capital as agents of production are capable of ownership. Ownership indeed is a primary requirement. Until land belongs to the actors in the drama of production it remains inert; it is there in the beginning, awaiting ownership and, pending the event, neither capital nor labour is expended upon it. Capital goods do not exist at all apart from ownership. They are not natural but are created by the use of land and labour, and their very creation is an expression of the ownership of the resources from which they are formed. This is more easily understood when we think of private capital, the means of acquiring wealth. It is true nevertheless of national capital or the total means of production[2] for national capital is an aggregate of the property of individual proprietorships. Individual proprietorship does not invariably imply ownership by real persons; it may extend to ownership by institutions, incorporate bodies, Government departments and other *persona ficta* of legal theory. Wherever we look, land and capital as agents of production cannot be dissociated from mine and thine.

The use of land and capital as agents of production in economic activity depends therefore upon the sanctions of ownership and upon an owner's understanding of those sanctions. How much economic progress is hampered by restrictive proprietary rights? What lost opportunities should be laid to the account of ignorant ownership? Economic activity lies in the cradle of proprietorship.

---

[1]Schumpeter, *History of Economic Analysis* (George Allen & Unwin), p. 554.
[2]Knut Wicksell, *Value, Capital and Rent* (George Allen & Unwin), p. 100.

Forms of ownership are institutional and on that account study of them does not attract the mind of the contemplative economist. Social institutions, ownership among them, are none the less a bridge spanning the realm of economic theory and the world of practical consequences. After all, the dynamic world of the owners of land and capital and the workers they employ is the origin of much economic theory. To think about the ownership of land and capital is not a base exercise but a returning to the well of ideas.

Estate capital

Capital and land can be related to each other in more ways than one. From the time of J. S. Mill economists have spoken of circulating capital and fixed capital. Circulating capital is defined as that 'which fulfils the whole of its office in the production in which it is engaged, by a single use'. Fixed capital 'exists in a durable shape and the return is spread over a period of corresponding duration'.[1] A classification, not usually made by the economist but dear to the heart of the lawyer, distinguishes fixed capital which is an integral part of land from fixed capital which is chattel property. Land to the lawyer is not the virgin, rent-bearing soil and other natural resources of economic theory. It is much more. It includes all corporeal things subjacent and superjacent to the soil and annexed thereto.[2] Thus, buildings, fences, roads, drainage works and such like, which to the economist are fixed capital, are to the lawyer land. The distinction has an immediate relevance to the proprietorship of land and capital. Capital which to the lawyer is part of land is subject to the laws of landright: in English legal form the law of real property. Fixed capital which is not land in the legal sense is owned as chattels: in English law as personal property. To borrow further speech from the lawyer, we can say that fixed capital of the former kind together with the soil to which it is annexed lies in an estate in land. The landright in the soil is the landright in the fixed capital. The status of tenure, or estate, is identical in both. Capital that lies in an estate in land is thus distinguished from other capital.

Economic theory, certainly in its early forms, keeps capital and land apart. From the viewpoint of a businessman, however, capital is all wealth devoted to earning an income either as money or its equivalent. Land and capital are one: 'land is but a particular form of capital from the viewpoint of the individual producer'.[3] But even for the businessman the distinction between capital which lies in an

[1]Marshall, *Principles of Economics*, p. 75.
[2]Cheshire, *Modern Real Property*, 7th edition, p. 99.
[3]Marshall, *Principles of Economics*, p. 430.

estate in land and capital which does not do so is valid, and we can speak of the fixed capital and the land to which it is annexed as *estate capital*. Estate capital is capital, as a businessman sees it, which lies in an estate in land. All enterprise in which estate capital plays a part is, to the extent of its dependence upon estate capital, cradled in an estate in land.

Agriculture dependent upon estate capital

Agriculture, of all industries, rests intimately in an estate cradle. Farming is governed directly by the extent of land, the natural qualities of the soil and its durable improvements, and by the degree and manner of providing what is now technically known as fixed equipment.[1] Agriculture is fundamentally dependent upon the provision of estate capital. This is so whether the farmer is tenant or landowner. All farms, the tenanted and the owner-occupied, lie in an estate cradle and their fortunes are radically governed by, although not wholly dependent upon, the provision of estate capital. In this, tenanted and owner-occupied farms are alike. The manner of the ownership of the estate capital is the essential difference. On a tenanted farm the landlord, as a general provision of the contractual tenancies of Britain, owns the whole or the major part of the estate capital. A farmer who tills his own soil provides both the estate capital and other capital needful to the farming enterprise. The estate capital of an owner of agricultural land will not always be wholly employed in agriculture. Investment in other activities, and the ratio the investment bears to the agricultural investment, are controlled by the character of the estate.

The foremost financial problem of modern agriculture is the provision of capital. It is a common problem. Highly developed countries advancing stage by stage towards a mechanised agriculture of utmost power are face to face with it, and also countries where the bonds of a primitive culture have but recently burst asunder. Many heads and wise are bent to seek solutions to it. It is comprehensive, the problem of a total industry, and belongs to the *mise en scène* of a nation's general economy. As such it should be studied and has been studied. The rate of capital formation in agriculture[2] as a whole; the need of the industry for investment in equipment, plant

---

[1] The Agriculture Act 1947, Section 109(3) describes 'fixed equipment' as including 'any building or structure affixed to land and any works on, in, over or under land, and also includes anything grown on land for a purpose other than use after severance from the land, consumption of the thing grown or of produce thereof, or amenity . . . .'

[2] cf. *Net Investment in Fixed Assets in the U.K.*, 1938–1953, P. Redfern, Royal Statistical Society, 1955.

and stock[1]; and the requirements of extensive agricultural areas for land improvement, are features of the national problem which have received recent attention in Britain. But the form of the problem, so expressed in comprehensive ways, is controlled immediately by the manner in which each farmer and each landowner experience it. Each farmer and landowner has a contribution to make to the total experience of the problem. And a proper understanding of the national problem cannot overlook these particular and personal contributions.

Estate capital by definition is the concern of individual proprietors of land. The study of its provision on agricultural estates is therefore a study of the national problem of capital provision to agriculture as the individual landowner experiences it. Secrets illuminative of deeper understanding of the national problem lie immured in the files and investment portfolios of the landowners.

Provision of estate capital

The provision of estate capital for agriculture in a particular case is governed by:

    (i) the landowner's estimate of what is required;
    (ii) the resources available; and
    (iii) the use and administration of those resources.

A landowner's estimate of what estate capital is required turns upon his ability to assess the potentialities of his land for agriculture and his knowledge of the technical processes of providing fixed equipment. To one man, the buildings and other equipment and the investment of capital in land improvement may appear adequate for full production. Another, with keener insight and wider experience, will see possibilities for investment which could expand output and enhance farming profitability. Landowners who agree over the wants of the land can differ in opinion over the means of supplying them. Each of the three little pigs in the nurseryland story provided for himself a house; but—straw, sticks, brick—how different were their ideas of construction! Judgement of what is wanting and of the means of providing it will be influenced by the extent to which landowners are technically competent, or seek and follow competent advice. Requests from tenants and the pressure of Government directives are also contributory factors of importance. When all is said and done, the estimate of need which forms in the landowner's mind, however other minds may think, measures the problem for

[1]Cheveley and Price, *Capital in United Kingdom Agriculture Present and Future*, 1956.

him and sets the bounds at that point to the demand of the industry for capital.

Sources of estate capital are the self-formed capital of the estate economy, other fortune of the landowner capable of conversion to estate capital, and funds not peculiar to himself but answerable to his command, such as Government grants. What a landowner has may differ from what he thinks he has. If he thinks he has more than he has in fact, no matter; the imaginative fortune is of no consequence. But the reverse may obtain. An owner's resources can be more than his estimate of them. Imagined limitations can be decisive. Fiscal policy designed to encourage private investment in agricultural land achieves nothing where a man is ignorant of its proposals, however well they might benefit him had he taken advantage of them. An estate in the ownership of trustees can be seriously undercapitalised if the beneficiary in occupation is ignorant of the financial powers available to him in the terms of the trust deed.

The use and the disposition of a landowner's resources and the place of agricultural estate capital in the general arrangement of them will depend upon his attitude to agriculture, to forestry and to landowning in general. A man passionately devoted to farming land is likely to dispose and arrange his fortune somewhat differently from one who sees an agricultural estate as one among many alternative forms of monetary investment. Even within the estate itself, preference and prejudice will decide priorities and places. A forestry enthusiast would probably allocate his estate capital between forestry and agriculture in shares unlike the corresponding ratio on an estate to whose owner trees and woodlands have no appeal.

A factual study of estate capital

Motives that determine the disposition of a landowner's fortune; his ability to measure correctly the extent of his resources; and his understanding of the capital requirements of agriculture and other estate enterprises are subjective and personal attributes. Although they must influence the level of estate capital investment, their very nature makes the study of their influence difficult, but not impossible. These subjective attributes can be identified only by knowledge of the intimate thoughts of landowners who are willing to disclose them. Motives and powers of comprehension cannot be objectively selected for study.

But these immediate, subjective attributes are not the only forces governing the level of estate capital investment. History can be conceived as playing a part. The will of a bygone age may tie the will of the present; a landowner who desires to make certain dispositions of his capital resources can be prevented from doing so by fetters clamped on his powers of ownership by predecessors in title. And the extent and other physical properties of the land can influence the pattern of capital employment; a landowner whose estate lies along the thousand-foot contour of North Britain is not likely to face competing demands for capital created by a need for modern accommodation to house combine harvesters and the opportunity to buy attractive shares on the equity market. Title, physical pattern and farming systems are features of estates by which one agricultural estate may be objectively distinguished from another in character. And these and other estate character traits like them, can be selected for study.

The theme of this book is a study of the provision of estate capital on estates of different character traits. Surveys[1] have been made of selected estates and measurements taken of the estate capital invested in them. Correlation of the evidence shows the degree, if any, to which estate character influences the formation of estate capital, the level of investment in fixed equipment, the ratio of estate capital to other capital and other aspects of the provision of estate capital. Wherever possible the cross-influences of motive and other subjective attributes are observed. The next chapter examines the idea of estate character traits and defines those which guided the choice of the estates for survey. Choice was hypothetical: there was no obvious correlation between the level of estate capital or any other feature of its provision and the particular estate character trait chosen. The facts of the survey test the hypothesis implicit in each choice.

[1]cf. Appendix

CHAPTER TWO

Estate Character Traits

Classification of estate character traits

AN estate in popular imagination is a thing of physical parts. It is land, mensurable in length, breadth and area. It is forest or factories or farmland. Its contours are high or low, undulating or even. It skirts the seaboard or is hugged by the city. It is simple, and uniform, or complex and multi-featured. We can visualise it. We can measure it. We can map it. But these physical attributes are only a skeleton. An estate has abstract qualities. Its skeleton is clothed by the formulae of legal and economic thought. The abstract qualities are not so obvious as the physical attributes but are equally important. Indeed, certain physical features cannot be identified without the aid of abstract ideas. Size and shape are examples. The size and shape of an estate are controlled by its boundaries, but what appears to be a boundary—a hedge or a river or a road—may give a false impression. A hedge lining a road is a commonplace, work-a-day boundary, but the law measures the estate to the middle of the road. The true boundary is the legal boundary. It has a precise physical location but the location cannot be identified apart from the abstract legal definition.

Physical boundaries are not the only limits circumscribing an estate. An estate extends in time as well as in space and boundaries in time provide an example of the wholly abstract qualities in estate character. An estate of inheritance may run back over many centuries and perpetuate itself until the heirs fail; or the duration of an estate may be limited to a lifetime or to a shorter period. Such temporal boundaries are created by law. They have no physical form; albeit they are essential features of estate character. A further illustration of the wholly abstract side of estate character is the pattern of land tenure. On a large estate the land may be parcelled among tenants. The form of tenure is an important feature of estate character; yet it is essentially abstract. The pattern of land tenure is not discernible by merely observing the physical features of the estate. No amount of topographical surveying can show whether the farms are occupied by what the Americans call sundown tenants or by families with tenurial chains ten generations long.

19

On its abstract side estate character is greatly influenced by the estate owner himself. The legal personality of the estate owner gives character to the estate, and so do his social status and economic circumstances. Strict settlements in the history of English law provide an illustration of this. At common law the main beneficiary under a settlement is barred from making full use of the timber and mineral resources of an estate. Forests, quarries and farmlands of such a place may resemble those of a neighbouring estate held by an owner in absolute fee simple. Physically the estates are identical, but hidden in their abstract nature is a fundamental difference. On one the rich resources are sterile; on the other they are prolific. The legal characters of the estate owners are responsible for the difference. Because one owner is a tenant for life under a strict settlement, cramped by legal restriction, the potentialities of the estate are reduced and its entire character adversely affected.

An estate, like the chameleon, matches its colour to its environment. A change of ownership can mean a radical change of estate character. An estate burdened with tax today may tomorrow be tax free as it passes into the hands of a charity or other institution exempt from tax. Physically nothing alters. The change takes place in the abstract character of the estate.

Estate character traits that are not immediately affected by changes in ownership may conveniently be termed primary traits, and those liable to change as ownership changes may be termed secondary traits. Primary traits are the ground character of an estate that passes from owner to owner. Thus, we may classify estate character traits as physical and abstract, primary and secondary. The physical and the abstract are reciprocal; and so are the primary and secondary. But the two pairs do not correspond exactly with each other; all physical traits are not in the primary class; nor are all abstract traits in the secondary class. Most secondary traits are abstract, although estate size and shape are notable exceptions.

Primary character traits are not constant. They are insensitive to change of ownership and only in this do they differ from secondary traits. Many primary traits are clay in the hands of the estate owner once an estate is acquired. During his ownership an owner may radically alter the lineaments of his estate. An estate that came to its owner subject to many tenancies may be deliberately altered to become an estate wholly in possession. Likewise, secondary traits are not constant. The character an estate acquired at the last change of ownership may alter with changes in the fortune and circumstances of the owner. A rich owner may suffer misfortune. Fate on its bright side will lessen his tax liability and his estate, burdened by the incidence and threat of heavy taxation from the day he acquired it, will be relieved. Although secondary traits may change as owner-- ship alters, it does not follow that they invariably do so. Duration as a secondary estate character trait provides an example. An estate of inheritance with an ancestral title may pass to the legal heir and retain its character as an estate of ancient lineage. If it had passed to another family a new estate would be created, and the estate of ancient duration would cease to be.

Estate character can appear ambiguous, as when character is concealed by an unintentional incognito. An estate of ancient lineage, for example, with a title running deep and unbroken into

TABLE I

CLASSIFICATION OF ESTATE CHARACTER TRAITS

NUMBER	ESTATE CHARACTER TRAIT	CLASSIFICATION			
		Physical	Abstract	Primary	Secondary
1	Size	Size			Size
2	Shape	Shape			Shape
3	Structure	Structure		Structure	
4	Holdings pattern	Holdings pattern			Holdings pattern
5	Tenure pattern		Tenure pattern	Tenure pattern	
6	Duration		Duration		Duration
7	Tenure		Tenure		Tenure
8	Ownership personality		Ownership personality		Ownership personality
9	Taxability		Taxability		Taxability

past centuries may change ownership not as a consequence of death or sale but by the creation of a trust or private estate company at the instance of the estate owner. He will become chief beneficiary or controlling shareholder. At law, the change of ownership will be an unquestionable fact and the estate character will suffer change. But to tenants and neighbours, friends and dependents, no vital altera- tion occurs. The squire still commands his estate; he has not sold his birthright; he is the scion of his line and lord of the land he enjoys. In one sense the character of his estate has changed; in another sense it endures.

Estate character traits can be denominated and classified in many ways. The observations of this book are based on a broad and comprehensive schedule set out in Table I.

The meaning of every term used in Table I is not obvious. Some terms are capable of more than one meaning and definite choice has to be made between alternatives to avoid ambiguity. Explanations and definitions are necessary. The definitions that follow are those used in the selection, preparation and presentation of the illustrative statistics of this book. In the main the definitions are general in form, but a few are specially adapted to the purpose of the surveys.

Size and shape

Size and shape are interdependent. The lands of one landowner may lie together in a compact block neatly ringed by a regular boundary. The lands of another may be scattered like an archipelago over far distances. Must we say of the owner of the single block: he owns an estate? And say of the owner of the scattered properties: he owns many estates? Or may we call both estates entire, and explain the differences between them as a difference of shape and not of number? The size of the estates turns on the answer we give. In area the lands of each owner may be equal. If we regard them as entire estates, we have two estates of equal size; if the contrary opinion is held, we have one large estate and many small estates.

A possible solution is to call in aid an abstract idea to interpret the physical fact. Scattered lands are subject to different systems of management. One owner, however widely dispersed his land, manages it as a single entity. Another regards his possessions as an empire of separate properties severally managed. Central control in one system can mean no more than a tenuous oversight little concerned with local policy and managerial details. In another system, central control may be restricted to financial policy and accounting. In a third, the scattered portions may be subject to constant and minute technical and financial control from the centre. Variations occur on these three alternative systems. For the purpose of defining shape a managerial criterion has been adopted. Scattered properties where local control is complete, or central control no more than an attenuated oversight are not regarded as a single estate, but as a group of separate estates. Scattered properties, however widely apart, subject to a genuine central control are accounted a single estate of scattered formation. Here and there a scattered estate, accounted a single estate by this standard, has one or more portions overseas; the alien portions are disregarded and the home parcels counted as the single estate.

To define the conformation of an estate does not wholly resolve the problem of estate size. What is the proper size of an estate? In the early days of English feudalism the word 'estate' denoted the social status of its tenant and the quality and duration of tenure. The physical size of an estate ranged widely; historians are hard put to it to discover the size of the typical manor of medieval England. Tenure and social status have long dissolved partnership; but something of the ancient glory still gilds the idea of an estate. Popular opinion today is inclined to think of a landed estate as property whose size and wealth are not unpretentious. This vague conception is out of keeping with the notion of an estate as the cradle of agricultural enterprise. To satisfy this idea, we must allow the word to embrace every property capable of carrying a farm somewhere on its surface. This passes the problem of definition to the question: What is a farm? We need not despair on that account. At least in English law there are legal definitions of farming and distinctions between farms proper and allotments.[1] So wide a usage of the word 'estate' includes the smallest holdings, even those that lie on the divide between farms proper and allotments. Smallholdings, however, have problems peculiar to themselves and have been deliberately excluded from this study of the agricultural estate; an arbitrary minimum of 100 acres has been adopted. No upper limit has been set. For the purpose of statistical comparison estates have been classified in size classes from 100 acres to over 10,000 acres.[2]

Structure

Estate structure is governed by land use and may be simple or complex. An estate of simple structure is one put to a single use. Agricultural estates are not necessarily simple in structure, although as a general rule small agricultural estates tend to be simple. In any event, the structure of an agricultural estate is not likely to be very complex. The degree of complexity is influenced by the manner in which we look at things; a dominant feature of land use overmastering other features will clearly stamp an estate with a peculiar character. The degree of dominance will depend upon how we measure the parts. Measurement may be either in units of area—acre for acre; or in units of value—£ for £. An upland estate of 13,000 acres, for example, having 10,000 acres of mountain sheep-farms, 3,000 acres of mature softwoods and 100 acres of valuable salmon fishing, is clearly agricultural in character if we measure the ratio of its parts in acres. But the ratio of the monetary values of its parts gives a different picture, when the value of the farmland is £15,000, the value of the woodlands £600,000 and the value of the salmon fishing £100,000.

[1] cf. Allotments Act 1922, Section 3 (7).   [2] cf. Table B, p. 200 post.

The estate as a cradle for agricultural enterprise is the focus of our attention, consequently area ratios have been adopted as the normal criteria of estate structure. All estates mentioned are agricultural estates in this sense. Differences in structure, from the viewpoint of value ratios, are specifically referred to as occasion requires.

The area principle is used also to distinguish between agricultural estates of differing farming systems. More than one system may be followed on an agricultural estate, but the system most extensively established, dominant acre for acre, sets the farming character of the estate. Definitions of farming systems are manifold. The six basic types of farming used as a foundation for the National Farm Survey made in Britain in 1946[1] have been adopted here.

A scattered estate may have a separate block wholly or mainly (according to area) given to a use other than agriculture. Where this is so, the block has not been regarded as part of the estate structure, but included among the external resources of the estate. There are extreme cases in which the acre-for-acre principle is questionable. An estate of 200 acres might comprise 80 acres of highly developed urban land and 120 acres of agricultural land. To count such an estate an agricultural estate would be a misleading pedantry. These cases are very rare. Under-developed land in a ring fence with urban property, although used for agriculture is likely to be influenced by development value and in that event is not acceptable as agricultural land proper. Proper agricultural land generally lies away from urban development and, on the principle just explained, is looked upon as a separate agricultural estate in itself, to the disregard of the urban property. On the rare occasion when this is not so, the structure of an estate has been judged by the values ratio, and if the urban element overshadows the agricultural the estate is not reckoned as an agricultural estate.

Another way of looking at estate structure is to regard it as built up of different types of functional units: farms, quarries, residences, woodlands and so on. This principle, as will be seen,[2] has a usefulness when making certain comparisons.

Holdings pattern

The farming system of an estate hints at the probable size of its typical farm where farming practice is technically associated with the size of holding operated. Mountain sheep-farming, for example,

---

[1]cf. p. 143 *post*; and *National Farm Survey of England and Wales*, H.M.S.O., 1946.   [2]cf. p. 143 *post*.

needs space. Although many hill farms in this country are comparatively small with wide ranges of common grazing, the association of hill sheep farming and extensive holdings is definite enough to support the supposition that an agricultural estate devoted to mountain sheep-farming will probably be an estate of large holdings. Similarly, although there are exceptions to the rule, an estate of intensely cultivated market-garden land will probably have small, compact holdings.

Size of holding is a distinctive feature of estate character but to rely upon the farming system of an estate as evidence of a particular pattern is unnecessarily crude. An attempt has been made to formulate a principle to distinguish estates according to the size of their holdings. The average size of holding is liable to be an extremely misleading pointer, for an estate of a few large and many tiny holdings would appear as an estate of moderate-sized holdings. What statisticians call the mode—the size of holding numerically preponderant—is a safer determinant. Unfortunately the mode is ineffective when the range of items is small, as is the case with the number of holdings on most agricultural estates of Britain. The expedient has been adopted of identifying estates with a preponderance of holdings below 100 acres. Pattern is determined by area, not numbers. An estate of two very large holdings and a few small-holdings, if numbers were decisive, would be counted among the estates of smallholdings and this would be wrong. Only estates where holdings of less than 100 acres account in total area for 50 % or more of the total area of the estate are reckoned estates of small-holdings; area means area of agricultural land and woodland and does not include areas used for urban or other purposes.

Tenure pattern

Ownership is the creation of law. Neither primitive custom nor sophisticated legal principle give full-handed the total rights of absolute ownership. Always there is limitation for the law that creates and upholds property rights sets bounds to those rights. Particular ownerships vary in power according to the bounds set by law; some are superior, others inferior. Owners of superior interests are, as a rule, permitted to create inferior interests out of them. In Britain, the freehold is superior to the leasehold and leaseholds are created out of freeholds. A freehold agricultural estate may have no derivative leaseholds, in which case the estate is said to be wholly *in hand* to the owner. Or the contrary can be true, and every farm, cottage, wood and acre of waste-land be let to tenants. Or the tenure pattern can be intermediate between these extremes.

We can quickly establish how much of an estate is in hand and how much has been let. As with the holdings pattern, the ratio can be expressed either in numbers of holdings or as proportions of total area. The latter principle has been adopted. Estates are classified as owner-occupied or tenant-occupied according to which of the two tenures is found over 50 % of the estate area.

The tenurial character trait of an estate can be much influenced by the principle which governs the calculation of acreage. The calculation may be comprehensive or selective. Selective calculations take into account only land of a particular type—agricultural land for example. The more complex the structure of an estate the more prone it is to this kind of influence. Agricultural estates are comparatively simple in structure.[1] Consequently the calculations were invariably comprehensive. Total acreages of all types of land use, agricultural, silvicultural, residential and otherwise, have been calculated and the proportions of let land and land in hand expressed accordingly.

Clear identification of tenurial pattern is often difficult, especially on small estates where vague family arrangements confuse the issue. Land is said to be let by wife to husband, by father to son, by aunt or nephew or cousin to others of the blood. These consanguineous arrangements are not proper tenancies at law, whatever the *soi-disant* landlords and tenants may suppose. Generally they are the joint investment arrangements of members of a family pooling resources and sharing profits. Estate tenure patterns ignore these bogus tenancies. On the other hand family arrangements frequently set up true tenurial arrangements among members of the family.[2] A common form is the private company. The owner of the estate freehold becomes chief shareholder with other members of the family, and the company takes a lease of the estate from the owner. Although his estate is wholly let, the close affinity between the landlord and the tenant company procures most of the benefits enjoyed by holding land in hand. Where the tenancy is of this or a similar kind, a tenancy valid at law, it is recognised as such and the estate accounted as a tenant-occupied estate.

Duration

The size of an estate in time, the temporal dimension, runs backwards into the past and forwards into the future. The backward measurement, from the present to the known origin, is implicit in the idea of duration. The measurement forward is marked by tenure and is dealt with in a later definition.

[1]cf. p. 23 *ante*. [2]cf. p. 171 *post*.

It has been shown how an estate of unbroken lineage can through change in ownership personality sever its ancient roots and become a new creation[1] although virtual control of it is not affected. The descendant of an ancient line who transfers the ownership of his land to a company or a trust usually does so with an eye to the continued enjoyment of the benefits of proprietorship. Legally the ownership passes from him but for all practical purposes it remains his. There is a conflict between legal principle and observable fact. This conflict has an immediate bearing upon the definition of duration. Does the estate remain one of ancient lineage despite the title recently vested in a company or trust? Must we in defining duration measure the root of legal ownership or the root of the blood tie which binds both kith and kin to the land? The second alternative is the wiser choice. By so defining duration, an estate of ancient title passing at the instance of the present owner to an estate company remains an estate with ancient title. Full justice is done to the legal root when defining ownership personality[2] which is sensitive of the strict viewpoint of the law. Thus, an estate of ancient lineage recently granted to trustees by the owner is in character an estate of ancient title owned by the trustees.

An estate may change character as it passes down a long line of descent. What was once a large estate may today be but a remnant of its former greatness; or on the contrary it may have multiplied its acres and increased its complexity. Must these physical changes be taken seriously, as the evolutionist takes mutations, so that we say something new emerges at each change? Or must the essential estate find its criterion of duration in the line of inheritance, no matter how changed in physical form it may be? Of these two alternatives, the latter is preferred and duration follows inheritance. Inheritance in this respect has a wider meaning than the lawyer's precise principle which recognises true inheritance only when an estate passes to the legal heir—"only God can make an heir!" The word here is used in the sense of continued family ownership, no matter how, on occasion, the title passes from successor to successor. Kith and kin are the bond. Duration is the length of time an estate has remained in the ownership of a single family, whether successive owners came to their titles through inheritance or testamentary disposition or purchase.

Estates with origins in the eighteenth century are old compared with estates newly sprung in the twentieth; but compared with estates whose duration runs back to Domesday Book, eighteenth-century origins are novel. Classification of estates into estates of old title and estates of new title is impossible without the aid of an

[1]cf. p. 21 *ante.*   [2]cf. p. 29 *post.*

arbitrary device. The advent of the twentieth century has been taken as the point of division: estates whose titles run over the century boundary are classified as old estates and those whose origins lie within the twentieth century are new estates. The turn of the century has been taken as the point of division because it is an event of ready reference and, what is more, it almost coincides with the date of the imposition of modern estate duty. Estates of old title have endured the whole gamut of the much spoken of and in places much lamented estate duty.

Tenure

The duration of an estate has just been defined as the period of unbroken succession by kith and kin from an original ancestor to the present owner. Where a family sells an estate or gives it away the duration of the estate terminates. But in legal theory the estate does not terminate. It continues into the future in the title of the new owner as it would have continued in the title of the previous owner had he retained ownership. Its capacity to do so, the probable span of its days, is the quantum of its tenure.

Common law in England recognises only two forms of tenure: the greatest estate, which lawyers call fee simple absolute in possession; and what is in common parlance a leasehold and in lawyers' speech the term of years' absolute. The leasehold is a lesser estate than the fee simple. Only long leases are significant for estate character, since they have an affinity with the superior tenure. Agricultural estates in Britain are not held on long leases and the leasehold as a possible form of tenure need not concern us. The ponderous phrase 'fee simple absolute in possession' denotes an inheritance, unconditional and potent to pass down the line of general heirs of the estate owner. It is only defeasible when there is none to inherit.[1]

Common law is not the only source of English law. If it were, the tenure character of estate ownership would clearly be uniform, for all owners would hold their land in fee simple absolute. In England there is a variety of interests in land, important for estate affairs which common law does not recognise. These interests are championed by equity, a source of law whose principles often run parallel with common law but nonetheless have a way of their own. In equity a man may hold a life tenancy or other lesser right in land. Equitable interests, as they are called, mar the simplicity of character promised by the simple legal estate. The law, however, helps somewhat by insisting on arrangements which 'keep the equitable

---

[1]Fee simple may be defeasible through failure to account for fee farm rent (cf. Cheshire, *Modern Real Property*, 7th edition, p. 110).

interest off the title'. Two contemporaneous titles exist—the legal title and the equitable title. The legal estate in the land is invariably held by trustees in trust for the owners of the equitable interests. Estate character is moulded by the form of the trust, for the fact of the trust determines the ownership personality, and the influence of equitable interests upon estate character in general is reflected in that character trait. Tenure, therefore, as an aspect of estate character is universally the fee simple absolute for all estates in England.

In Scotland tenure differs in fundamental principles from English tenure although its impact on estate character has a practical similarity. The tenure of highest status is the fee or inheritance. This is analogous to the English fee simple but in many cases is an inferior cast, unknown to modern English law. A fee in Scotland may be an inferior or vassal tenure dependent upon and derived from a tenure of superior status: the owner of the fee is feuar of the superior owner and generally the inferior fee is burdened with feu duty in favour of the seignorial or superior estate. Again, Scots law recognises an interest analogous to the equitable tenancy for life in English law; this it calls a life rent. Unlike England, the life rent in Scotland need not be kept off the heritable estate by the device of a trust.[1] In earlier days these proper life rents were frequent. Modern times, however, have preferred the cover of a trust and the fee is vested in trustees to hold it for the provision of a beneficiary life rent for the life renter. Leaseholds in property are real property if terminable; for estate character they have the practical insignificance of the English leasehold and, like the English leasehold, need not concern us here. The superior feudal tenure does not give the right of possession and for that reason has no bearing upon estate character apart from the burden of feu duty it imposes upon the inferior fee. As proper life rents are almost a thing of the past and the existence of beneficiary life rents is implicit in the trusts that protect them in fee, tenure, as an aspect of estate character in Scotland, is tenure in fee, save for rare exceptions.

Ownership personality

The personality of the owner of an estate is not the same thing as ownership personality. This phrase has been invented because an estate may be owned by a single person or by two or more persons associated together. Proprietorship by a single person needs no comment. Plural proprietorship has different forms. There are three main forms in Britain: joint owners, corporations and trustees. They

[1]Gloag and Henderson, *Introduction to the Law of Scotland*, 4th edition, p. 485.

are not entirely exclusive of each other. Ownership personality can be a dual personality or even a trinity. Trustees, for example, can be a trust corporation; in this event the ownership personality is a duality of trustees and a corporation.

In English law an estate owned by joint owners invariably means dual ownership personality. Joint owners may be joint tenants or tenants in common. Joint tenancy arises when two or more persons own an estate indivisibly. Joint tenants must hold an estate as trustees upon a trust for sale.[1] If the two or more owners have divisible or separate shares, the ownership is said to be a tenancy in common; and again, a trust arises. The legal estate is not held as a tenancy in common but by certain persons as trustees holding in joint tenancy.[2] In Scotland an estate may be held jointly or in common but no consequential trust is created.

For the purpose of estate character, trustees fall into two distinct classes: trustees whose existence is necessary to give effect to the ownership of land by an unincorporate association; and trustees owning land in order to execute specific beneficial trusts in it. To the latter class belong the trustees of settled estates and trustees of trusts for sale of land. These trustees of beneficial interests in land fall into two minor but important classes: tenants for life under settlements, who are strictly tenants for life, and other persons not strictly tenants for life who have been given a like status;[3] and trustees who are not tenants for life in any sense but are statutory owners who have been given the powers of a tenant for life. The practical difference between these two minor classes lies in the relationship between the beneficiary who occupies the land and the trustees. A tenant for life, or person of like status, is both trustee and beneficiary. He is in occupation of the land, can exercise certain powers of management and disposition and does not have to seek the sanction of an independent body of trustees to his actions. Where the trustees have not the status but virtually the powers of a tenant for life, the beneficiary in occupation of the land is largely subject to their sanctions in the management and disposition of the land. Life renters in Scotland are in a position somewhere between these two minor classes.

An unincorporate body of trustees acts together by the individual decision of each member in concert with the others. A corporation differs from this. It is an association which has unity in itself, created one body by an act of incorporation. It is a fictitious person. It owns and manages land in its own name and capacity. Corporations are created for divers reasons. Some are hoar-headed and have existed

[1] Law of Property Act 1925, Section 36 (1).
[2] Law of Property Act 1925, Sections 34 to 38.   [3] *Ibid.* Section 20.

for generations, the embodiments of many traditional social institutions—colleges, cathedrals, cities, charities and others of similar company. A form of corporation peculiar to modern history is the joint stock company operating for financial gain. Companies may be public or private. All types of corporation are significant for estate character, in especial the private company. In contemporary Britain, many estates are owned by estate companies formed for the sole purpose of owning and managing the estate. Estate companies should be distinguished from private companies of a general kind operating for profit and owning an estate as a collateral or incidental interest to their main concern.

Taxability

Taxability as a feature of estate character denotes the incidence of tax on an estate, the total annual imposition and the total capital levy which the estate has to bear. It must not be confused with tax liability, because tax liability is peculiar to the person of the taxpayer and is not an attribute of taxed wealth. Taxability of an estate is nevertheless largely governed by the liability for tax of the estate owner and serves to emphasise the close bond binding estate character to the personal circumstances of the estate owner.[1] On the other hand, certain types of property, especially agricultural land, receive preferential treatment and the taxability of an estate is controlled by the proportions of privileged land to normal tax-bearing land within its boundaries. Estate structure evinces *prima facie* evidence of taxability. If it told the whole story there would be no need to introduce taxability as a distinct estate character trait. As far as structure does affect taxability it can be left to do so.

Taxability as a distinct character trait means the total estate tax burden consequent upon the personal liability for tax of the estate owner. Taxability so regarded divides estates in Britain into two basic classes—the taxed and the untaxed. Principles of tax exemption and tax privilege are somewhat complicated by niceties of legal interpretation. Broadly speaking, the income tax statutes have wholly or partially relieved from tax liability what are called 'charities', provident associations, mutual societies, trade unions, clubs and other social institutions. Where estates are owned by these tax-relieved bodies the estates are regarded as tax-free or tax-privileged estates. To facilitate simple classification privileged estates are referred to as 'Charity Estates'. The majority of charity estates are owned by charity trusts, corporations or similar institutions whose

[1] cf. p. 20 *ante*.

existence is not dependent upon the life of their members. These owners stand in the paradoxical shoes of the great immortals of the past who held land by the dead hand of mortmain. The estates they own are beyond the toll of death duties. Charity property owned by personal trustees or by an officer of the charity in the capacity of his office is expressly exempt from estate duty as it passes to a successor at the death of the trustee or of the holder of an office.[1] Estates classified as charity estates on account of income tax privilege can as a general rule be regarded as wholly immune from death duties.

Estates owned by joint stock companies are exempt from death duty because the company is an incorporate body and never dies. Estate duty nevertheless is levied on the shares of its shareholders. Estate duty on shares is of no consequence to public companies whose capital is subscribed by the general public. A heavy toll of estate duty on the shares of a majority shareholder in an estate company or other private company can provoke a serious financial problem especially if the value of the shares is computed on the market value of the land and other assets and not upon the market value of the shares *per se*. Estates owned by private companies whose shares from estate duty is exigible on the death of the holders are regarded as tax-prone estates.

Character traits in the main sample

The main sample of estates was selected at random to give a balanced representation of estates of different character traits. As explained later,[2] it was not possible to represent in this balanced sample all the estate character traits defined in this chapter. The character traits represented are size, shape, tenure pattern and taxability. It does not follow that the other traits have been overlooked. Where they have occurred due notice has been taken of them. Their presence is fortuitous and this is the main point which distinguishes them from the character traits of the estates in the balanced sample, which have been deliberately selected.

[1]Finance Act 1894, Section 2 (1).   [2]cf. Appendix, p. 199 *post*.

CHAPTER THREE

Measurement of Estate Capital

Market value the principal measurement

THE influence of estate character upon the provision of estate capital cannot be considered until we have decided how to measure the degrees of that provision. We can add up the acres, the improved and the improvable, and number the buildings and articles of equipment. That is one way, the way of the stocktaker in all business, whether he counts aniseed balls or steam engines. It is a physical census and has practical merit. Estate capital measured in this way will enable the technically competent agriculturalist to compare the productive potential of what is, with the productive potential of what should be. But mensuration by this principle will not enable the amount of estate capital to be compared with the amount of other capital. Acres of newly won hill land, lengths of road and ditch and fence, and itemised cottage bathrooms cannot be compared in sum with a portfolio of Stock Exchange equities or other alternative investments which might have attracted an estate owner's capital. Feature will not compare with feature. There is no congruity. For comparison's sake we must invoke money, the genie of the economic world who introduces like to unlike and makes of a multitude of incompatibles one pattern of prices and monetary values. The monetary value of estate capital can be compared with the monetary value of other investments.

The monetary value of estate capital has more than one face. We must choose the countenance we think most fitting. An estate owner who tots up the prices he paid when he purchased the several portions of his estate and adds to the sum the outlays he has subsequently made to provide new buildings and alterations will not in the total have an infallible figure of the current monetary value of his investment in the market. The price which the open market would give for the land and buildings might be a much lower figure. Which of the two is the monetary value of the estate capital? Is the monetary value of estate capital the cash value of capital transferred to the estate from elsewhere as it appears on the occasion of purchase or improvement; or the market value of the land and buildings at a given time? If the cash value of the capital at the point of transfer is the answer,

33

it leads to the paradox that the estate capital of an inherited estate has no monetary value. Again, the monetary value of an estate to an owner who would be willing to give more to retain possession of it than the open market would give to purchase it is another measurement of the same order but distinct from the monetary value in the open market.

Of the possible choices of monetary value, the open market value at a given time is preferable to other measurements. Value to the owner is too subjective for precise survey and study. Cash value of transferred capital runs up against the difficulty of inherited capital; although to some in the modern debate on the just remuneration of estate capital investment it is the preferable determinant. Remuneration, so the argument runs, should be related not to the market value of the estate capital but to the contributions to estate capital made by the estate owner and their cash value when contributed. The gravamen of the argument is what is the due of the one who inherits an estate: he has provided nothing himself and has no just claim to remuneration. The argument is not a persuasive one. It touches the morality of inheritance but never goes deep enough to reveal the fact. Patently, if inherited land has no just right to earnings, then farming stock and chattel capital in industry are in the same case: a son who inherits his father's farming stock must not complain if the farm profits are too meagre to pay interest on the market value of the working capital. The argument ignores the principle of substitution; an estate owner who inherits his estate can substitute another investment for it, if it is marketable. And on this count alone current market value commends itself as a measurement of estate capital.

Methods of measurement

The path is not easy to tread even after we have decided to adopt current market value as a standard measure of estate capital. Empirical evidence of market value is hard to come by in Britain, for there is no national statistic of property values. Knowledge of local market prices is possessed by surveyors and valuers, but estimates of value, even when made by informed professional opinion, are uncertain judgements because orthodox valuation method [1] fails to analyse satisfactorily the prices of agricultural land in the post-war market. Agricultural estates are in strong demand, although remuneration from income is very low and on occasion without positive value. Hence it is difficult and at times impossible to relate prices to estate

[1] The basic principle is the product of rental value, less outgoings and repairs, and a selected Y.P. figure representative of the estimated risk-status of the property as an investment.

income and interest rates, and to judge values accordingly. When orthodoxy was reliable a qualified surveyor could value an agricultural estate with some degree of accuracy wherever the estate was situated. Nowadays local expert knowledge is essential and, at best, is hesitant in its opinions. What is true of the valuation of agricultural land and estates is doubly true of the valuation of improvements. Insufficient study has been made of the effect of improvement upon the market value of the land and until the relationship between cost of improvement and the consequential change in the value of the land is better understood, prudent professional valuers will be slow to speak confidently of the contribution of improvements to land value. Valuation principles need rethinking; a new methodology is required.

Dissection and dispersal

Another difficulty which the market value standard meets is the " whole-and-the-pieces " conundrum. An agricultural estate may be worth more in small pieces than entire. It must be decided whether the value of estate capital shall be the market value of the estate entire, or the sum of the values of its several parts. To the estate owner *per se* an estate disintegrated is a nonentity. Looked at with an investor's eyes, the value of estate capital is the realisable value of the estate; and this is the sum of the values of the parts of an estate partitioned to fetch the best prices. Very few large estates in the property market of Britain are sold in a piece and evidence of entity values is scanty. It is equivocal too. Capacity for reliable judgements of value is developed by comparing like with like. Large estates are more complex than small estates and the greater the complexity of an estate, the less does it lend itself to comparison with other entire estates. Lack of correspondence makes such prices as there are of doubtful worth as standards of comparison.

Value of the entirety has a certain logical appeal as a measurement of estate capital but the practical difficulties of its use are great. The alternative, the portions principle, is no paragon. Not only must the value of each portion be estimated but the manner of dissection itself can be no more than a working postulation. Whoever appraises the value of the estate must postulate a plan for carving the body into *disjecta membra*. How far shall the anatomist go? It is possible to imagine a large estate with many let farms divided farm by farm, and each holding sold to its sitting tenant. The tenants will probably buy at a price somewhere between the market value of let farms and the market value of farms with vacant possession. Chopping an estate up too minutely can glut the local land market and reduce the

---

[1] cf. *The Paradox of Rural Land Investment in Britain*, Land Economics, Vol. XXXII, No. 2, (1956) p. 109.   [2] cf. p. 193 *post.*

market value of the portions. A principle of division must be established if the market value standard of measurement is to be applied.

Dissection is distinguished from dispersal. A large agricultural estate is unlikely to be agricultural in all its parts. Dissection for valuation will probably separate like from unlike; farms from residences; residences from village shops. But portions not agricultural must be included in the aggregate and not dispersed. Completeness must be preserved. An agricultural estate is one entity not because it is wholly given to agriculture but because in area it is preponderantly agricultural.[1] Timber, minerals and game raise a nice question of dispersal. Are they within the embrace of estate capital? Or are they more properly external resources? If they are estate capital, they will be included with other portions of the estate in a complete valuation. The degree of their development is a reasonable test. Timber, mature and ripe for marketing; minerals surveyed, measured and exploitable; game and fishing rights, clearly identifiable should be excluded from estate capital. They count as resources separate from the land, despite the legal definition of land. Immature timber, and minerals and sporting rights vaguely identifiable should stand part of estate capital.

Disrepair and market value

The little understood equation between improvement cost and the market value of improved land has been mentioned. There is a counterpart: the effect of disrepair upon market value. This enigma is perhaps the greater. An estate whose buildings are in sore need of repair may not as a consequence suffer loss of market value, if the owner can offer vacant possession on a property market where farms with possession are in strong demand. Market value is not depressed by dilapidation in such a case. Had the estate been one of let farms and vacant possession was not available, the market price would reflect the dilapidation more faithfully. On the other hand, an owner in occupation of an estate who can offer an open door to a purchaser will have to bear the cost of rectifying disrepair himself should he retain ownership and occupation. To him the measure of his estate capital will be the value of the estate with vacant possession less the expenditure he must incur in repair. The open market value of estate capital and the value to the occupying owner are not identical in these circumstances. Which of the two must be taken when measuring estate capital? The peculiar viewpoint of the owner-occupier is analogous to the personal viewpoint of the estate owner

[1]cf. p. 24 *ante.*

who inherits his estate and is said to have made no personal investment. In such a case the open market value is preferable to the
individualistic conception'.[1] Similar preference should decide the
present choice. It must not be concluded that no account whatsoever
need be taken of disrepair. Measurement must follow the market.
The disrepair to take note of is that which affects the market value
of the estate, with or without vacant possession, as the owner is
able to offer it. It is not a simple cost measurement—the cost of
making good the disrepair. Repairs in the course of routine maintenance never affect value. And the market is insensitive to accumulated
disrepair when premises are obsolete and redundant and when market
price is contingent upon a change in land use to which the premises
are unfitted.[2]

Latent value

Neglected repair or want of improvement may reduce the production
potentialities of a holding and depress its market value to a greater
extent than the cost of making good the disrepair and want of
improvement. Repaired and improved, the value of an estate may
be enhanced beyond the cost of rectification and improvement. This
margin of enhancement is termed latent value. Repair and improvement reveal it. A neglected estate does not lose it; it is but temporarily hidden. It is a permanent element of estate capital. But
latent value realised, and latent value anticipated, can greatly differ
in value; indeed, the market can be entirely insensitive to latent
value since the value of an estate can be depressed by neglect to an
extent greater than the cost of remedy. However aware a particular
owner may be of latent value in his land, it will be inconsistent to
take his peculiar viewpoint when measuring estate capital. The open
market value is the standard.

Need for statistics and records

Reliable facts about estate capital, especially monetary values, are
not available in Britain from national statistics. Until the statistical
gap is closed, factual studies of estate capital and associated ideas
will at best be fragmentary. Greater practical wisdom would be
gained if estate accounting recorded the value of estate capital and its
changes in an accounting period.

[1] cf. p. 34 *ante*.
[2] This is not likely to be a significant factor in the valuation of estate capital
in agricultural estates.

Definition of the measurement used

In the light of these remarks, measurement of estate capital in the illustrations that follow is based upon the open market value of the estates in the condition in which they stood at the time of survey. The portions principle is adopted, but to a limited degree; farms let are not the subject of supposed sales to sitting tenants. Mature timber, minerals and sporting sufficiently identifiable to be valued are excluded from the aggregate value. Many sources of opinion were consulted. Some figures are owners' estimates;[1] some are the opinions of professionally qualified local men; some are recent valuations for probate or other purposes; and a few the market prices of the estates, declared by recent sales.

Net estate capital

The definition just given is of gross estate capital. On an estate mortgaged or otherwise pledged as security, the amount of the pledge must be allowed against the gross figure to obtain the value of net estate capital. Allowing the mortgage debt thus does not contradict the principle of the personal viewpoint previously accepted. Admittedly, a mortgage is personal and particular. But there is a clear distinction between the thing valued and its value. Just now we were concerned with the value of estate capital, not with its substance, and the open market opinion was preferred to the opinion of a particular owner. Mortgage reduces the very substance of estate capital, value it how we will. The net value of estate capital is no more than the value of the right to redeem a pledged possession. This is well expressed as the market value of the estate less outstanding mortgage debts and similar charges.

Expenditure needed for improvement of land and buildings is not taken specifically into account in the measurement of estate capital. The expenditure, if made, would probably enhance in some respect the market value and the cost of the improvements deducted from the enhanced market value would give a logical figure for estate capital. The principle is not followed as a method of measurement for two reasons. Should the cost of making improvements exceed the resulting increment in the market value of the estate, the deduction of expenditure from the estimate of the value of the estate improved would depress the estimated value below the current market value of the estate in *status quo*. The value of the estate unimproved is the maximum measure of estate capital and the true

---

[1] i.e. the owner's estimate of the open market value, not his estimate of the value of the estate to himself.

index. Should the cost of the improvements be less than the increment in value, the value of the estate improved would contain an element of latent value; but this would not be realisable until the money for the improvements was found and invested. The open market value should in theory give a similar result; in practice it will do so only to a limited extent and precise calculation on this principle may emphasise latent value beyond the recognition given it by the open market.

Measurement of deficiency and excess

Nevertheless, the amount of capital required to improve land and buildings and reap the full rewards of potential production is a figure of paramount significance for estate capital. It is one of the points where landownership and agriculture part company. Improvements to land which increase agricultural output may be uneconomic to the landowner. What is remunerative in the hand of a particular farmer may be profitless in the hands of the general run of farmers. Landowners with an eye on the land market cannot afford to overlook its general verdict. Capital requirements from the standpoint of agricultural production are not invariably wholly within the economic margin of a landowner's total investment.

Deficiency in fixed equipment and want of land improvement can be measured in monetary terms: pounds sterling per acre of estate area, or other physical unit. With certain reservations measurements of this kind can be expressed as percentage deficiencies of an estimated ideal total estate capital. Changes in land value and in the cost of buildings and land improvement can alter the percentages without alteration of the actual physical amount of equipment and capital investment; this is a weakness of monetary measurements. Moreover, monetary measurements of capital deficiency are not articulate expressions of agricultural needs. Where water supply schemes are of greater consequence to agricultural production than implement sheds and cost half as much to finance, to provide water will reduce the monetary measure of capital deficiency by a third while in fact it advances to a far greater degree investment in effective capital.

An attempt has been made to measure deficiency of fixed equipment and improvements in practical terms. What is wanting in items of fixed equipment and land improvement is ascertained and stated in concrete terms as a basic measurement. The unit employed depends upon the type of equipment and land improvement. Buildings of distinctive types are counted and the deficiency stated numerically, unless the buildings provide accommodation mensurable per capita or by some other simple standard (e.g. standings in cow houses), when the lesser unit is used. Deficiency in land improvements is usually measured per acre—deficiency in land drainage is an example; other measurements are lineal—yards of road, chains of fencing and so on. Degrees of deficiency in each item are calculated as percentages of an ideal; a farm wanting standings for fifty cows and having accommodation for only forty is 20 % deficient in that item. Equipment and improvements are classified according to the grade of their consequence for agricultural production and the farming economy in the circumstances of the estate: lack of cottages on an estate hard against a market town will not be so serious a deficiency as a similar lack on a remote, extensive arable estate. Percentages of deficiency are averaged in each class and the results weighted according to the competence grading of the class. Class averages are themselves averaged to give a general percentage deficiency. Certain items do not lend themselves to numerical calibration—sanitary standards in farmhouses are an example. Where this is so, a straight quantitative judgement is made of the percentage of deficiency.

Measurement of capital earnings

Thoughts about the measurement of the corpus of estate capital will be somewhat incomplete unless they turn also to the problem of measuring its earning power. Estate capital earns estate income. Estate income is derived from estate revenue. What is estate revenue is a question that attracts different answers from place to place. An estate owner may farm land in hand, exploit minerals and convert trees to timber. Revenue from these enterprises and from rents added together will in one place be taken as the aggregate estate revenue. There is no accepted standard. In another place estate revenue will be limited to rents; and timber receipts and the earnings of farming and other enterprises will be treated as separate revenue. When this happens the land in hand, farmed, quarried and used for the separate businesses, will render rent to the rental revenue of the estate.

Estate revenue in this book corresponds to the definitions of estate capital. It is confined to rental earnings. Revenue from the profits of farming, forestry and other enterprises is disregarded. Aggregate rental revenues are composed of actual rents received and the estimated rental values of farms and other lands in hand. Except for estimates of farm rents, the estimates of rental value follow the assessments of the properties to income tax.[1] Income from land and

[1] Cottages and offices occupied by estate staff are excluded unless their assessments are included in the items of the maintenance claim.

buildings is assessed to income tax at the rent the properties would render under specified terms of tenancy. Assessments in England and Wales for lands in hand [1] are a long way out of date; all assessments are low. The estimates of estate revenues used in these pages have therefore a bias towards understatement; the degree of bias is *pro tanto* the number of properties in hand, other than farms, and the total of their assessments. Farms in hand are the subject of special rental estimates. The principle of valuing farm rents is a topical problem in Britain just now. Agricultural rents have been in the main the most depressed item in the national economy throughout the post-war inflation. Gradually they are picking up. When farms become vacant they are often relet at rents far above the level of the rents of the sitting tenants. Estimates of rental value of farms in hand are difficult judgements to make when, as often happens, comparable farms are let at widely varying rentals on the same estate. High extremes are probably the outcome of recent lettings; and low extremes the light rents of traditional tenant families. As a general principle estimates lean towards the lower figure. Bidding for new rents is sometimes high in the knowledge that landlords can be forced to revise their rents before an arbitrator within a few years of the creation of a new tenancy. Arbitrators are wary of what they call premium payments and are suspicious of these high rents.

What appears as rental revenue in the accounts of an agricultural estate is not true rent as the classical economists see it.[2] In theory rent issues from the land; and from the land alone. A large proportion of actual rental revenue today is interest payment for landlords' capital invested in buildings and durable improvements. It is quite common for a tenant to make two payments: one rent and the other interest. Interest is added to rent payment in the measurement of estate revenue.

Rent is determined by the inherent qualities of the land. But these are not the sole criteria. Of equal weight are the terms of the tenancy. Two identical holdings may differ widely in rent because on one the tenant accepts full liability for repairing the premises, and on the other the burden falls across the shoulders of the landlord. No attempt is made to adjust the rental revenues, given as illustrations, to a common standard. Explanatory comment is made where necessary. The figure which expresses the earnings of estate capital is estate income, not estate revenue and calculation of estate income takes account of expenditure on repairs, and this expenditure reflects the reciprocal responsibilities of landlord and tenant for repair of the demised property.

[1] Lands let are assessed on actual rents.
[2] cf. Marshall, *Principles of Economics*, p. 639.

Estate income is rental revenue less the burdens of maintenance, depreciation and outgoings and is the true earnings figure of estate capital. Outgoings in contemporary Britain have many forms which differ in amount from estate to estate: common forms are tithe redemption annuity, land tax and owners' rates. Maintenance is a comprehensive term for expenditure on repairs, management and insurance. Management cost should allow an estimate of salary where the estate is managed by its owner, although as a general rule this is not done. Depreciation of capital equipment is inevitable. Wear and tear of the years is relentless however well and diligently premises are repaired. Estate accounting in Britain is not familiar with depreciation allowance *per se*. The nearest the common form of account comes to it is expenditure on renewals caught up in the yearly average repair costs. But the practice of depreciating new buildings and equipment is taking hold. Where this is done, care must be taken not to allow renewal costs and depreciation for the same items in a calculation of estate income. Maintenance expenditure on some estates includes in addition to renewal costs expenditure on estate improvements. This expenditure is not strictly a current outgoing: it is capital expenditure and should not appear as an item of maintenance, deducted from revenue to compute estate income. Where such expenditure is included, the maintenance costs appear abnormally high on account of it. It has not been possible to detect and extract anomalous expenditure of this kind from the maintenance costs on the estates surveyed. Whatever comprises maintenance costs on the specific estate has been accepted as such. Nevertheless, the presence of an element of improvement expenditure in the maintenance costs is apparent when for each estate, revenue, income and improvement expenditure are compared.

CHAPTER FOUR

Estate Capital Formation

Estate income: a means of capital formation

RECENTLY the British people have been exhorted by a homily on
the hoardings to look to their weekly budget. 'Do not spend in a
week all that you earn in a week' runs the homely caution. The
advice is sound economic wisdom if what is saved becomes true
investment. For a community at large, all saving is investment, as
Keynes observed. But money saved by an individual person is not
capital investment as economic theory sees it. It is truly invested
when it is used to create production capital. Nevertheless from the
viewpoint of the businessman, money saved is capital. The two viewpoints can be reconciled somewhat if we think of money saved from
the profits of an enterprise as a token of the power of that enterprise
to create or acquire new capital goods and hence of the capacity of
the enterprise to form capital from its operations.

In this manner we may approach the formation of estate capital
from estate income. Estate capital comprises land improved and improvable and its fixed equipment. Land cannot form land, but the
employment of land and the fixed equipment upon it can earn
estate income by which additional equipment is created and acquired
and estate capital formed.

Improvement expenditure measures estate capital formation

A logical way of demonstrating the competence of estate income to
form estate capital is to show by historical analysis the extent to
which the items of estate capital economically effective today have
been paid for from estate income in the past. Exhaustive historical
and economic analysis of this kind was far beyond the capacities of
the surveys. An alternative method of demonstration is the replacement principle. By this the yearly replacement cost of existing equipment is compared with yearly estate income. This method is somewhat unrealistic. In the normal course of events entire replacement
of equipment and land improvement does not take place and estate
income is never required to satisfy such a demand. A third alternative is the comparison of recent yearly expenditure on estate

43

capital equipment and land improvement with the yearly estate income.

This is the method followed here. Ten years from 1945[1] have been taken as a basic period. Total expenditure on estate improvement during this period is spread over the ten years to give an average yearly figure. A ten years' principle was adopted not because ten years is likely to be the period of effective usefulness of the items of improvement. Little is known of the economic life of buildings and land improvements. The simple rules of thumb used for calculating the life of farm buildings for mortgage security suggest twenty years as a conservative general estimate. But we are not concerned with the capacity of estate income to repay mortgage loans by instalments.[2] We are concerned with the power of estate income to effect saving and provide funds for capital improvement. We must have regard to the practical requirement of saving method. An estate owner, liable to estate duty, who attempts to accumulate funds over twenty years for the capital improvement of an agricultural estate is running a grave risk. The fund may be impoverished by a heavy imposition of estate duty before it is used. The shorter the period, the less the risk. This only affects estates whose size makes it impracticable to finance improvements by a regular yearly expenditure. Estates of this kind are an exception to the general rule. Apart from these exceptions, a savings period of ten years is a more practical basis of calculation than a period of twenty years and this is the main, primary reason for choosing a ten years' principle.

A secondary reason, and one why the year 1945 suggests itself as a suitable point of departure, is the Government policy of income tax rebate on capital investment in agricultural improvements. In 1945 the Government introduced an income tax rebate[3] on capital investment in agricultural improvements. The rebate is granted on a tenth of the cost of the improvement for each year of a ten-year period immediately following the execution of the work. Since making the surveys the ten-years principle has been adopted as a basis of a bold and invigorating policy of providing Government financial aid for the renewal and improvement of fixed equipment on the land.[4]

The income tax rebate policy bears upon the provision of estate capital from another direction: it carries a definition of improvements. In attempting to measure capital formation by the cost of

---

[1] In a few cases the ten-year period was 1946–56.

[2] To do so would presuppose a capital loan and therefore the financing of improvements from external sources.

[3] Income Tax Act 1945, Section 33 (re-enacted by Income Tax Act 1952, Section 314).　　　　　[4] cf. Cmd. Paper 53, 1956.

improvement, evidence is not limited to improvements which attract the income tax rebate. Nevertheless these improvements have influenced the definition of improvements in general. Whatever is acceptable as an improvement to the tax authorities is looked upon as improvement in the survey and in this respect the Inspector of Taxes is allowed to draw the distinction between improvement expenditure and maintenance expenditure. The word 'improvement' has a Janus face; it looks two ways. What is an item of improvement expenditure on one estate is an item of maintenance expenditure on another. No attempt has been made to reconcile differences in a common definition; the usage of each estate has been accepted as the criterion. The result is a conservative measure of the burden of capital formation, because many estates exclude from their account of improvement expenditure the cost of the provision of equipment which undoubtedly contributes to capital formation but has been included among the items of current maintenance and repair.[1]

The possibility of difference is not as serious for the results as might at first appear. We are concerned with the relationship of estate income to improvement expenditure. Improvement items included among current maintenance costs swell the total maintenance outlay of an estate and thereby reduce its income; but at the same time and to the same extent inclusion of these items among maintenance costs reduces the total improvement expenditure which is the measure of the task of capital formation. Income and improvement expenditure drop by like amounts. And in any event we are addressing ourselves to the problem of capital provision from the personal viewpoint of the specific estate owner.

Cost of improvement may appear to be a measurement of estate capital out of step with the market value measurement previously defined.[2] This previous definition is the standard adopted to measure total estate capital at any given moment. We are now considering not the ultimate end of capital formation but the processes that lead to it. Improved land and buildings are the real contribution to capital formation. Without the money to pay for these improvements the work could not have been done; hence the capacity to find the cash is a logical indication of the capacity to form estate capital, whatever the subsequent market value of the capital may be.

One out of two estates incompetent to form estate capital

Evidence from the tenanted estates of the main sample is arranged in Table II. Competence to form estate capital from estate income is given as the percentage by which estate income actually contributed

[1]cf. p. 42 *ante.*   [2]cf. p. 33 *ante.*

TABLE II
COMPETENCE OF ESTATE INCOMES TO FORM ESTATE CAPITAL

COMPETENCE CLASS	SIZE CLASS						% of total numbers	% of total acreage
	100–249 acres % of class	250–499 acres % of class	500–999 acres % of class	1,000–2,499 acres % of class	2,500–9,999 acres % of class	10,000+ acres % of class		
100 %	18	—	4	31	48	22	21	14
50 %+	14	4	18	10	4	5	9	2
50 %−	5	14	14	18	4	5	10	5
Nil	31	59	42	31	40	68	45	78
Unknown	—	—	4	—	—	—	—	} 1
Tenant sole contributor	23	9	14	10	4	—	10	
No expenditure	9	14	4	—	—	—	5	
Number of estates	22	22	22	22	23	22	—	—
Acreage	3,731	7,887	16,424	32,275	123,583	1,219,628		1,403,528

to improvement expenditure or was capable of doing so if *wholly* expended to that purpose. The more direct information, the percentage actually contributed, comes only from let estates of the central survey.[1] Potential competence of the larger estates is measured by estimating actual estate income from the evidence of rental revenue and outgoings averaged over the immediately preceding five years.[2] The two forms of evidence are compatible although evidence of actual contributions does not show what margin of estate income, if any, remains after financing improvements. This is the only difference between the results of the two forms of evidence and is of no consequence to the present purpose.

Of the tenanted estates 45 % are incompetent to form estate capital from estate income. In contrast to this manifestation of weakness, 21 % of their number are wholly competent and capable of financing from estate income all recently formed capital. An interesting feature of these stalwart estates is the high proportion of them among the larger size classes. A reverse tendency is shown by the estates whose incomes are only partially competent; the larger size-classes have very low intermediate percentages and appear to be either wholly competent or incompetent.

The not insignificant tenants' contributions are noteworthy. It is also of interest that some capital has been formed since 1945 on a large majority of the estates; only 5 % of the total number had no improvement of any kind. These improvident few are among the smallest estates and the sum of their acreage is less than 1 % of the total area of the estates in the sample. In other words, 74 % of the estates in the sample, covering 1,205,734 acres or 85 % of the total area, have been wholly or partially improved by finance from external resources. And this figure does not allow for those estates whose improvements were paid for from temporary capital loans raised on external securities and repaid from estate income.

The whole burden

So far we have taken capital improvement actually made as the measure of capital formation. The whole burden of capital formation on estates is greater than this. Its full weight is the sum of what has been done and what needs to be done.

On the larger estates an attempt has been made to measure this full burden. The estimated cost of outstanding improvements is

[1]cf. Appendix p. 194 *et seq.*

[2]On a few estates a five years' average was not possible for one reason or another; e.g. recent changes of boundary or alteration of accounting system had broken the continuity of the evidence.

TABLE III

COMPETENCE OF ESTATE INCOMES TO FORM CAPITAL AND MEET INTEREST

PERCENTAGE OF THE SAMPLE

COMPETENCE CLASS	A Past improvements	B Past improvements + 5 % interest	C Past and outstanding improvements	D Past and outstanding improvements + 5 % interest	E Past and outstanding improvements + 5 % interest on estate capital and outstanding improvements
	% of estates in sample	% of estates in sample	% of estates in sample	% of estates in sample	% of estates in sample
100%	42	39	23	10	
50%	4	7	16	18	
50%	5	5	12	23	51
Nil	49	49	49	49	49

reduced on a ten years' principle to a yearly figure and the result added to the yearly cost of past improvement. In each case, the estimate of need is a judgement of the estate owner or his professional advisor. This measurement of the total burden assumes that the cost of improvement and the level of estate income will remain unaltered for ten years.

The effect on the competence of estate incomes to carry the total burden of capital formation is shown in Table III. Competence to carry the burden of past provision is compared with the competence to carry the total burden. On a few estates no improvement is outstanding and the competence of the estate incomes is unaffected. In general there is notable change in the pattern of competence. The percentage of wholly competent estates drops from 42 % to 23 % under the greater pressure. The greatest change is in the class of intermediate percentages: the percentage of estates of partial competence jumps from 9 % to 28 %.

Interest on capital weakens competence to form estate capital

Although we have imagined estate income contributing to improvement expenditure we must not lose sight of the fact that this expenditure is a capital investment from the viewpoint of the estate owner. An estate owner with income to spend on improvement may invest it elsewhere. By improving his land he is denying himself the interest the money could earn in an alternative investment. Earnings thus foregone should be made good from the income of the estate investment. Estate income as defined earlier and used for the illustrations so far given makes no provision for reimbursement of this kind. To do so weakens the competence of estate income to form capital. This is also illustrated in Table III. The Table shows how the pattern of competence alters if, in addition to forming capital on the ten-years principle, the estate income provides interest at 5 % per annum[1] on the cost of the capital formed. The percentage of estates wholly competent to form estate capital, measured in terms of improvement done, falls from 42% to 39%; and the percentage of those strong enough to meet the whole burden falls from 23 % to 10 %.

We must go further. Capital formed as improvement of land and the provision of fixed equipment becomes part of the entire estate capital. Not only does the definition of estate income allow no interest on recent capital formation, it makes no provision for interest on the entire estate capital. Estate capital is defined as the current marketable value of the estate. An estate owner who regards

[1] 5 % is used as it is a fairly common rate of interest charged to tenants in post-war years on landlords' improvements; cf. p. 61 *post*.

4

his estate as an investment will look for remuneration from income. If estate income is to contribute dividends on the entire capital, its competence to form fresh capital will be impaired. What this means for the estates surveyed is again illustrated in Table III. The Table shows the effect upon competence of charging against estate income interest at 5 % on the value of the estate capital and interest at the same rate on the cost of outstanding improvements; improvement already made stands part of existing estate capital and is therefore reflected in its current value. The once-bold 42 % of wholly competent estates falls to nothing. In fine, of fifty-six estates covering 1,347,700 acres, not one is competent to form capital entirely from estate income and in addition pay interest at 5 % on the total capital investment; and none is competent to make such an interest payment and at the same time form over 50 % of the necessary capital.

Where the fault lies

The cause of incompetence in estate incomes may be either inadequacy of the income itself or a high rate of capital formation. Comparison of incomes and improvement burdens indicates where the fault lies.

Before we attempt this diagnosis the figures of Table II call for closer examination. A relatively high percentage of the estates over 1,000 acres are wholly competent; 34 % of their number are capable of financing from estate income the whole of the recently formed capital, while the corresponding percentage among the smaller estates is 7·6 %. This contrast may be due to a difference in the extent of improvement; the wholly competent estates may appear to be competent because they have carried a lighter task. Capital formation, on which the figures are based, is measured by the extent of past improvement. An estate little improved would on this account appear to be more competent than one whose standard of improvement had been high. If the general standard of improvement of the competent estates is low it could account for the high percentage of wholly competent estates among the larger sizes.

Now, if this were the reason for the seeming competence, the standard of improvement of the incompetent estates and of the partially competent would be markedly better than the standard of improvement of the wholly competent estates. Fortunately we can test this in some measure by the estimates of the cost of improvements still required. On the wholly competent estates the average is £9 8s. per acre; on the estates over 50 % competent the figure is £8 10s. per acre; on the estates less than 50 % competent the figure is £6 4s. per acre; and on the incompetent estates £7 6s. per acre. By this showing it appears that the boasted competence of many of the larger estates is consequent upon a lower investment in improvements. The strength of their incomes is illusory; they appear strong because they have tackled a light task. It may be, however, that the cost of outstanding improvements is not a reliable guide in the matter, because the standard of equipment on the competent estates may be higher than the standard on the others.

It is well therefore to go further. Later on, the level of investment attained by recent capital formation is measured by relating past investment to total demand. Total demand is measured as the cost at current prices of providing the past improvements and the outstanding improvements.[1] Past improvements at current cost expressed as a percentage of this sum gives an indication of the relative supply of capital answering the total demand. When the accomplishments of the tenanted estates are measured in this way it is seen that the competent estates have average percentages below the averages of the partially competent estates, and even below the average percentage of the incompetent estates. The average achievement of the competent estates is 35·2 %; of those over 50 % competent, 60·4 %; of those less than 50 % competent, 60·3 %; and of the incompetent estates 47·8 %.

Evidence from the estates of the central survey in a different form supports this verdict. On these smaller estates an attempt was made to measure the amount of fixed equipment required at the time of survey for maximum production within the capacity of the estate owner and his tenants. Measurement was not monetary and based on the cost of providing what was required, but was a measurement of the physical quantities of equipment item for item. The results are given as percentage deficiency in an ideal inventory of equipment. Results range from perfection to a 25 % deficiency. The wholly competent estates have an average deficiency of 9·4 %; the estates that have financed over 50 % of capital formation from estate income have an average deficiency of 6·9 %; the estates that have financed less than 50 % of capital formation have an average deficiency of 6·5 %; and the average deficiency of the incompetent class is 6·6 %. These figures run parallel with the above monetary measurements in the competence classes. It can be said that the competent estates are the least satisfied with their investment achievements. And this can mean poorer achievement in an absolute sense. On the other hand their dissatisfaction may be due to inordinate ambition. It may be that they are aiming at higher standards of equipment.

Further diagnosis can be made by studying more closely the figures for the larger estates. Almost half their number are wholly

[1] cf. p. 81 *post*.

incompetent because they have no income whatsoever from rental revenue. Obviously the cause of incompetence on these estates is weakness of income. No matter what the outlay on improvements may be, it cannot affect the total failure of estate income to contribute to capital formation. Failure is absolute. And the fault lies on the income side, not with the rate of capital formation.

Now estate income is rental revenue minus outgoings. A weak estate income may be the consequence of either low revenue or high outgoings. Conversely, a competent estate income may have its virtue either in a high rental revenue or in low outgoings. Table IV

TABLE IV

DEVIATIONS OF COMPETENCE CLASSES

Competence class	Percentage deviation from mean revenue		Percentage deviation from mean outgoings		Percentage deviation from mean improvement expenditure	
	+	−	+	−	+	−
100 %	18			28		57
50 % (+ or −)	24		19			14
Nil		16	21		54	

compares rental revenue, outgoings and improvement expenditure of the wholly competent, the partially competent and the incompetent estates. Average revenue and expenditures of the estates in each competence-class are compared with the overall averages. The results are given in the Table as percentage deviations, either plus or minus, from the overall averages.

Yearly revenue from all the estates averages £1·29 per acre; outgoings average £1·26 per acre; and yearly improvement expenditure averages £0·35 per acre. Revenue from the wholly competent estates is on average 18 % higher than the overall average, and the average revenue on the partially competent estates is on average somewhat higher still, 24 %. Revenue of the incompetent estates is on average 16 % lower than the overall average. Outgoings on the competent estates are 28 % lower than the overall average. On the partially competent estates they move in an opposite direction and are 19 % higher than the overall average. On the incompetent estates they are higher still, but only slightly so, a deviation of 21 % above the overall average. Average improvement expenditure on the wholly competent estates is 57 % lower than the overall average; and on the partially competent estates it is 14 % lower than the overall average. Improvement expenditure on the incompetent estates is as much as 54 % higher than the overall average, a point referred to later.

This relatively high level of capital formation on the incompetent estates is not the cause of incompetence. Income has failed absolutely: that is the cause of incompetence. It is tempting to suppose that the high improvement expenditure betokens a high repairs outlay; for the costs of many quasi-improvements are caught up in the repairs expenditure. This supposition is reasonable but it is not supported by the evidence of Table IV; the outgoings of the incompetent estates do not rise much further above the overall average than the outgoings of the partially competent. The revenue of the partially competent, on the other hand, is 24 % higher than the overall average, while the average revenue of the incompetent estates is 16 % lower than the overall average: for every £1 of incompetent revenue the partially competent estates have £1 10s. Surely it is here where the fault lies. The revenues of the incompetent estates are too low and have rendered their incomes incapable of contributing anything to capital formation.

Further comparison of the deviations of Table IV confirms the relatively low achievement of the seemingly wholly competent estates. Undoubtedly with the majority competence is due to a low improvement expenditure. Average improvement expenditure is very far below the mean for the sample. A sidelight is thrown on to this condition by the figures for the average outgoings. Not only do the wholly competent estates display relatively low improvement expenditure, their outgoings are also far below average. Now a low improvement expenditure and low outgoings could be mutually supporting evidence that the demand for capital investment on these estates was low because the requirement of fixed equipment per acre was slight. If this were so, the estates would be genuinely competent. But it has been shown that on these competent estates past improvement falls short of total demand, and this would not be so if the total requirements were relatively slight. It would appear that the low outgoings are in character with the low improvement expenditure and indicate low standards of maintenance and improvement. It would be wrong, however, to conclude that every competent estate is in this case. Revenue is above average, an indication of a competence not altogether specious.

We have seen that if the seemingly competent estates had financed outstanding improvements in addition to past improvements from estate income more than half of them would not have remained competent. And if the strength of the estate incomes that makes competence possible is due to skimped maintenance, it is reasonable to suppose that had proper attention been paid to repairs and maintenance very few if any of the competent estates would be able to finance both past and outstanding improvements from estate income.

The wide deviation from the mean of improvement expenditure on the incompetent estates is due to the influence of two estates with exceedingly high improvement expenditure. If the undoubtedly anomalous evidence is excluded, the improvement expenditure on the incompetent estates deviates from the mean by a positive 5 %. The overall mean is of course reduced by this adjustment and its reduction alters the deviations of the improvement expenditure of the partially competent and wholly competent estates. Expenditure on the wholly competent estates is still much below the mean, but is now 21 % and not 57 %. The greatest change takes place in the deviation of the improvement expenditure of the partially competent; from a negative 14 % it becomes a positive 58 %. Admittedly the rental revenue of the partially competent estates is above the average, but when its positive deviation is compared with the positive deviation of the rental revenues of the wholly competent estates and the insignificant difference is seen in the light of the positive deviation in improvement expenditure, the cause of partial incompetence is plain: rental revenues have not kept pace with investment.

In sum, the estate incomes of the tenanted estates of the main sample, with very few exceptions, are incompetent to form over a ten-years creative period the capital demanded by their respective estates. And, so far as the larger estates give evidence, the cause of incompetence is the inability of rents to keep pace with outgoings, and the cause of only partial competence is the inability of rents to keep pace with investment demands.

Income from improvements

Incomes of the tenanted estates would have been weaker had not the improvements themselves contributed to their strength. The manner of this contribution differs. On some estates it is impossible to identify the contribution; at the time the improvements were made, no interest on the capital outlay or similar charge had been levied from the tenants by the estate owners. Rental revenue has increased since the improvements were done but their contribution to the increment cannot be distinguished from the beneficial influence of a strong market and other factors affecting the level of rent. On other estates the contributions from improvements can be identified up to a point; when the improvements were made the estate owners charged the tenants yearly payments for them. Usually the payment is looked upon as interest, and no more than that, on the landlord's capital commitment. On occasion it is more than this and though calculated as a percentage of the cost of the improvement, is in fact interest plus a sinking fund to amortise the capital outlay over the period of the estimated life of the improvement.

Specific yearly payments of this kind are significant. They are accepted as rent. And where they occur on the estates of the survey they have been included in the rental revenues. An improvement that attracts interest payment is paying its way to some extent and if in addition it earns sufficient to cover the cost of its own amortisation, it cannot be accused of burdening the existing estate income with the task of capital formation. And if, despite this self-forming capacity of improvement capital, the total estate income is incompetent or only partially competent, the fault must lie with the revenue or outgoings of the estate; that is to say, with the existing income and not with the rate of capital formation.

Some knowledge has been gained of the contribution of improvements to the estate incomes of certain[1] of the tenanted estates. Some 18 % of these either have made no improvements or the tenants have provided the capital. Of the remainder, 42 % do not charge the tenants interest on improvements made by the landlord; 40 % recover interest or specific payment of some kind from all landlords' improvements; and 18 % charge the tenants payment for selected improvements but not for all. In every case payment is calculated as a specific percentage of the capital outlay. On those estates where the policy of payment is consistent and all improvements are subject to payment, the percentage rates vary from 4·5 % to 11 %; the average is 6·6 %, and the mode 5 %.

Although during the earlier years of the post-war decade money could be borrowed on first mortgage secured against rural land at a lower rate than 5 %, this percentage may be regarded as a reasonable average return on landlord's improvements during the decade. Where it or something lower is charged, the income provides nothing by way of amortisation of the improvement. If interest is foregone and the entire payment put to a savings account over a ten years' period in accordance with the principle adopted above[2] as a criterion of capital formation, it would provide no more than half a replacement fund; and if tax were levied on the payments at approximately 10s. in the £,[3] only a quarter of the task would be accomplished. To form

---

[1] i.e. 111 of the 133 tenanted estates of the main sample.   [2] cf. p. 44 *ante*.
[3] 10s. in the £ is suggested as this allows for a modicum of surtax in addition to an income tax in the neighbourhood of 9s. in the £.

a savings fund over ten years from taxed income (at a rate of tax in the neighbourhood of 10s. in the £) would require a payment of 20 % on the landlord's capital, wholly devoted to the fund. The nearest rate of payment to this on the surveyed estates is 11 %; and so high a charge was made on only one of the estates. If interest on the yearly contributions to the savings fund were added each year to the fund so that it accumulated at compound interest, a charge of 8·9 % would be required to make good replacement over ten years, supposing the rate of accumulation to be 2·5 % tax free.

A redemption fund over a much longer period could of course be provided. Or tenants' payments for improvements could be used to defray repayment instalments of loans raised to finance the improvements. These possibilities are not considered further here. The calculations based on a longer period would be incongruous with the general argument of this chapter and the principle of saving earlier adopted. The practical significance of both possibilities is dealt with later in a more convenient context.[1]

If the interest payments made by tenants are accepted for what they are, they bring a useful contribution to estate income and at least pay the landlord for the employment of his capital. Of the fifty-six estates of Table III, forty-six are receiving from estate income a deliberate and definite contribution towards capital formation in the form of interest payments by tenants on the landlords' improvements. Although the improvements of these estates did not enhance their income sufficiently to meet the cost of a ten-years' amortisation, they brought a definite contribution to estate revenue and thus assisted the competence of estate incomes at what appears to be one of two weak points. It is noteworthy that of the incompetent estates whose weakest point is revenue, 82 % receive benefit in this way. The benefit is not peculiar to them. Among the wholly competent estates 81 % benefit; and each of the few partially competent estates benefit.

These percentages include those estates whereon some improvements are allowed free to the tenants while others are subject to interest payments. Were interest charged on landlords' improvements on every estate and charged consistently at 5 % on all improvements, the number of incompetent and partially competent estates would be markedly lower. What the enhancement of estate incomes in this way would mean is demonstrable. There are forty-three incompetent estates and partially competent estates[2] among the larger tenanted estates. Only twenty-six of these require interest payment on all

[2]i.e. with incomes incompetent to form all the capital required for past and outstanding improvement.

improvements. Interest at 5 % on all improvements done and outstanding would enrich the estate incomes of the others and lift six
estates, now incompetent, into the partially competent class and four
estates, now less than 50 % competent, into the over 50 % competent
class.

Estate capital formation by the tenant

All that has been said so far presupposes the financing of estate
capital formation from estate income. Estate income is immediately
dependent upon rental revenue rendered by tenants. A tenant can,
however, contribute to the formation of estate capital in a direct way
by providing fixed equipment and undertaking land improvement
at his own expense. Capital formed in this way is truly estate capital
when it vests in the estate owner as landlord. Common law in Britain
does not favour the tenant who improves the landlord's reversion.
Whatever is affixed to the soil becomes part of the soil and is the
property of whosoever owns the fee or superior estate: *quicquid
plantatur solo, solo cedit.* Statute law has intervened to give the
tenant the right to claim compensation from the landlord for tenant's
improvements made to the freehold during the tenancy. The law
virtually creates a proprietary right in tenants' improvements which
it vests in the tenant. Capital thus formed is not estate capital; it
belongs to the tenant so long as he has a right to claim compensation
for it from the landlord. Once compensation is paid, or for some
reason the tenant loses his right to claim compensation, the improvements vest in the estate owner and become estate capital.

Not all tenants' improvements that attract compensation contribute to estate capital. Some, although costly, have a short effective
life and are more akin to farming stock than estate improvements.
A landlord who compensates his tenant for them will either pass the
ownership of them on to succeeding tenants or, if the holding is not
relet and he takes possession of it himself, will retain the interest in
them as part of the trading capital of his farming enterprise. Improvements of this kind need not concern us further.

A fundamental difference between these short-term improvements
and long-term improvements which can contribute to estate capital
formation is the influence each has upon the capital value of the
estate. Short-term improvements have no influence. Long-term improvements have it in their nature to enhance the capital value of
the farm or holding, although in a particular circumstance they may
not do so. Statute law[1] recognises the distinction: tenants are com-
pensated for short-term improvements on the basis of their value to

[1] cf. Agricultural Holdings Act 1948, Sections 48 and 51.

an incoming tenant; long-term improvements attract compensation commensurate with the increase in the capital value of the holding as an investment.[1]

Long-term improvements made by tenants alleviate the burden of estate capital formation on estate income. If the tenancy outruns the period of the effective usefulness of the improvement, the improvement will not increase the capital value of the holding at the termination of the tenancy and so will not attract compensation. The tenant will then have provided funds for the improvement, executed it and enjoyed it to its exhaustion, and the estate income will have been entirely relieved of the burden of its formation. Tenants' improvements whose period of efficiency outlasts the term of the tenancy relieve estate income of part of the burden of estate capital formation. During the tenancy the tenant provides and maintains the improvement. It is not estate capital. At the end of the tenancy compensation is paid for such virtue as remains in the improvement and enhances the value of the holding. The amount of the compensation is the measure of the capital formation that falls upon the estate resources.

Where an improvement reveals latent value, a landlord may find himself paying away to his tenant as compensation a sum which represents the latent value in his own freehold. This can happen when the increment in the capital value of a holding consequent upon an improvement is greater than the cost of making the improvement. This somewhat unjust compensation can be avoided. A landlord should either do the work himself; or, when he gives consent to his tenant to make the improvement, he should, as a condition of the consent, require that the compensation ultimately payable should be either the cost of replacing the improvement at the end of the tenancy or the increase in the capital value of the holding, whichever is the less.

An appreciation of the practical value of a tenant's direct contribution to capital formation is gained if we look once again at the tenanted estates in their respective competence classes. On at least 47 % of the 133 estates capital has been formed by tenants' improvements. The favoured estates are not confined to the wholly competent class. Of the incompetent estates 50 % have benefited from tenants' improvements; and of the partially competent estates 60 % have benefited. Whether or not this tenant-formed capital will ultimately burden the estate resources with claims for compensation cannot be foreseen. The significance of the figures for the incompetent and partially competent classes is that although estate income

[1]This is not so in Scotland where compensation is measured by the value of the improvement to an incoming tenant.

has not fully financed the formation of estate capital, the tenants by directly financing potential estate capital have assisted capital formation in a manner not reflected by the evidence of the estate incomes.

The way the incompetence of estate incomes can hide the tenants' contribution to potential estate capital is further demonstrated by the average amount of the contributions in the competence classes. The average amounts move in an opposite direction to the competence of the estate incomes. On the wholly competent estates the tenant's average contribution is 18·7 %; on the partially competent estates the contribution is higher, 24·58 %; and on the incompetent estates it is higher still, 29·8 %. These figures exemplify the practical benefit of tenants' direct contributions. They go further and suggest that where the estate income is too weak to form capital, tenants are more inclined to help themselves.

The average contribution by tenants where the facts are known on the smaller estates is 29·9 %. The figure is somewhat misleading because half of the number of these estates lie at the two poles; either no contribution has been made by the tenant, or the tenant has contributed 100 %. Normally the tenants' contribution lies between 1 % and 10 % of the total capital formation. Nearly one in ten of all the tenanted estates have all their capital financed by the tenants. The majority of these are estates where there is a close affinity between landlord and tenant.[1] Nevertheless, what some can do, others can be encouraged to do.

[1]cf. p. 171 *post.*

CHAPTER FIVE

Consociate Capital

Consociate capital supports estate capital

THE incapacity of estates in the main sample to form estate capital from estate income raises the question, from what sources are capital funds obtained? The question is pertinent to the past and the future. Estates that have improved their equipment and land condition at a cost beyond the capacity of their estate incomes must in the past have drawn upon external resources. And if their poverty continues they will need similar support in the future. Other estates which in the past have financed from estate income their recently formed capital but will not be competent from that source to meet the demands of future capital formation will also need support from outside. Even if capital formation is financed from loans secured on the estate capital, the finance *per se* comes from beyond the estate and in that sense is external to it. A proper understanding of estate capital cannot be incurious about these funds associated with estates and strengthening their weakness.

And besides these causes, there are other reasons why we should seek information about what may be termed *consociate capital*. Agricultural estates competent to form estate capital from estate income require certain monetary funds to support their financial mechanism. Farms on the majority of tenanted estates in Britain are held by some form of contractual tenure which reserves a monetary rent to the landowner. Rent is paid at six-monthly audits. Revenue therefore is spasmodic over the short term. Outgoings on the contrary, especially running repairs, are normally continual. Consequently during the short term a monetary reserve is necessary to float the finance on an even keel. Over the long period rental revenue is continual, a six-monthly cyclic inflow, but expenditure is often spasmodic because renewal and replacement of buildings and other equipment and land improvement schemes, unlike running maintenance costs, make heavy demands upon the estate exchequer at irregular intervals. A well-run estate therefore requires a monetary fund to support its finances in the short period and a fund of quickly realisable assets to finance improvements and renewals in the long period.[1] These funds may be built up by a contribution from estate income, but once created, they must either be held as liquid cash or invested; and in either event become external to estate capital, although closely associated with it.

Other reasons why agricultural estates need consociate capital are the consequences of peculiar quirks in the present taxation policy in Britain. An estate is assessed to income tax on its rental revenue less certain outgoings and the actual expenditure on repairs and other costs of maintenance. The allowance for maintenance expenditure is not the *de facto* expenditure of the year of assessment, but a yearly average over the immediate past five years. If this average in any year is greater than the estate income, on property other than agricultural property, the allowance is limited to the amount of estate income; but on agricultural property the overplus can be set off against 'other income' enjoyed by the landowner. A landowner who has no external resources to provide him with other income is at a disadvantage. His agricultural estate will from its own capital resources have to finance the overplus of maintenance expenditure which would have been met from untaxed income had there been adequate external funds. Furthermore, in addition to the five years' average maintenance allowance an estate owner can claim the tax rebate on capital expenditure. Although a landowner receives a tax rebate on his capital expenditure, he has to wait ten years for its full benefit. In the meantime he has to find the money for the capital expenditure either from taxed estate income or external resources. When the competence of the estate incomes of the main sample was assessed it was supposed that the incomes had received the benefit of a full tax rebate on improvement expenditure. If this rough assumption had not been made the incomes on many of the competent estates would have been greatly weakened. In the world of real circumstance, the full tax rebate has to be waited for and the estate owner, even of a competent estate, may need temporary funds to finance his improvements.

Apart from these considerations, wealth consociate with estate capital provides an economic environment for the estate, which influences its character traits. A landowner's total fortune, for example, governs the taxability of his estate. Moreover, the role of an estate in the general investment and financial policy of a landowner cannot be understood unless the estate is seen in association with the whole wealth of that landowner. Agriculture supported by estate capital that is the subject of a carefully planned and balanced

[1]The fund for the short period has been termed the Reserve Fund; and the fund for the long period the Capital Works Fund (cf. *Reserve Fund and Maintenance Funds*, Department of Estate Management, Cambridge University, 1954.)

investment policy, is likely to be more stable than an agriculture whose land and buildings are looked upon as incidental items of a farmer's trading stock, of no greater consequence in the farming economy than the rusted muck-rake in the cobbled corner.

The dividing line

The dividing line between consociate capital and estate capital is suggested by the definition of estate capital. Estate capital comprises the land and fixed equipment upon it owned by the estate owner. Chattel property, farming stock, timber hauling equipment, quarrying machinery and so forth, even the vehicles and other gear of the estate yard, heirlooms and household effects, are not estate capital, however intimately they are associated with the estate and its economy. On tenanted land the dividing line is more easily identifiable than on owner-occupied estates, especially small ones; estate capital comprises the reversionary interest in land and buildings—nothing more. Tenants' fixtures and improvements, although affixed to the soil and therefore in one sense part of the land, in fact belong to someone else and hence do not come within the definition either of estate capital or consociate capital. Woodlands and quarries present a difficulty. Stone and other mineral wealth leased or quarried as a distinct estate enterprise are regarded as consociate capital and not as estate capital. It is not possible to draw precise definitions between consociate capital and estate capital in timber; as a rough guide timber that can be valued in the market is accounted marketable and designated consociate capital, and all other timber is accepted as part of estate capital. Sporting rights are ignored unless they are so clearly identifiable that their capital value can reasonably be appraised, when they join the items of consociate capital.

Adventitious capital

The term consociate capital has been coined to express the fact that the total wealth of an estate owner may marry estate capital and other private capital in a common ownership. Estate capital and consociate capital are alike in so far as both lie in the same hand of ownership. Their identity is not an identity of legal rights of ownership; rights of ownership in real property and personal property are distinct forms. Identity is in the person of the proprietor. He who owns the estate capital owns the consociate capital.

Now, it can happen that an estate will lie under the beneficent wing of other capital which is not consociate with its estate capital because this other capital is not owned by the estate owner. Yet there is an affinity between the estate owner and the owner of this adventitious fund; an affinity that cannot be ignored. An example of this relationship, frequently met with, is an estate owned by a private estate company whose chairman and principal shareholder has a substantial fortune in his own name. The company is the estate owner. The only consociate capital is the assets of the company other than the estate capital. Nevertheless, the principal shareholder is there supporting the company if need be with the bulwark of his private fortune. Another example, also frequently found, is the relationship between trustees and the creator of the trust. An estate owner creates a trust in landed estate and a specified supporting fund. The trustees become the estate owners and the owners of the supporting fund; the supporting fund is consociate capital with the estate capital. But the creator of the trust stands at the trustees' elbow and the fortune that financed the supporting fund can augment it. Yet that fortune is not consociate with the estate capital, since there is no identity of ownership. The trustees and the creators of the trust are distinct persons. Fortune collaterally linked with estate capital in this way but not consociate with it is referred to as *adventitious capital*.

The pattern of investment

The practical benefit to estate income of these external resources depends as much upon their structure as their size. Obviously the greater the fund the greater its power of support, other things being equal. But if other things are not equal, if one fund differs from another fund in the pattern of its investments, a smaller fund may well be of more practical use than a larger. A modest fortune readily realisable is of greater use as consociate capital backing up estate capital than an extensive fund in the shares of a private company which is incapable of realisation unless the company is wound up; or a fortune in other real property whose realisation means prolonged and anxious waiting upon the whims of a sluggish property market.

The surveys have attempted not only to obtain knowledge of the size of consociate and adventitious funds supporting estate capital but to go further and learn something of the manner in which these funds are employed and invested; to discover both the capacity of the funds and the pattern of their investment. Results vary. On some estates the survey is complete and it is possible to relate the total consociate capital and other external funds to the amount of estate capital and to present, with more or less precision, the ratios in which the funds are distributed among an array of investments and

other employments. On other estates the size of the fund is revealed
and the principles of the investment pattern, but not the proportions.
Less successful results give only the simple ratio between estate
capital and other funds. On a few estates calculations of the probable
extent of external resources had to be made from information about
the ratio of total income to estate income. On the least successful of
all, information is limited to the sources of finance for past improvements.

Coefficients of support

We are disregarding just now the motives that move an estate owner
to spend money, which his estate income has not earned, on the
betterment of the fixed equipment of the estate and the improvement
of its land; and the reasons why he may hesitate to do so. The
restraints that check and the inducements that impel are considered
in subsequent chapters. Here we are merely observing the facts of
the fortunes of estate owners. Our purpose is to see how far, if at
all, agricultural estates have other wealth at the back of them;
capital funds potentially available. It is logical, therefore, to look at
an estate owner's fortune as a whole, where our data make it possible
to do so, and to express the external funds as a ratio of estate
capital; to see how many times a £ of estate capital is covered by a
£ of other fortune. And these ratios we will call *coefficients of support*.

Some estates in the sample are mortgaged or have other charges
secured against their titles. For the purpose of expressing the ratio
of external funds to estate capital a transfer must be postulated. We
must suppose that all debts secured against the title of an estate are
transferred to the consociate fund and redeemed by it. This principle
is necessary in order to ensure a universal standard of reference to
which the ratios are related. If debts were deducted from the value
of the estate capital and the external fund expressed as a ratio of
the result, the ratio would have no point of general reference. It
would depend upon particular circumstances—the indebtedness of
the estate. By transferring the debt to the external fund and calculating the ratio between the net fund and the estate capital as the
coefficient of support, we link the coefficient to the market value of
the estate. Every estate has its market value. Market value is public
knowledge and hence the trend of ratios is related to a patent
standard and not to a standard unknown and unknowable apart
from knowledge of the special circumstances of a particular estate.

Mention has already been made of the practical importance of
funds easily and quickly used. We must distinguish between those
parts of an external fund that are monetary or quickly convertible

TABLE V

EXTERNAL FUNDS SUPPORTING AGRICULTURAL ESTATES

SIZE CLASS (acres)	PERCENTAGE OF CLASS HAVING CONSOCIATE CAPITAL %	PERCENTAGE OF CLASS HAVING ADVENTITIOUS CAPITAL %	CO-EFFICIENTS OF SUPPORT						
			Consociate capital					Adventitious capital	
			Net total fund	Net liquid fund	Gross total fund	The average percentage of estate capital and gross consociate capital	Percentage of group represented	Gross total fund	Percentage of group represented %
100–249	90·4	15·4	2·39	0·93	2·48	1·24	90·4	3·03	13·5
250–499	92·3	25·0	1·67	0·64	1·79	0·90	92·3	5·52	21·2
500–999	96·2	36·5	1·21	0·38	1·36	0·82	94·2	1·35	30·8
1,000–2,499	63·6	36·4	1·48*	0·81	1·56	0·83	59·1	1·99	27·3
2,500–9,999	56·5	26·1	0·30	0·12	0·43	0·37	39·1	0·80	26·1
1,000 +	81·8	54·5	1·03	0·24	1·08	0·71	77·3	0·50†	40·9
Average of all classes	80·1	32·3	1·35	0·52	1·45	0·81	75·4	2·19	26·6

* Excluding an anomaly of 11·7.   † Excluding an anomaly of 29·7.

to money and those parts that are not. For the purpose of analysis monetary funds, Government stock and shares quoted on the Stock Exchange are regarded as readily available and distinguished from other capital by referring to them as liquid. This distinction must not belittle the importance of the other portions of a capital fund. Liquid funds have a special faculty as reservoirs of finance for regular cyclic expenditure, for which funds only infrequently converted to cash are cumbersome and somewhat unreliable.

The coefficients of support for the majority of estates in the main sample are set out in Table V. Consociate capital and adventitious capital have been measured as the sum of the values of the component parts of the funds, so far as it was possible to ascertain the values at the time of the survey. Prices of stocks and shares are not quotations current on the precise day of enquiry; the value used is the last quotation the estate owner had available.

The first three columns of Table V show simply the numbers of the estates in the various size groups that have consociate and adventitious funds to support them. There is no attempt to express the ratio of these funds to estate capital because the sum of the capital fund is not known on a number of the estates represented. The Table shows clearly in two other columns the percentage of the number in each size group for which information is sufficient to compute coefficients of support.

In one form or another, the estate capital of 80 % of the estates in the main sample is supported by an external fund in the same ownership as the estate itself. A minority of the estates in the main sample are without measurable consociate funds. The consociate funds are not entirely liquid. Only 47 % of the estates have liquid consociate funds. Liquidity does not appear to be peculiar to any particular size class; estates with no liquid consociate capital are found among the small estates of 100–500 acres and as frequently among the largest estates.

In addition to the consociate funds, 32 % of the estates are supported by adventitious funds. These funds with their affinity of title tend to be a feature of the larger estates. It is not possible to tell the extent to which they are liquid. All that need be noted at this stage is the percentage of estates in the sample that benefit from collateral capital of this kind: a percentage of numbers that represents 59 % of the land area of the estates of the main sample.

Detailed information is available of the size and structure of a fair proportion of the consociate funds and the information allows coefficients of support to be calculated. Results can be given in a number of ways. Each estate can be considered separately and the value of consociate capital divided by the value of estate capital to give the co-efficient of support. Co-efficients calculated in this way can be averaged for the whole sample and for size-classes and other divisions. This has been done and the results are given in Table V. Distinction is drawn between liquid funds and others, and between gross and net funds. What is meant by a liquid fund has already been defined. A gross fund makes no allowance for outstanding mortgages or other charges. A net fund as explained above is the balance of consociate capital after deduction of mortgages and charges for which the estate owner is liable whether secured on the estate or not. Another measurement is the co-efficient of support given by the ratio between (a) the average percentage of consociate capital in total fortune and (b) its reciprocal, the average percentage of estate capital in total fortune. Measurements of this ratio are also given for the various size-classes in Table V. These measurements approximate to the statistical mode and are therefore a more sober presentation of the facts than the picture given by the other averages.

The evidence indicates that estates in the neighbourhood of 100–250 acres tend to be supported by gross consociate funds of twice the value of the estate capital; for every £ of estate capital there are approximately £2 in the external fund. The larger estates, up to 1,000 acres, are less well supported. Estates over 1,000 acres are the worst off proportionately; their consociate support funds tend to equal the estate capital—a £-for-£ ratio. It is perhaps significant that the largest estates of all appear to be better endowed than the smaller estates of the over-1,000 acres class.

The pattern is but little altered when gross consociate funds are reduced by outstanding mortgages and other charges. The sum of the evidence suggests that in the majority of the cases, something between a half and a quarter of the consociate fund is liquid and in a form readily available to build up estate capital. Strongest support from liquid funds is given to the estates in the 100–249, and 1,000–2,499 size-classes; the significance of this is commented on later.

The size of the total net funds looks somewhat smaller if the mode of the co-efficients in each size-class is used as a measure and not the arithmetical mean; and the figures are more regular. Hardly any difference is displayed in the modes for the three size-classes within the range 100–1,000 acres; most frequently occurring net funds are in the region of half the value of the estate capital, and vary between a third and three-quarters of that value. The modes of the size-classes of the larger estates are also close together, but are half of the size of the others; on these extensive estates the most frequent form of consociate fund is no more than a quarter of the value of the estate capital.

The average percentage of consociate capital in total fortune is very similar for each size-class from 100–1,000 acres and approximates to 50 % ; the other 50 % of the fortune is estate capital ; the support co-efficient of these averages is therefore 1. For estates over 1,000 acres, the average percentage of consociate capital in total fortune in each size group is 39 %; the reciprocal 61 % is estate capital ; and the support co-efficient is 0·64.

When calculating the averages of support co-efficients and the average percentage of consociate funds in total fortune, two glaring anomalies in the figures were removed from the calculations where it was thought they would unduly bias the result. Thus, the figures for the estates from 1000–2499 acres give an average support co-efficient of 1·48 for the net total fund. The range that gives this average has a mode of 0·70. Among the figures is an estate with exceptionally high consociate funds; estate capital is covered 11·7 times. The other serious anomaly is a co-efficient of 29·7 as a measure of the support given by adventitious capital to one of the estates in the over-10,000 acres size class. These gross anomalies have been omitted and the figures adjusted to those given in the Table.

Where figures of adventitious capital are available the ratio between the funds and estate capital is expressed in Table V as average[1] co-efficients of support. For all size-classes these adventitious funds tend to give a twofold cover to estate capital. Representation in the size-classes is small. Looked at overall, the figures illustrate a tendency for the larger estates to be better supported by adventitious capital in frequency of occurrence but the smaller estates to have the advantage of larger funds.

Too much must not be asked of the averages of Table V. Differences between mode and mean point to a fair range of inconsistency. The averages suggest that an owner-occupier of a 200-acre farm might have £2 10s. tucked away in Stock Exchange investments, farm stock or some other employment, for every £1 in the market value of the land and buildings. The mode cautions us to be less sanguine. Its evidence suggests that while the £2 10s. is by no means improbable, the actual amount of external capital is likely to be nearer 10s. for every £1 in the market value of the estate.

The figures are of value as relative measurements and illustrate general tendencies. Small estates appear to be better provided for than larger estates. If the value of agricultural land per acre were to remain constant for all sizes of estate, the evidence points to the probability that the larger the estate the more thinly per acre will

[1]The averages do not take account of the estates that have no adventitious funds.

consociate capital be spread. In fact, the value of agricultural land per acre does not remain constant for all sizes of estate. Market values per acre tend to be less on the larger estates. It follows that the amount of consociate capital acre for acre is doubly likely to be less on larger estates than on smaller estates; consociate funds are lower £ for £ for value, and the number of £'s in the value of an acre is less. On the other hand, a large estate is more likely than a small estate to have a second line of reserve in the form of adventitious capital.

TABLE VI

ESTATE COMPETENCE AND CONSOCIATE CAPITAL

COMPETENCE CLASS	AVERAGE CO-EFFICIENT OF SUPPORT FROM CONSOCIATE CAPITAL		
	Gross total fund	Net total fund	Net liquid fund
100 %*	1·65	1·61	0·73
50 %* (+)	0·60	0·54	0·23
50 % (−)	0·64	0·61	0·51
Nil*	1·28	1·21	0·42

* Excluding one extreme anomaly in each competence class.

Competence and external funds

An estate unable to form capital from estate income must have consociate capital to support it, if it is to survive. Logically it could be supposed that the greater the degree of incompetence the stronger would be the support from consociate and other external capital.

An arrangement of the evidence confounds this presupposition. In Table VI the average co-efficients of support are worked out for estates arranged in competence classes. Contrary to expectation the wholly competent estates are far better supported than the partially competent and the incompetent by consociate funds, gross, net and liquid. The support given to the incompetent estates is much greater than the support behind the partially competent. In this respect the facts support the postulation. Only by the support of strong consociate and other external funds can an incompetent estate continually improve its fixed equipment and land. The marked disparity between the size of the funds supporting the wholly competent and the size of the funds behind the partially competent supports still further the supposition that the competence of the wholly competent is mainly hollow. The figures give the impression that the partially competent have transferred money from consociate funds to estate improvements to supplement finance from estate income, and that the competent estates have marked time. Hence they have today a greater demand than the partially competent for investment while boasting more substantial consociate funds.

Sources of external funds

So far attention has been mainly directed to the size of external funds. In distinguishing liquid funds from funds less readily available some indication has been given of the way in which the funds are built up. We must now look a little closer at this aspect of them and try to discover what sources contribute to them. Our investigation can be made in two ways: a direct analysis of the investment patterns of the external funds; and an analysis of the sources that have financed past improvements. Evidence from the finance of past improvements is not an index of the structure of existing funds, but is valuable testimony to the sources of finance that have supplied postwar agriculture with capital through the estate system.

Structure of consociate funds is shown in Table VII. Funds have been analysed and the elements of each expressed as percentages of the total. The Table gives the average figures for the size-classes.

Certain principles stand out clearly. Timber and farm stock are prominent sources. For the small estates timber investment is insignificant; but farm stock is of notable proportions. On the larger estates the reverse obtains. A broad reading of the figures suggests that the proportion of external funds employed in farming enterprise on smaller estates is put into silviculture on large estates. Correlation between size-classes and percentages is most regular; there is a continuous drop in farm stock investment as size increases; and a corresponding rise in the percentages of timber investment. Land investment other than the estate in question is fairly constant both for agricultural land and other real property, although a significant change in the pattern of figures occurs in the evidence for the largest estates of all. This is due to the definition of an estate. The largest estates generally have the most highly organised systems of management and what would on a smaller estate be classed as other agricultural land or other land, on the larger estates becomes part of a

TABLE VII

STRUCTURE OF CONSOCIATE CAPITAL

SIZE OF ESTATE (acres)	AVERAGE PERCENTAGE CONTRIBUTION TO CONSOCIATE FUNDS						
	Timber %	Farm stock %	Agricultural land %	Other land %	Stocks and shares %	Monetary funds %	Other sources %
100–249	1·5	32·1	3·1	12·4	27·9	5·8	17·2
250–499	1·7	35·6	4·5	8·1	32·2	4·5	13·4
500–999	3·8	33·1	8·1	5·3	31·4	1·8	16·5
1,000–2,499	22·2	9·8	4·7	18·4	35·7	0·8	8·4
2,500–9,999	18·5	5·0	12·9	19·3	34·9	—	9·4
10,000 +	44·2	6·3	—	6·0	30·4	1·7	11·4
Average all size classes	15·3	20·3	5·5	11·6	32·1	2·4	12·9

scattered unity.[1] The tendency to absorb detached parcels into the body of scattered estates is shadowed in the figures which compare the structure of consociate funds supporting scattered estates and the structure of the funds supporting compact estates; the percentage of other land in the consociate funds of the scattered estates is lower than the corresponding percentage in the funds supporting compact estates.[2]

A remarkable feature of the figures is the consistency in the percentages of investment in stocks and shares among all size-classes; the percentage for the largest estates is slightly less, as might be expected from the evidence of Table V, for the proportions of liquid funds. In general the evidence points to a third of the consociate funds of all sizes of estate being invested in Government stock and share equities. Relatively high percentages of monetary funds in the smaller size groups are congruous with the high percentage of capital in farm stock; the monetary funds are mainly cash deposits used in farming enterprise. Other contributions to the consociate funds are collected together in a class of miscellaneous items. A noteworthy feature of these percentages is the relatively high percentage of miscellaneous contributions to the funds of the smallest estates; the reason for this is life insurance. Many owners of these smallest estates have funds in life insurance which in themselves are not exceptionally large but their prominence is due to the relatively smaller total fortunes of the owners whose estates are in this class. Many miscellaneous contributions are investments made by estate owners in business enterprises other than farming. Mostly, the sources in this miscellaneous class are not liquid and are of little moment.

Analyses of the sources that have financed estate improvements in the past are given in Table VIII. There are certain differences in general character between these sources and the contributory sources of consociate funds. Income cannot be an ingredient of consociate capital; nor can consociate capital include Government grants. And borrowed money, *per se*, is not a logical item. Among the sources that have financed past improvements room must be made for contributions from income, Government grant and loans. Farm stock provides another point of difference. An owner farming his own land is not likely to sell farming stock to finance improvements to it unless the stock were surplus to requirements, in which event the transfer would be the rectification of a bad investment policy and not a calculated funding of improvements from wisely handled funds. Another difference is the possibility of financing improvements by selling portions of the estate; other land may contribute to consociate

[1]cf. p. 22 *ante.*   [2]cf. Table XVIII p. 140, p. 167 *post.*

TABLE VIII

PERCENTAGE CONTRIBUTIONS TO FINANCE OF PAST IMPROVEMENTS

AVERAGE PERCENTAGE CONTRIBUTION TO FINANCE OF PAST IMPROVEMENTS

SIZE OF ESTATE (acres)	Timber %	Estate land %	Other land %	Stocks and shares %	Grants %	Loans %	Income		Other sources %
							Rents %*	Other %	
100–249	—	1·8	—	16·8	6·6	0·2	18·3	51·6	4·7
250–499	1·8	3·3	0·5	9·7	5·8	4·0	4·4	63·9	6·6
500–999	3·0	3·6	—	8·8	6·6	13·4	13·1	48·9	2·6
1,000–2,500	12·7	35·5	7·4	15·6	4·2	—	20·5	4·1	—
Average all size classes	4·4	11·0	2·0	12·7	5·8	4·4	14·1	42·1	3·5

* The average percentages of this column are weighted to allow for unequal representation of owner-occupied and tenanted estates in the size-classes.

capital but the land of the estate itself is excluded by definition. Because of these differences in the nature of the contributory sources it is not possible to compare item by item the analyses of consociate capital and the sources of past improvement finance.

The figures show that the greatest contribution among the smaller estates came from income other than rental revenue. On the estates in the size groups 100–1,000 acres, 'other income' is largely farming profits, and the high percentage of contribution from this source corresponds with the high percentage of farm stock in the funds of consociate capital in these size classes. Unfortunately details of the finance of past improvements were not obtained from the extended survey and hence information is limited to estates from 100–2,500 acres. The evidence is sufficient, however, to show how the larger tenanted estates have had to rely on sales of estate land, timber and stocks and shares to finance improvement; contributions from rents vary little from the rental contributions made on the lesser acreages. Contributions from Government grants are fairly consistent but on average amount to no more than 5·8 % of the total expenditure. Rental contribution is remarkably consistent except for estates of 250–499 acres. In this size-class other income makes a preponderant contribution and rental revenue is of no consequence; the higher percentage of other income is due almost entirely to a greater contribution from farming profits. It is noticeable that among estates from 500–999 acres, where farming income is less significant and where size probably makes the sale of land and timber a limited source of supply, loans have played a relatively important role. In sum, farming income, sales of land and timber and the realisation of stocks and shares have provided the bulk of the improvement finance.

CHAPTER SIX

Investment Level

Provision and need

BRITISH post-war legislation subjects the landowner to what it terms the rules of good estate management. To honour the rules the landowner provides the land with fixed equipment necessary to enable an occupier to maintain efficient production. Perfect compliance means the provision of capital in fixed equipment exactly answering the agricultural production capacity of the estate; a state of affairs in which the level of investment of agricultural estate capital is at the optimum. Imperfect compliance means investment at a different level.

So far attention has been directed to the capacity of estate income to form capital, and to the support of external funds. Both capacity and support are means of provision. They are not concerned with what is provided of capital to meet a given demand. They show where the springs rise, but of the depth of the reservoir fed thereby they tell nothing. Yet the story needs to be told. We must look at the reservoir. We must consider the investment level, the extent to which actual provision of estate capital satisfies the demand for it.

Estate capital of an agricultural estate can be more than the land equipped for agriculture. It is comprehensive of all developed land whether used for agriculture or not. Measurement of the level of estate capital investment should be similarly comprehensive. It should take account of houses and cottages, or roads, stores, offices, buildings and equipment of every description whatever their purpose or use. While the comprehensiveness of estate capital must not be overlooked, the theme of this book is concerned with the manner in which estate capital finances agricultural needs. Agriculture lies in an estate cradle. The cradle may provide the needs of agriculture and none other, or it may have features of no consequence to the industry. We are interested solely in the investment level of estate capital directly employed in agriculture.[1]

Methods of measuring investment levels have already been described. Either monetary or physical standards can be used. In one

[1]The figures for the estates of the extended and previous surveys include a vestige of expenditure on past improvement of woodland.

respect, there is no difference between the two methods for monetary measurement stands upon prior physical estimates of need. The two methods differ in what each can achieve. Measurement of physical items is the only satisfactory way of gauging the absolute provision of estate capital in farm buildings and other fixed equipment; the absolute level of investment is the extent to which the sum of what has been provided meets what is required. Monetary measurements can at best only be relative. They take cognisance of the amount of capital recently formed and relate this to a monetary estimate of what needs to be formed. Monetary estimates of the extent of absolute provision of estate capital are impossible. Wants would have to be related either to the replacement cost of all equipment and land improvements, or to the market value of estate capital. Replacement cost is a false standard, for farmsteads are not replaced entire in the normal event. And at present the market value of fixed equipment cannot be distinguished from the market value of land and equipment combined.

Detailed physical measurements of capital equipment and land improvement take time; consequently physical measurements were made only on the central survey. Monetary measurements, however, were taken on all estates. Provision and need are presented as the ratio between the cost of capital formation since 1945 (adjusted to current prices) and the estimated cost of providing outstanding improvements.

Costs and the physical dimensions of existing equipment are facts. Deficiencies are matters of opinion. The estimates of deficiencies are based on the opinions of landowners or their professional advisors,[1] and thus reflect the problem of capital provision as the estates experience it. Standards differ. A well-informed highly skilled farmer inspired by a vision of the ultimate capacity of his holding, well-equipped with modern buildings and plant, will assess its needs on an entirely different plane from the viewpoint of the eternal peasant, whose unchanging world opens no window upon new horizons. High estimates may be the expression of a visionary, or the sombre cost of restoring derelict holdings to a semblance of respectability. All perception of potential improvement is born of vision to some degree. A farmer who would light all his buildings with electricity differs in outlook and awareness of need from one who is content to plod evermore beneath the guttering wick of a hurricane lantern even when electricity is available.

Physical deficiency can be presented in two ways. Two farms each wanting a Dutch barn are not on that account equally deficient in

[1]They are compared later with estimates given by tenants: cf. p. 165 *post, et seq.*

equipment. The missing items are the same, and the cost of their provision may be the same, but one farm may require a Dutch barn merely to complete a battery of four, while the second farm has no barn at all. In the second case deficiency is 100 %. The need for a companion barn to complete an ideal foursome in the other is a 25 % deficiency. Deficiency can thus be presented as a percentage deficiency. It would be misleading to make a simple quantum measurement of this kind without adjustment. A Dutch barn may be a novelty on the farm which had none, and yet compared with an open yard be of secondary importance to the farming economy of the place. A fourth barn on the other farm might be of third-rate importance. When measuring percentage deficiency each item on the farmstead has to be graded according to its consequence for efficient production. Deficiency percentage in items of first consequence must be weighted more heavily than deficiency percentage in a class of less consequence when computing a figure for general percentage deficiency. Another way of presenting physical deficiency measures the complement of fixed equipment and land improvement item by item and expresses deficiency numerically, as so many cottages, cow stalls, loose boxes, reclaimable acres and so on. Deficiency measured in this way is designated item deficiency and so distinguished from percentage deficiency.

Deficiency measurements from the central survey are given in Table IX. The figures express what is wanted of equipment and land improvement. No account is taken of restoration needs or of disrepair whose rectification requires capital expenditure. However, the cause of physical deficiency is not enquired into. Implement sheds or other buildings may be wanted because old buildings have collapsed. Gaps so created are counted among the physical deficiencies. Moreover, the method does not exclude the enlargement of buildings or the need to provide higher standards. Where standards are inadequate, the sub-standard installation is reckoned as a percentage contribution towards an ideal and the reciprocal percentage given as the measurement of percentage deficiency. A farmstead wholly devoid of T.T. accommodation but with perfectly sound cow houses capable of conversion is not regarded as 100 % deficient; the utility of the existing structures is regarded as a basic percentage and its reciprocal as the percentage deficiency. Water and electricity supplies, sanitation and other services incapable of itemised enumeration are judged directly as providing a percentage contribution towards a perfect standard. Perfection in water supply, for example, is defined as a piped supply from a water main and a cottage or farmhouse with well water piped to the premises is looked upon as 50 % deficient.

TABLE IX

PERCENTAGE DEFICIENCY AND ITEM DEFICIENCY
IN FIXED EQUIPMENT AND LAND IMPROVEMENT

SIZE OF ESTATE (acres)	PERCENTAGE DEFICIENCY					CO-EFFICIENTS OF ITEM DEFICIENCY								
	In general	According to graded consequence				Housing	Dairy stock accommodation	Yards and boxes	Barns and stores	Implement accommodation	Land improvement	Reclamation	Services	Average co-efficient
		First	Second	Third	Fourth									
100–249	7·06	4·87	11·12	6·04	6·74	16	11	41	44	30	58	2	67	47
250–499	7·45	6·64	8·79	7·58	4·93	41	21	58	73	33	126	13	271	96
500–999	6·47	5·45	7·00	7·52	6·18	24	27	68	62	68	86	24	225	92
1,000–2,500	7·00	7·55	7·27	6·46	4·09	33*	33*	128*	128*	33*	77*	14*	166*	76*
Average all estates	7·00	5·78	8·86	7·01	5·83	29*	22*	82*	85*	44*	96*	14*	241*	93*

* Weighted average to allow for a relatively small number of estates in the size-class 1,000–2,500 acres.

Percentage deficiency

The percentage deficiencies are surprisingly modest. Over the full range of the estates of the central survey, the percentage deficiency for housing, farm buildings and land improvement averages 7·00 %. Average percentages in different size-classes deviate little from this general figure. Within the narrow limits of difference, the larger estates are better equipped than the smaller. Estates from 250–499 acres have the greatest need with an overall average deficiency of 7·45 %. Not a few estate owners consider their properties to be fully equipped. Here and there are exceptions, but on no estate is the general percentage deficiency more than 40 %. Of the 167 estates, three have percentage deficiencies between 30 % and 40 % and five, deficiencies between 20 % and 30 %, and every one of these abnormally deficient estates is in the smaller size-classes.

The need to classify equipment and land improvement according to its consequence for efficient production has been mentioned. Table IX arranges the evidence for percentage deficiency in four classes of graded consequence; deficiency in the first class is of graver consequence that deficiency in the second, and so on. Greatest deficiency is found in equipment of secondary consequence and least deficiency in the primary class. This overall pattern is not paralleled among the size-classes. Estates of 100–249 acres distinguish themselves by being abnormally deficient in equipment of secondary importance. Estates above 500 acres and below 1,000 acres are the best equipped. Their worst deficiency is in equipment of third-rate consequence and is not likely seriously to impede farming, although if it were made good production and efficiency would be enhanced. Greatest fluctuation occurs in the deficiency figures for items of least consequence, and the most stable figures are those for items of third consequence. In sum, the evidence indicates a strong tendency to give first consideration to the provision of items of prime consequence to farming needs.

Item deficiency

We cannot say from the figures for percentage deficiency what kind of equipment is deficient more than another kind; an estate with a 10 % deficiency may lack cottages and another estate with a similar deficiency may be in need of loose boxes. Table IX by means of co-efficients,[1] shows the frequency of deficiency in specific items of equipment and land improvement. The items are presented under

[1]The value of the co-efficients is calculated from the formula $100(s/e - 1)$,
 where s = number of estates in sample,
  e = number of estates in sample supplied with the particular item.

eight heads. Housing is inclusive and covers farmhouses and cottages. Dairy Stock Accommodation is comprehensive of all buildings essential to dairy farming. Piggeries are included in the term Yards and Boxes. Barns and Stores is comprehensive of Dutch barns. Implement Accommodation covers implement sheds, fuel stores and workshops. Land Improvement denotes a wide range of improvements inclusive of roads, tile drainage and field water supply. Reclamation is another extensive term and is used of scrub and bracken clearing, and the reclamation of land from forest, fen and woodland. Services is comprehensive of water supplies, electricity installations, sanitation and like attributes of good living standards in farmhouse and cottage.

Throughout the estates at large, the most frequently occurring deficiency is sanitation, piped water supply, electricity and other services to farmhouses and cottages. Land improvement is the next most seriously deficient item; although there is little to choose between it and deficiency in barns, yards and boxes. At the other end of the scale is reclaimable land, dairy stock accommodation and housing. It is significant that deficiency in housing is comparatively slight, while services to cottages and farmhouses is the most deficient item of all. Deficiency in dairy stock accommodation is influenced by the naturally low requirements of farms other than pasture farms and mixed farms. Pasture and mixed farms occupy approximately three-fifths of the total number; if they are considered alone, the co-efficient for all size-classes moves from 22 to 32.

Item deficiency is not uniform among the size-classes. It agrees with the evidence for percentage deficiency in presenting the estates from 250–449 acres as the most needy. A notable feature of the estates in this size-class is the relatively low standard of housing. Among the other estates, abnormally frequent deficiencies in services are counterpoised by comparatively infrequent deficiencies in housing. The somewhat prominent deficiency in yards, boxes and stores on the largest estates is in keeping with their size. Lack of ten boxes on an extensive estate could be no more than a 10% deficiency; on a smaller estate a similar want could be a 50 % deficiency. The co-efficients of item deficiency measure the frequency of wants occurring in the sample, and the chances of a 10 % deficiency occurring are far greater than the chances of a 50 % want. There is no defect in the method of measurement. The figures simply mean that the very nature of the larger estates makes it more probable that they will experience more frequently than the smaller estates deficiencies of this kind.

The figures of item deficiency contradict the evidence of percentage deficiency in the tale they tell of estates from 500–999 acres. According to the item deficiency measurements, these estates follow the starved 250–499 acre estates, and yet the measurements of percentage deficiency show them to be the least deficient. The explanation lies in the deficiency of services on these estates. Item deficiency magnifies this lack because its method measures the frequency of occurrence and the evidence shows that lack of services is by far the most frequent deficiency on these estates. Measured as a percentage deficiency of the total quantity of equipment, lack of services would never contribute impressive figures. Hence these estates have a 6·47 % deficiency and a 92 co-efficient of item deficiency. Otherwise the verdict of the evidence for item deficiency confirms the showing of the percentage deficiency figures, that the provision of equipment and land improvement on the estates of 500–999 acres is in general at a high level.

Monetary measurement

Monetary measurements of the level of investment have a limited use. We cannot add the cost of providing necessary fixed equipment and other items of estate capital to the value of what now exists and reach a sum expressive of the complete estate capital investment: a wholeness of which the cost of providing what is now lacking can be expressed as a percentage deficiency. The most we can do is to go back a few years, notice what capital has been formed, calculate what the formation would cost today, and add this to an estimate of the cost of meeting present wants. The sum of these two figures can be taken as a monetary measurement of the demand for capital over the particular period. Present cost of past provision as a percentage of the sum of the two figures gives a reasonable monetary measurement of the level of present investment.

Measurements after this manner have been made on all the estates in the main sample. The results are given in Table X. The period from 1945 to the date of the survey was taken as a basis for the calculations. It varies slightly from estate to estate, but with very few exceptions it is a period of ten years. The average level of investment is 55·2 %. Should the past rate of formation continue and the amount outstanding represent a true bill of wants and no further needs arise, the present demand for capital would be met in a little under ten years. Past provision over the period at current prices averages £15 14s. per acre and the average estimated outstanding need is £10 2s. per acre.

We must not associate the cost of providing outstanding improvements and the physical percentage deficiency. An average physical deficiency of 7 % and an average outstanding improvements cost of

6

£10 2s. do not point to a total value of capital in fixed equipment of
£140 per acre.[1] What is significant and noteworthy is the relationship
between the figures for physical deficiency and the rate of capital
formation. On the smallest estates, 100–249 acres, the rate of capital
formation was above the average for all sizes. Over the ten-year period
70·1 % of the total estimated need has been provided. Other estates
have not done so well. The figures for item deficiency agree with this
verdict, but the measurements of percentage deficiencies contradict it;
a 70 % supply over the past ten years leaves the estates 7·06 % short

TABLE X

PERCENTAGE OF TOTAL REQUIREMENT
PROVIDED BY PAST IMPROVEMENT

Size of Estate (acres)	Cost of past improvements per acre (at current prices) £	Cost of outstanding improvements per acre £	Past improvements as percentage of total costs %
100– 249	38·1	16·2	70·1
250– 499	22·5	15·6	59·0
500– 999	17·6	11·3	60·8
1,000–2,499	7·9	7·5	51·2
2,500–9,999	2·3	3·1	42·5
10,000+	6·3	6·9	47·7
Averages	15·7	10·1	55·2

of physical requirements. On estates between 500–999 acres the
average provision has been 60·8 % of total need, but the percentage
deficiency is only 6·47 %. Estates of 250–499 acres have provided on
average 59·0 % of their requirements and have a 7·45 % deficiency.
Estates above 1,000 acres and below 2,500 acres have achieved an
investment of 51·2 % of total need but display a percentage deficiency
of 7·0 %

We have seen that incongruity between the figures for percentage
deficiency and the figures for item deficiency is due to differences in
type of equipment. Small frequently occurring wants will give a

[1] i.e. 100/7 × £10·1.

high item deficiency but a low percentage deficiency. Incongruity between the monetary measurements of deficiency and the physical measurements arises because the most important items of equipment or those most frequently missing are not necessarily the most costly to provide.

The smallest estates of all may be used as an example. According to the figures for percentage deficiency they are among the most needy, and yet item for item they are the best off, a fact borne out by the monetary measurements, which show the achievement of these small estates as the highest. Table IX shows that want of land improvement, next to services, is the most frequent need among them. Land improvement compared with re-equipping a farmstead is not costly in the normal event but it can contribute much to general farming economy. Hence lack of land improvement would tend to give a relatively high figure for item deficiency and relatively low figures for percentage deficiency and the cost of outstanding improvements.

Other incongruities reveal differences in the standard of provision. Estates of 250–499 acres are the worse off on all counts among the estates of less than 1,000 acres, and yet the cost of providing what improvements are needed is lower than the cost of providing the needs of the well-equipped smaller estates. It is reasonable to conclude that the standard of equipment and land improvement, taken over all, is higher on the smaller estates.

The general impression given by the figures of Table X is that the smaller the estate the more rapid the pace of capital formation. At past rates the smallest estates, 100–249 acres, could fully meet their outstanding need in another six to seven years, while the larger properties would require ten to fifteen years. The correlation between size of estate and rate of investment is in fact somewhat illusory. The influence behind the sequence of percentages in Table X is tenure pattern and not size. The low achievement of the larger estates is due to the preponderance of tenanted estates among them.[1]

Transposition

A rise in the level of investment, either physical or monetary, does not invariably increase *pro tanto* the net value of the estate capital. Disparity may be due to the relationship between cost and value—an expenditure of £5,000 on new equipment that increases capital value by only £2,000. Or the difference may arise from transposition of capital resources. This happens when existing estate capital is mortgaged and the loan invested in new fixed equipment and land

[1] cf. p. 150 *ante*.

improvements. Part of the unencumbered estate capital in land and buildings is virtually transposed as newly formed capital in equipment and land improvement. Should the cost of the new equipment and improvements exactly correspond to the increase in capital value resulting from them, the net value of the estate capital would not be altered; the increase in value consequent upon the investment is discounted by the decrease in value occasioned by the mortgage.

Transposing capital resources is infrequently used in agricultural estate finance. Among the rented estates of the main sample only 30 % have mortgaged their title deeds. Only three have a greater debt than the traditional 66 % of market value, and only four are mortgaged above 50 % of market value. Frequency and extent of mortgage vary among the size-classes. Estates over 10,000 acres are the most frequently mortgaged. The 250–499 acre class are the most indifferent. Extent of encumbrance does not follow suit. The highest average, 31·6 %, is characteristic of the 2,500–9,999 acre size-class, and the lowest average, 15·1 %, belongs to the largest estates.

Reluctance to transpose estate capital is understandable. Ever present is the risk of capital loss: decrease in value consequent upon mortgage may not be matched by a corresponding increase in value. And mortgaged land to many is a *pis aller*, only to be contemplated when all else fails.

Pledging unencumbered estate capital as security for improvement loans would probably be more popular if income from agricultural estates were stronger, and capable of redeeming the land of mortgage within a reasonable time. Formation of estate capital has been envisaged as the accumulation over a ten-years period of a money fund from income and the investment of the fund in equipment and land improvement. Formation of capital by the reverse process of borrowing money to finance the provision of new equipment, and redeeming the loan from income was purposely not considered. Of the two policies it is the more practical. Consideration of it was postponed until now because its essential principle is a transposition of estate resources and is best considered in the same context as investment levels.

The figures portraying the competence of tenanted estates to form capital from estate income reveal a high proportion of estates quite incompetent of any process of formation. Partial competence depends upon how the task of formation is envisaged. If the yearly burden of redeeming an improvement loan were lighter than the burden of capital formation over the ten-years period, formation by the reversed process would lead to greater competence. But if in fact the reversed process meant a lighter task, the impotence of the incompetent estates would not change; they have no income and can no more subscribe to mortgage redemption than they can to a capital reserve fund. Rather than investigate the competence of existing incomes to effect mortgage redemption it seems wiser to consider the extent to which rental revenues must expand to enable the estate incomes to meet a yearly redemption charge.

Generous terms for long-period loans are offered by the Agricultural Mortgage Corporation. The Corporation advances loans repayable by half-yearly instalments over a period determined by the type of work financed; periods vary from ten to forty years. Title deeds are not always lodged with the Corporation as security, but a yearly rent-charge covering interest and repayment is created in the land. Existing encumbrances on the land nevertheless govern the extent of an advance as with all prudent lending from whatever financial source.

The infrequency and extent of mortgages on the estates of the survey have been mentioned. Table XI shows the incidence of the loans as percentages of estate capital. The figures spread the burden of the burdened over the unencumbered, and indicate the general load of indebtedness and its average incidence among estates of different size. Average indebtedness is only 6·1 % of estate capital. Estates from 250–499 acres whose investment level is lowest are the least indebted. And estates from 500–1,000 acres whose level of investment is high are the most indebted. The burden on each estate determines its capacity to borrow. Nevertheless, these figures of overall indebtedness and the details of encumbrances opposite given show clearly a substantial security margin.

If the entire cost of providing outstanding improvements were met by mortgage loans, and the loans so raised were added to the existing encumbrances, the average total indebtedness would not amount to more than 18·1 % of estate capital. There is very little variance in the averages of total indebtedness for the different size-classes. It is interesting to note that the regular inverse ratio of cost per acre and estate size so patent in the figures of Table X is not repeated when these costs are expressed as percentages of capital value. The highest percentage is suffered by estates from 500–999 acres, although the cost of outstanding improvements per acre is much lower on these estates than on the smaller estates where the percentage figures are lower. The outstanding improvements are in this sense a greater burden on these estates than on the others. Moreover they have the least security margin to offer after existing encumbrances are added to the costs of providing outstanding improvements.

The yearly charge depends upon the period of redemption and the rate of interest. Before the recent exceptional rise in the Bank

TABLE XI

RENTAL INCREASE REQUIRED TO MEET IMPROVEMENT LOANS

| Size class (acres) | Percentage of estate capital | | | Annual improvement loan repayment (per acre) £ | Rental revenue (per acre) £ | Rental increase to meet loan repayment % |
	(a) Current mortgages %	(b) Outstanding improvements %	(c) Total %			
100–249	7·9	12·0	19·9	0·74	2·3	32·2
250–499	2·8	14·4	17·2	0·64	2·2	29·1
500–999	8·1	15·2	23·3	0·58	2·1	31·1
1,000–2,499	6·9	12·2	19·1	0·40	1·9	21·1
2,500–9,999	5·6	7·0	12·6	0·17	1·7	10·0
10,000+	5·5	11·2	16·7	0·07	0·8	8·8
Average all size classes	6·1	12·0	18·1	0·43	1·8	22·1

Rate, the Agricultural Mortgage Corporation were asking $4\frac{1}{2}$ % interest on loans. At this rate, yearly interest and repayment over a period of thirty years[1] amounts to £6 2s. 2d. per £100 of loan. The costs of meeting interest and repayment instalments on loans sufficient to finance the provision of outstanding improvements on the tenanted estates are given on an acreage basis in Table XI. As would be expected the figures move in regular inverse ratio to the size of estate.

Average costs of interest and repayment are related to the rental revenues to show the percentage increment required to meet them. Rental revenues themselves also move in inverse ratio to estate size. But they move at a different pace. Hence a much higher rental increment is necessary on the smaller estates than on the larger. On the smallest estates the increase required is in the neighbourhood of 33%, while on the largest estates a 10 % increment or less would suffice. The average increment required is 22 %. The figures presuppose the additional rent to be relieved of income tax and surtax and wholly available for mortgage repayment and interest.

These percentages can be reduced to cash terms. On the estates 100–1,000 acres, a rental increase from 12s. to 15s. per acre would suffice over thirty years to redeem a mortgage sufficient to finance the provision of present outstanding improvements. On the larger estates the rental increment required ranges between 2s. to 8s. per acre. Again, these figures only hold true in so far as the enhanced income is tax free. Moreover they suppose an interest rate of $4\frac{1}{2}$ %. At current borrowing rates[2] the rental increments would have to be on average 26 % higher than current levels before they were competent to meet the mortgage repayments and interest. And if the redemption period were shorter than thirty years, rental increments would have to be correspondingly greater.

[1] A period of thirty years is the second longest of the four alternative periods of loan, and provides a reasonable basis for the present purpose.
[2] Christmas 1956.

CHAPTER SEVEN

Restraints

RICH men in tatters incite curiosity. We want to know what happens to their money. Agricultural estates can do the same. Among the properties of the surveys are estates wanting improvement and well endowed with capital funds to pay for it. Money to match the need is not used to dispatch the need. On the face of it, a logical economic process is restrained. Furthermore, some estates have incompetent incomes, but no attempt is made to better their power of capital formation. Their owners seem inert. What restrains them?

Motives, especially financial ones, are usually hidden from public ken. Nevertheless, many estate owners whose lands were surveyed spoke freely of the incentives that hold them to the land, and of the restraints that check the flow of capital to estate improvements, and hinder the advance of estate incomes. A variety of opinion was expressed. One man would echo another man's thought in description and phrase peculiar to himself, but common themes ran through the miscellany of comment.

However a particular restraint may be explained, whether it be a sole motive or an accomplice of mixed motives, it will either be a restraint of law, beyond the power of the restrained to oppose, or a restraint of free choice, a preferred alternative action. Ownership is the creation of law, and restraints in the use of property may be the direct or indirect prohibitions of positive law. During the late war period and for some time afterwards, in Britain, the formation of estate capital in improvements and new buildings was directly controlled by Government licence. An illustration of indirect restraint through positive law, is seen in the law which gives security of tenure, in an agricultural holding so unprofitable that the meanness of its livelihood robs the tenant of all incentive to co-operate with a landlord willing to improve the land.

Both economic and moral forces influence free choice. An estate owner free to employ his wealth in the formation of estate capital will not do so if economic expediency or the whisper of a tender conscience restrain his action. What I would, and could not; must be distinguished from, What I could and would not.

RESTRAINTS ON INVESTMENT OF EXTERNAL FUNDS

Better alternatives

Landowners like everyone must have money to live on. If their estates bring them little or no monetary reward, who is to blame them if they put such external resources as they have into more remunerative investments? The reason why an external fund is not used to improve an estate may lie no deeper than the homely problem of making ends meet: the estate owner cannot afford to improve the estate. To do so will deprive him of a necessary means of livelihood, when nothing is earned from the investment of capital in the improvement of his agricultural land.

How far the lure of a better investment will restrain the employment of capital funds in agricultural improvement will depend upon the standard of living of the estate owner and the earnings of the alternative investment. The estate owner's attitude to landownership will also influence his decision. One who regards his agricultural estate strictly as an investment will weigh its earnings against the yield of possible alternatives. An attractive line in equities can temporarily, perhaps permanently, deflect a capital fund away from investment in agricultural estate. It must be borne in mind that we are considering estate capital. Estate enterprises on the estate itself are among possible alternative investments. Instead of putting money into buildings and land improvement, the estate owner uses his wealth to finance farming, or forestry, or quarrying. Timber conversion, petrol stations, housing development, a great variety of enterprises suggest themselves to resourceful owners of resourceful estates. Of the many alternative estate enterprises, farming is the most frequent cause of deflection of funds. Landowners are taking land in hand to farm it when tenancies terminate because reletting will lock capital away in an unremunerative reversion over which landowners feel they have lost all control of management.

The pull of an alternative investment, especially the development of a farming enterprise, is not invariably stronger than the attraction of investment in agricultural improvements. Fair rates of interest and amortisation allowance can alter the prospect. And for those who can win to it, there is always the harvest of hidden fruit in the garden of tax concessions. When all is considered, an agricultural estate looked upon as an investment and competing for external funds with alternative investments will not attract capital for improvement with the ease of an estate whose character is less emphatically the character of an investment.

Spreading the risk

An estate owner may invest capital funds away from the estate not because alternative investments are more remunerative. His motive may be to spread the risks of failure. However much he may love the land, he is not prepared to commit his wealth entirely to its bosom. His savings are given into the keeping of many hands and this limits what he can spare for the estate.

Rate of capital formation

Capital transferred to agricultural improvements is liable to drop immediately in value owing to the paradoxical state of the property market in Britain—the cost of erecting buildings and other fixed equipment can be far greater than the combined market value of land and buildings when erected. Because of this, estate owners are wary of investing entire capital funds in land improvement. An owner willing to forego income to improve his estate will not surrender his capital also. In these circumstances capital for improvement will have to be formed from income; either from the income of the estate solely or from that income and income from external funds. If the cost of outstanding estate improvement at the beginning of a year is greater than the income expendable on improvements in that year, the paradox will ensue of an adequate capital fund not being employed to finance outstanding improvement. Provided the accumulation of income over the long term is greater than the initial cost of improvement and the cost of making good depreciation, the estate will make steady progress towards full improvement. The rate of investment will depend upon the strength of the total income to form capital year by year.

Within an inflationary economy the process of capital formation from income slows up in time, unless changes in income keep pace with rises in building prices and other costs of improvement: a most unlikely contingency in Britain today unless rental revenues change character for the better. Taxation aggravates the problem and retards the process of capital formation. The British tax system attempts to relate the actual income of estates to taxable income by allowing the estate owner a deduction from the gross assessment of income in respect of repair and maintenance costs. The deduction is not the very costs incurred in the year of assessment. It is an average figure, the average cost over the previous five years. This maintenance claim, as it is called, supposes that excessive expenditure one year will be offset by low expenditure another. In days of continuous inflation this is not so. Costs of maintenance rise year by year, and the maintenance claim never catches up.[1] Consequently an owner has to pay income tax on an income he never receives, a refinement of torture especially irksome to estate owners struggling to finance capital improvement from income.

Unwilling tenants

An estate owner with let farms cannot improve the land and its capital equipment without the concurrence of his tenants, for he has no right of entry upon the land.[2] Good farms can have bad tenants. A tenant of a potentially productive holding may not be inclined to improve the land and better his lot. Fault is not with the farm but with the farmer. On the contrary, an inherently poor holding can cloud a man's vision and crush his hope. Whatever effort is put into its husbandry the land can never earn an income capable of maintaining the farmstead. Tenants of such places do not welcome modernisation and other improvements, if they mean interest payments on the cost, but a landlord is likely to help a tenant in this plight by making improvements free of interest, before helping the indifferent and the lazy. Not all landlords can afford to improve holdings and ask no reward, save the satisfaction of seeing the land well preserved. Some who can afford to do so and for their own part wish to do so, refrain lest they should embarrass neighbouring landowners who cannot afford to be so liberal; their generous improvements would make discontents of a neighbours' tenants.

For the benefit of agriculture the fixed equipment of these holdings needs to be adjusted to the farming capacity of the land. The ratio of fixed equipment to land area should be reduced, boundaries altered and farmsteads demolished. Landowners seeing this and willing to spend their fortune to achieve it, cannot act because rigid security of tenure binds a hopeless tenantry upon the land. To modernise the superfluity of steadings and houses is to send good money after bad. It is better to leave external funds where they are.

Management restraints

Security of tenure can petrify an estate layout set in uneconomic holdings. The landowner's impasse is sad but not altogether unreasonable. But when security of tenure protects indifferent and unimaginative tenants so that productivity is paralysed and estate improvement frustrated the case becomes unanswerable. On its face

[1]cf. *Estate Incomes* (Department of Estate Management, University of Cambridge, 1955).

[2]Unless the tenancy agreement or lease reserves to him a right of entry for this purpose.

the law is intolerant of the bad farmer; it provides the State with power of ejection[1] and lightens its grip on the landlord's arm.[2] But practice makes pretence of its precepts. Too often the bad tenant is cosseted by administrators of the law who have power to eject him and uphold a landlord wishing to terminate the tenancy.

Landowners are naturally disinclined to invest capital where bad farmers are secured in tenancies by State protection. This is not the only manner in which the strict security of tenure deprives agriculture of estate capital. Security of tenure virtually vests a life interest in the tenant of an agricultural holding in England and Wales, and an inheritable proprietorship in the tenant of a Scottish holding. The estate owner loses his sense of responsibility for the management of his estate, and is provoked to seek ways and means of regaining control of it.

Landowners who want to see their farms let to good tenant farmers are loath to offer them for hire when in the rare event they obtain possession. A farm relet means land lost to the control of its owner. Land is therefore taken in hand. This shortens the supply of farms to let and diverts capital from let land needing improvement. Instead of improving the let farms a landowner husbands his capital resources to buy farm stock for his farming enterprise. On one of the estates surveyed, it is very significant that the amount of capital recently put into farm stock (some £55,000) exactly corresponds to what the agent estimates should be spent on the general improvement of the agricultural lands of the estate.

An estate owner with an irregular and awkwardly shaped property in full control of his estate could adjust the boundaries of his domain by terminating tenancies, exchanging farms through the property market and reletting the land. Without freedom of management the process is much slower and can be detrimental to the land. The landowner marks on a map or determines in another way the line of his ideal boundary. Farms on the thither side of it he will sell away; farms on the hither side he will retain. The process may be very prolonged. Farms with vacant possession tend to be more valuable than let farms. Markets for let farms are slack. The landowner will not be prepared to sell a let farm at a relatively low price and buy a substitute with possession at double or treble the figure. He may be fortunate and exchange let land for let land; it is unlikely. So he must bide with patience until he can offer his own farms with vacant possession. In the meantime, and it may be a very long meantime, the improvement policy of the estate concentrates attention upon the hither farms, to the detriment of those marked off for sale.

[1]cf. Agriculture Act 1947.
[2]cf. Agricultural Holdings Act 1948, Section 24 (1) (c).

Estate duty

Curtailed powers of management are not alone among the irritants
that harass the landowner and dam the flow of capital to the land.
Death duties are if anything more deleterious. Generations back,
wealthy landowners were inspired by the prospect of estates handed
down to posterity, immaculate and supported by endowments
sufficient to carry into effect a planned future. Today landowners
well able to do as their forefathers did turn their fortunes to other
ends. The threat of an annihilating estate duty casts a sombre
shadow over the future. In its shade vision turns to despair. What
is the point of saving and planning and building for posterity? The
next heir, let alone succeeding descendants, will only get a fraction
of what now is.

To think of the long future and provide for it seems futile. Yet
practical steps are taken to mitigate the effects of estate duty. These
in themselves can rob the land of capital before its time. Attempts
are made to build up monetary funds from income to meet the long-
dreaded estate duty. Life insurance is a frequent form of this saving.
However the saving is done, it reduces that income which could
be used for capital improvement. Another form of saving diverts
income and capital funds from agriculture to develop silviculture,
on the ground that the law gives concessions from estate duty to
timber which are more attractive than the concessions it allows
agricultural land.

On some estates the threat of estate duty prompts the owner to
take land in hand. Farms offered for sale with possession are more
readily marketable and possession is an advantage if sales have to
be made to meet estate duty. In the meantime the farms have to be
stocked and funds are drawn away from the formation of estate
capital.

Settled estates and other estates owned by trustees can suffer from
similar restraints upon the expenditure of funds. As farms come in
hand to the trustees, they are let to the main beneficiary in possession.
The land becomes subject to a tenancy, and on that account is likely
to be of less value for probate than land with vacant possession. In
fact the farms are no less marketable because of the tenancy. The
tenant for life, or life renter, or the personal representatives at death,
who hold the contractual tenancy from the trustees will surrender
it in their own interests and offer possession to a prospective purchaser of the freehold. The estate suffers deprivation of capital
because the main beneficiary uses adventitious funds to stock the
land he hires instead of making the funds available as loans to the
trustees for the betterment of the estate as a whole. Moreover, since

the land let to the beneficiary is held ready for sacrifice, a ransom to redeem the land of estate duty, it is likely to be preferred for capital expenditure before other lands of the estate; and this unequal sharing of external funds can unduly starve of capital the ill-favoured portions of the estate.

An estate in trust supported by an external fund held in the same trust may suffer deprivation from the threat of estate duty. When mortgages have to be raised the trustees are tempted to pledge the external fund as security rather than the agricultural land; to pledge the agricultural land reduces the proportion, in the total fortune, of property that attracts a 45 % estate duty concession. Swinging a mortgage debt on to the consociate fund can cripple its effectiveness and dam the flow of liquid capital to the estate. Improvement programmes suffer in a way they would not do, if the fund had remained unencumbered and the loan were raised on the security of the land.

This temptation besets all owners of estates supported by consociate funds; trustees are no exception. And there are other temptations like unto it. Because consociate funds do not attract the estate duty concession of the agricultural land they support, owners, trustees among them, are sorely pressed when age advances the threat of estate duty to invest the fund in other agricultural land. When this is done the support which the fund should give to the original estate is temporarily withdrawn. There is no point in pouring the fund out in a spate of premature works on the original estate. Much of the expenditure would be redundant, and once the fund was totally sunk in the original estate it could not be resurrected at a later day without partitioning the estate.

Adventitious funds that in the natural course of events would be used to support an estate company are denied it because of the baneful threat of estate duty. An estate owner who transfers his estate to an estate company is not encouraged to supply the company with funds from his personal fortune in exchange for debentures or preference shares or other holding in the company yielding a reasonable return. At death the erstwhile owner who does so becomes liable for estate duty on the value of a proportion of the assets of the company. The proportion is not calculated on a capital basis, according to the ratio between the capital supplied from the adventitious fund and the value of the total capital assets. The calculation is made according to the value of the yearly benefit received and the proportion it bears to the total income of the company.[1] An estate owner who after transfer takes preference shares will be liable for duty on that portion of the capital assets of the company that bears

[1]Finance Act 1940, Section 46.

the same ratio to the total assets as the income from the preference shares bears to the total income of the company. When the income from an agricultural estate is low, as so frequently it is, the proportion of total assets attracting estate duty may be out of all comparison with the proportion of the sum subscribed from the adventitious fund to purchase the preference shares. This inequitable rule is depriving estate companies of the support of the personal fortunes of erstwhile owners who created the companies and assigned their estates to them.

Tax rebate

Estate companies were popular prior to 1940. By surrendering his title to a corporation an estate owner could save his land from death duty. The estate owner became a shareholder and death duties were levied on his share capital. The value of shares in a family company is their worth to a specified range of possible purchasers and is usually much lower than the realisation value of the company's assets they represent. So by transferring his estate to a company the estate owner reduced his liability for death duties and freed the land entirely. In 1940 the dark shadow of estate duty lengthened and extinguished this ray of hope. The Finance Act of that year[1] introduced the inequitable principle just mentioned, of assessing liability to estate duty according to the proportion of yearly benefit to income, and went further: it required that the value of shares in a private company, in certain circumstances, should for death-duty purposes be ascertained according to the market value of the assets they represent, and not their exchange value. Land transferred to a company lost its advantage; an estate owner who retains shares pays estate duty on the market value of the land they represent. What is more, he pays in full, for the property that passes at death is shares and not agricultural land with its special estate-duty concession.

Many estate companies formed before 1940 have been wound up. Those that remain encumber the land. They deprive it of capital, and the erstwhile owner of tax concession. It happens this way: a past owner whose income is subject to a high surtax cannot gain surtax rebate by improving agricultural land because he no longer owns it; the company is short of capital and has nothing to spare for improvement; an injection of fresh capital from the personal fortune of the past owner will not gain surtax rebate and will probably magnify estate-duty liability, for the reasons explained above. This predicament is not peculiar to estate companies formed prior to 1940 to mitigate the impact of estate duty. Any estate company that has

[1]Section 55.

insufficient consociate capital will be in the same plight if he who formed it is a man of large private fortune.

All estate companies with insufficient consociate funds are liable to suffer in another way. Not only is the previous estate owner prevented from gaining tax rebate on agricultural improvements, but the wretched company cannot receive a full income tax rebate because the company's income is too exiguous to contain the maintenance and improvement expenditure; to the extent of the margin of excess the tax rebate is lost. Where this is so, expenditure on improvements is often curtailed to bring potential tax rebate into line with the actual tax paid.

Restraint in this form is not peculiar to estate companies. It hovers over all lands where the owner is liable for income tax and surtax. Whenever tax rebate on capital expenditure is the prime inducement to investment in agricultural improvements expenditure on improvements is trimmed so that the amount of tax rebate earned does not exceed the amount of tax paid. The estate owner expends his capital fund in agricultural improvements up to the point where tax is recoverable, and no further. Location of the point depends on the earning capacity of the capital fund and of the estate. The higher the ratio of income to capital the greater will be the amount of capital the owner can afford to transfer.

On some estates the restraint is made more severe by limiting improvement expenditure to an amount that will earn tax rebate commensurable with the actual tax paid on the estate income. Setting off improvement expenditure against other income is an advantage deliberately thrown away.

Tax rebate can influence the expenditure of external funds in another way. Wherever an estate income, enhanced though it may be by the beneficent effect of capital improvements, is insufficient to take the yearly offset of improvement expenditure and reap a full tax rebate, the fund of consociate capital must be kept intact to provide the necessary income.

Title to funds

A tenant for life in possession of an estate is not encouraged to spend free capital, the adventitious fund, on the improvement of the estate. Similar discouragement besets the life renter in Scotland. When a life tenant, or his counterpart in Scotland, improves the trust estate there are no means of separating the capital so invested from the legal estate of freehold—in Scotland the heritable estate. Capital improvements pass to the trustees. Nothing analogous to tenant-right between a landlord and tenant of an agricultural, contractual tenancy secures rights of compensation in the improvements in favour of the tenant for life or life renter. A tenant for life may loan free monies to the trustees; but this is another matter. Failure to secure a personal interest in improvements financed from free capital can deter beneficiaries from improving the trust estate by the use of adventitious funds.

Estates in Scotland where the beneficiary in possession holds an alimentary life rent suffer exceptionally. Free capital invested in the heritable estate becomes part of the heritage; and over the heritage the alimentary life renter has no right of disposition. He cannot even alienate his life interest in the estate to another. Investing capital in the heritable estate means for the life renter binding his capital in fetters that have probably exasperated his family for a generation or more. Free capital is best kept free.

Hidden charges

A consociate fund can be a hollow elm, much weaker than it looks. If it is pledged to secure a mortgage or other loan, its weakness is patent, open to the world. But there can be hidden charges. These weaken the fund and are the reason why it is not employed more liberally in the improvement of the estate. In the hands of trustees a consociate fund frequently carries the burden of finding capital portions from its substance for beneficiaries of the trust. Payment is usually contingent upon a named event, and the fund must be kept sufficiently intact to meet the obligation when the occasion requires it. A peculiarly subtle hidden charge is an annuity out of trust income. Capital invested in the improvement of the agricultural estate may be capable of earning enough to maintain the trust income and pay the annuity, but the trustees deem it unwise to make the investment because of the threat of estate duty. At the death of the annuitant estate duty is levyable on that part of the trust property that bears the same ratio to the total trust property that the annuity bears to the total yearly income of the trust. If the consociate fund has been transferred in part to estate improvements so that the estate duty at the death of the annuitant is greater than what remains of the fund, the agricultural estate may have to be partitioned to discharge the duty.

Physical limitations

Rome was not built in a day. Capital improvements to land and buildings take time, and one reason why improvements are outstanding on some agricultural estates is shortage of time. Another

7

reason is lack of facilities. These are physical limitations and they take many different forms. An estate staff can only work to its capacity; if well-managed it has a planned schedule to follow and usually but not invariably, repair work takes precedence over improvements. Again, certain improvements cannot be contained in a yearly programme of expenditure and, between making spasmodic improvements, funds are allowed to accumulate.[1] On remote estates work remains undone for want of building contractors in the vicinity to do it. Paradoxically, estates near populous towns are sometimes in like plight. Builders prefer urban work, especially housing, and when a housing drive is in progress the countryside suffers. On one estate the owner could not improve his cottages because he wished to take advantage of the housing subsidy. No builder would tender and without two or more tenders the owner could not submit a valid application for subsidy. Builders were not prepared to tender merely to support applications for grant; the business prospect was too remote.

Miscellaneous

Motives are difficult to classify. The classification used in this chapter is wide enough to allow much variety in each class, but the experiences of a few landowners defy even this broad classification. These anomalies are jumbled together in a happy miscellany as a residue class. Differences are great but the total contribution does not amount to much. Most frequent among these anomalous restraints are arrangements with tenants to undertake all improvements and relieve their landlords. One landlord is waiting on his tenants' initiative; no request for improvements has been received and so nothing is done. Threat of compulsory purchase checks investment on a few estates. Inflexible funds restrain it on others. And old age and sheer indifference account for the remainder.

Frequency of restraints

The restraints described above are representative of the experience of 159 landowners whose estates cover a total acreage of 1,850,000 acres. The number of estates falls short of the total of the main sample, mainly because it was not possible to obtain the opinion of the majority of landowners whose estates were in the previous survey.

Some landowners are influenced by two or more restraints; for example, a landowner who finances improvement from the joint

[1]cf. n. p. 61 *ante*.

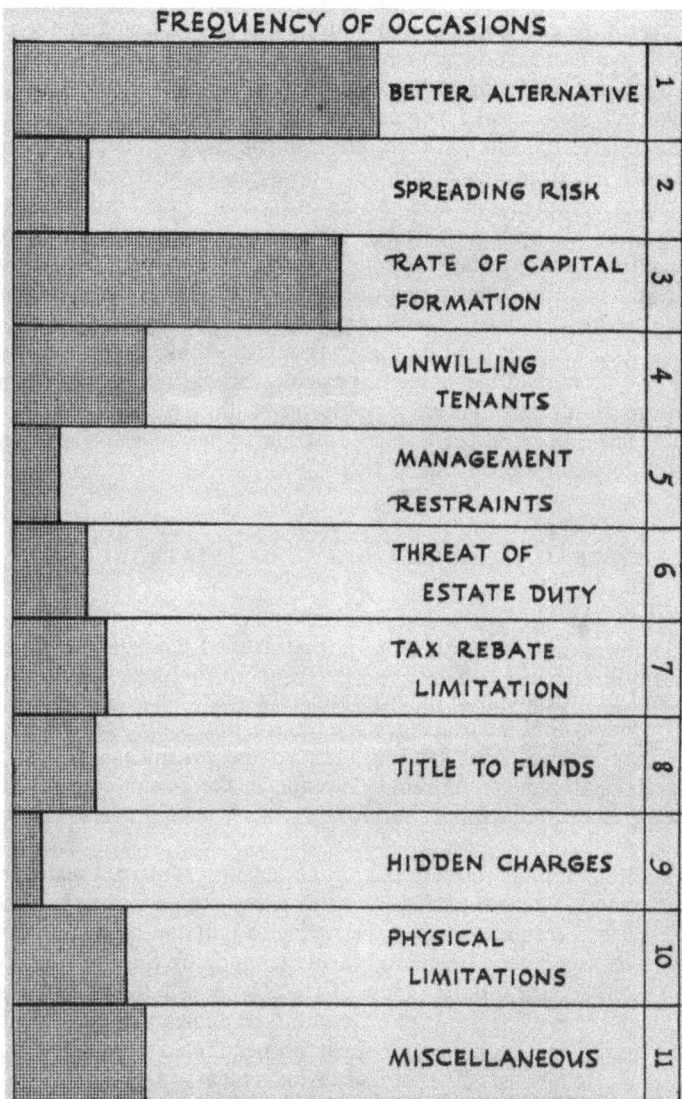

FREQUENCY OF OCCASIONS

BETTER ALTERNATIVE	1
SPREADING RISK	2
RATE OF CAPITAL FORMATION	3
UNWILLING TENANTS	4
MANAGEMENT RESTRAINTS	5
THREAT OF ESTATE DUTY	6
TAX REBATE LIMITATION	7
TITLE TO FUNDS	8
HIDDEN CHARGES	9
PHYSICAL LIMITATIONS	10
MISCELLANEOUS	11

DIAGRAM 1. RESTRAINTS ON INVESTMENT IN LAND IMPROVEMENT: FREQUENCY OF OCCASIONS

income of the estate and external funds will be restrained by the pull
of better alternative investments and the rate of capital formation
from income. The number of restraints that influence the investment
policies of the surveyed estates is therefore greater than the number
of the estates themselves. Diagram I shows the frequency of occurrence of the restraints described. The evidence is overweighted in
favour of the smaller estates, the significance of which is commented
upon later.[1] Subject to this bias the general picture shows better
alternative investments and rate of capital formation as the two
restraints most frequently encountered. The Diagram is too crude to
show the frequency of occurrence of varieties of restraint described
in the text. The headings of the Diagram are those used in the text
and give an idea of the range of possible variety; under the heading
'Title to funds' are placed in addition to the restraints described
under that caption in the text, all restraints upon investment arising
from inter-family problems of title.

RESTRAINTS ON BETTERMENT OF ESTATE INCOME

To avoid arbitration

Agricultural rents in Britain are not controlled. Landlords of agricultural estates are free to negotiate rent and rental revision with
their tenants and no statutory maximum limits the rent per acre
they may receive. And yet the tenor of the evidence of Table IV
suggests that paucity of rental revenue is the prime cause of incapacity in estate incomes. Surely the remedy is plain: raise the rent
and strengthen the income.

This suggestion is too glib. Although farm rents are not restricted,
the common law right of a landlord to terminate a tenancy has been
modified by Statute. A landlord's notice to quit can be rendered in-
operative, and a tenant secured in his tenancy by State protection.
Before this security, policy rents of farms were usually revised when
the farms were relet. Security of tenure now denies the landlord this
opportunity. Revision of rent must be negotiated with the sitting
tenant secure against all threats of dislodgement.

The law that brings security of tenure prescribes also a method of
settling rental disputes. A landlord at variance with his tenant over
rent can insist on referring the cause to an independent arbitrator. In
England and Wales arbitration is the only course; in Scotland the
landlord may choose the Land Court instead of an arbiter. Arbitration is not popular with estate owners as it estranges the tenants.

[1]cf. p. 135 *post*.

Rental revenue on many estates would be much higher if the land-lords had not assiduously avoided arbitration by keeping rents low. When speaking of rental policy not a few landowners expressed dissatisfaction with the awards of rental arbitrations and the judgements of the Land Court. They are bewildered. The logic of the issue seems so clear to them: the market is willing to offer advanced rents for the land, a fact reinforced time and again by their experience, and yet, arbitration awards appear oblivious of market opinion.

The subject is not so straightforward as it appears. Arbitrator and Land Court have to decide what the law means by a *proper rent*. The gravamen of the argument is whether market value is a true criterion. Legal decision[1] and authoritative professional opinion[2] reject it. Land Court precedents lay down that a proper rent is the fair rent from the standpoint of a sitting tenant and not the rent in the open market. It does not follow that rental value to a sitting tenant is invariably less than the rental value in the open market; it can reasonably be thought to be higher, but the inference of court judgements and of authoritative, professional opinion is to the contrary. And this view of the meaning of a proper rent goes a long way to explain that which bewilders the landowners : the discrepancy between rents freely negotiated and the rents of arbitration awards.

Low rent policies

Low rents on some estates are intentional. Mental attitudes behind the rental policies vary widely from altruism to apathy. The altruistic attitude adopts low rents, or rather declines to press for the highest rent, lest a general lift in farm rents should lead to higher prices, bigger subsidies, and weightier taxation. But on some estates low rents are thought to be advantageous. It is argued that they tend to keep company with low repairs. When the rent is low and undisturbed the tenants, the best of them at all events, quietly do their own repairs and improve the holdings. This policy tends to catch the landowner in a cleft stick. He leaves so much to the tenant that an attempt to raise the rent appears to ask the tenant to pay rent for improvements which he has made at his own expense. The conscientious landowner is loath to press for an increase, and the rent remains unchanged from year to year.

Low rents born of apathy are an unhappy thing. In some places a sense of futility prevails: rents are low, nothing can be done about it, arbitrators are deaf to reason—*laissez aller*! This frame of mind never

[1] cf. J. E. Guthe and G. Broach: 1956 SLT 170 (1st Division).
[2] cf. R. C. Walmsley, *Farm Rents*, *Chartered Surveyor*, Vol. LXXXVIII, No. 9 (1956), p. 502.

mends matters. Capital is deliberately withheld from the let land and expended on the land in hand. On one estate in the melancholy of apathy, the landowner never contemplates any improvement of the let land. Interest payments, he argues, however modest, are taken as rental increments and accepted only on pain of the landlord undertaking extensive repairs, whether he is liable for them or not. The repairs cost swallows up the interest and leaves a gaping hole in the estate income. A state of unhappy truce ensues. Rents remain low. Repairs are done grudgingly and only when necessity presses, and no expenditure whatsoever is made on improvements. The owner of the estate is confident that if he could bargain with his tenants in an open market, economic rents would be agreed and justify improvement expenditure and a sustained repair programme.

Tradition

Farm rents are low in some parts from neither expediency nor indifference. The land is ancestral, it has been owned for generations, perhaps centuries, by one family. Tradition has established a way of life. Strictly business between the squire and his tenantry is an abhorrent notion. The castle has always smiled upon the land it dominates: it must ever be so. On these estates, despite the dwindling capital of a straitened fortune, rents remain unaltered. Should income appear to rise, the upward movement is often in effect downward, for the landlord, jealous of family tradition, gives more than he takes. Modest rent changes are accompanied by unstinted repair and improvement programmes beyond, at times, the limit of prudence.

Repairs leniency

Country landowners, especially the owners of ancestral estates, sometimes indulge their tenants. Tenants are not required to honour the repair obligations of their tenancy agreements. The landlord spends revenue upon repairs that are legally the responsibility of the tenants and at the termination of the tenancy the same leniency is countenanced. Inadequate claims are made against the outgoing tenant for dilapidations to the landlord's reversion, and the tenant quits leaving an entail of heavy disrepair. Post-war insistence on a landlord's good estate management, rental depression and inflationary repair costs are having a hardening effect. Landlords now read the letter of tenancy agreements more closely and expect their tenants to do likewise. Here and there, the old sentiment, quite indefensible, still persists and reduces fair rental revenues to weak and incompetent estate incomes.

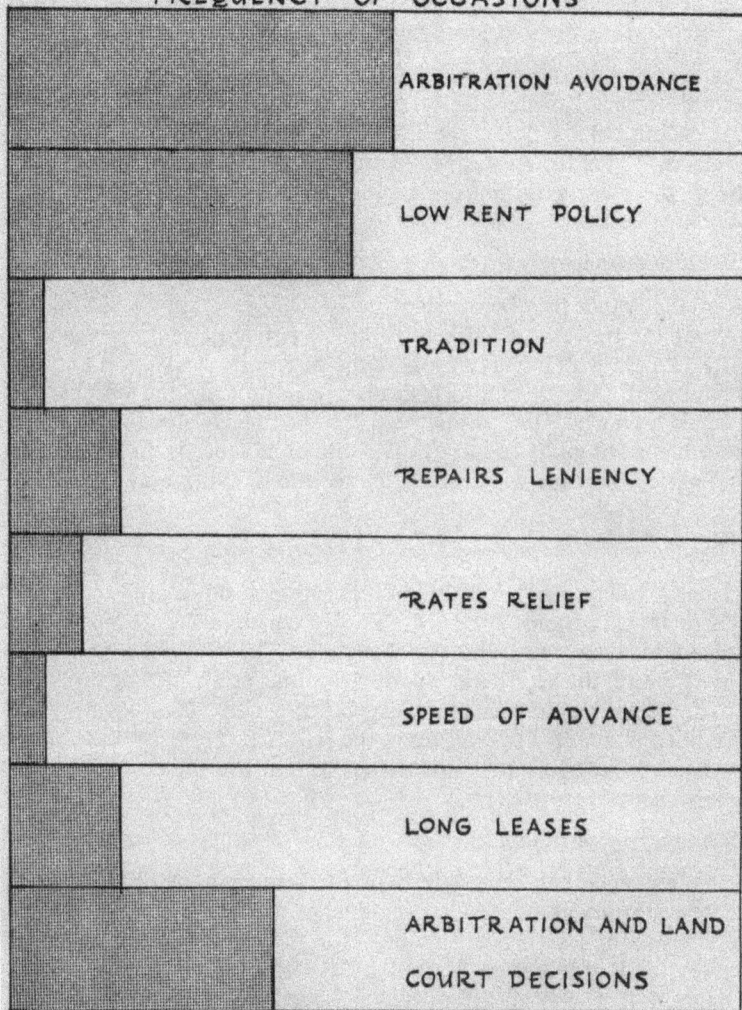

FREQUENCY OF OCCASIONS

ARBITRATION AVOIDANCE

LOW RENT POLICY

TRADITION

REPAIRS LENIENCY

RATES RELIEF

SPEED OF ADVANCE

LONG LEASES

ARBITRATION AND LAND
COURT DECISIONS

DIAGRAM II. RESTRAINTS ON RENTAL REVENUE

Rates relief

In Scotland both the tenant and the landlord had until recently made contributions to local rates. New legislation[1] has relieved the estate owner of owner's rates. Revision had been long mooted and the promise of it softened the attitude of estate owners towards rental revision. Relief from rates would augment the estate income. On this hope, the owners did not pursue policies of rental revision.

Speed of advance

Rental advance may be constant but slow. The larger the estate, the slower the movement is likely to be. A policy of rental revision is often linked with a heavy programme of repair, renovation and improvement. One by one farmsteads are improved; and one by one rentals advance. Time strengthens the income. A slowly advancing revenue is not guilty of inertia. The rate of advance is the restraining influence, and time will remove the restraint.

Long lease

Usually today agricultural holdings are let on yearly tenancies. There are exceptions. Estates are known where farms are let on long lease. This system restrains rental advance. The landlord cannot raise the rent until the lease expires and, meantime, estate income threatens to drop, as repair and other expenditure rises. Consequently the landlord is tempted to wait upon the termination of the lease and a revision of rent before he undertakes to improve the holding.

Frequency of restraints

Some evidence has been gained of the frequency of occurrence of these restraints on estate income advance. The evidence is not comprehensive; it was procurable only for the estates of the extended survey, and is therefore biassed on the side of the larger estates. Diagram II shows the frequency of occurrence of the restraints. Avoidance of arbitration is in the van, but low rent as the consequence of predetermined policy is a close runner-up. Third for place is the influence of arbitration awards, and the decisions of the Land Court in Scotland. A greater weight of opinion is prepared to confess to a desire to avoid arbitration, for fear of disturbing harmonious relations with tenants, than to say that the growth of income is stunted by the influence of arbitration awards and the decisions of the Land Court.

[1]Valuation and Rating (Scotland) Act 1956.

CHAPTER EIGHT

Inducements

RESTRAINT on the investment of capital in agricultural land is a prominent feature in the picture of agricultural estate capital. But it is negative. Without inducement to landowning and investment there would be no picture at all. Inducement is the positive pole over against the negative pole of restraint. Provision of estate capital is dependent upon the decisions of estate owners who acquire or inherit titles in agricultural land. What induces these decisions? The foregoing evidence shows clearly how often estate income fails to bring an adequate reward to estate capital investment. Yet the agricultural estates of Britain do not go begging for want of buyers or stand derelict for want of funds.

Attention has been paid to the motives that induce estate owners to purchase agricultural estates and retain a title to them after inheritance, and to invest money in land improvement. Unfortunately this study is not entirely a parallel of the study of restraints. Most of the information comes from case-studies of the larger estates in the main sample. Case-studies of other extensive estates have been added to the general evidence; in all a contribution from thirty-seven estates covering 1,744,214 acres. It is not possible to say how far, if at all, similar motives induce owners of small estates, although a certain degree of common experience is a reasonable postulation.

INDUCEMENTS TO LANDOWNERSHIP

Residence

An Englishman's home is his castle is a trite adage. Turned about it touches a nobler truth: an Englishman's castle is his home. From the days of the Norman kings in England, when the manor hall became a centre of social and economic life in the countryside, the agricultural estate has been something other than a sphere of economic enterprise. It has a spiritual quality. The hall and its land, however wide or narrow, are caught up together in the single conception of home.

The residential ethos has developed with the passage of time, and never more so than in the eighteenth and nineteenth centuries. Today this distinctive quality is still characteristic of many rural estates. The great mansion may not be vital with life as of old. Cold, endless corridors lined with treasures white-shrouded from the sunlight lead to state rooms freighted with the heavy silence of disuse. Yet, somewhere in the greyness is a patch of light and warm homeliness, a portion of the mansion set apart as the home of the owner of its land. Great mansions in some places stand entirely abandoned and the seat of residence on the estate is removed to less commodious quarters. Or the mansion is shared: what is home to the estate owner is school or training college to some of the rising generation. And not to be excepted are mansions today occupied and maintained in the dignity and quietude of the traditional great houses of England.

However it is, the estate owner's lands are his home. The attraction of the residential is distinct from ancestral responsibility and social status that can also bind a man to landownership. As home, the estate exercises a magnetism over an owner who has no roots of inheritance in the land or standing in the local community. What baffles economic analysis is the mystery of unity binding house and lands. Without its lands the house loses some, if not all, of its residential enchantment, although it is the same house, no whit diminished in size or splendour. Divested of land, it becomes a place out of keeping with itself, incongruous, an emblem of greatness in a lesser world.

Inheritance

A strong historical sense secure against the inroads of the modern mood possesses the mind of an estate owner whose land title sets him in the seat of his ancestors. Especially so, when the lands of its possession have given the family its name and distinction, and where the relationship of family and land is eponymous. Roots of title on some English estates run back through many centuries, even beyond the cataclysm of the Norman conquest.

Scions possessed of the lands of their ancestors are often burdened in conscience. What has come to them from the past must by them be handed on to posterity. Battlement and bookshelf bear eloquent testimony to the difficulties and desperate days through which the land titles have descended. Economic straits today are a challenge. He who now holds the heritage is loath to be the last of the landed line.

Impulse of inheritance has brought men, long alien to their family lands, home to ownership and responsibility. Cousins collateral in

descent have relinquished their collateral name and adopted the
family name, and grafted thus into the main stem of the genealogical
tree continue the inheritance. A sense of inheritance comes quickly.
Owners of the third generation have acquired it. It is not peculiar to
titled families after the form of the British convention, the noble
and aristocratic. A family name of renown can heighten the historical
sense and liven the conscience towards the past. But the impulse of
inheritance is a common experience: perhaps the prerogative of
primogeniture. The impulse is far above mere acquisitiveness. He
who inherits often has more to give than to gain. Nothing in the
sentiment is base. It is noble, and strong enough to draw fortunes
small and great to the support of unrequiting agricultural land.

Social responsibility

Landownership in rural Britain for long past has draped the shoulders
of estate owners in a mantle of social responsibility. The idea is no
platitude. Archbishop Temple, a man not given to platitudes, once
wrote:[1]

> "The rural landowner discharges many social functions, and
> ownership of agricultural land, subject to consideration of the
> public welfare, should not be subject to the same restrictions
> on ownership as industrial stocks and shares."

Unfortunately, Temple did not realise how dependent the ownership
of agricultural land is upon the ownership of industrial stocks and
shares. Many a rural landlord could not continue to own land and
discharge the social functions in the manner Temple applauds were
his fortune in stocks and shares not put at the disposal of his landownership, as that landownership is devoted to the service of society.

Noblesse oblige is foreign to our cities and our day. Nevertheless,
its high principle based on property although ill-fitting the temper
of modern social thinking, has not died in the countryside. Owners
bind themselves to their lands from a sense of social obligation. To
sell the land, cash it in, and live remote from its calls and cares is
breaking faith with neighbours whose families had been the concern
of their fathers for generations. And the countryside expects them
to continue and to serve. Squire and laird are the subject of clacking
criticism if for long they forsake the mansion or the castle. Squire-
archy has its satisfactions. Men can still:

> "Scatter plenty o'er a smiling land,
>   And read their history in a nation's eyes."

[1] *Christian Faith and Life*, p. 47.

Status, the true reward of service, is a prize men reach after and to gain the bare opportunity of winning it sacrifice their fortunes to the land.

Amenity

Sheer enjoyment of rural pleasures is another inducement to the ownership of agricultural estates. A man can enjoy the countryside, follow its pursuits, shoot its game, fish its rivers and hunt the fox without owning broad acres. Ownership of land seriously undertaken carries a burden of responsibility, but not to the exclusion of the amenities of rural life. Indeed, ownership of a large estate is usually a means of primary access. What need is there to purchase or rent rights of fishing and fowling when the waters and the game preserves are within the compass of one's own free tenure? The sporting side of country life is not its whole enjoyment. For some the superior pleasure is in the mode of living: a house dignified and apart, spacious architecture set among glades of parkland and the nearer grace of gardens, an ensemble of quiet splendour in a wider embrace of field and coppice, of hills or endless moor. All is amenity. We must not botanise its inwardness too readily lest its flower should fall apart. It is a wholeness, a true experience attracting those who can afford to respond, and making of them landowners possessed of agricultural estates.

Love of the land

Another pleasure and inducement to landownership is love of the land. Perhaps the truth is nearer if we speak of the lure of the land. To some its seduction is almost irresistible—the pure passion of a pursuit, followed for its own sake. Its mystery lies deep in the human soul. One never hears of the lure of the factory or of the ways of the professions. It is as the lure of the sea and the wanderlust of travel. There is no taint of avarice in the love of the land. Men are content to divide the land, work it, plant it, give to it again and again and ask as reward the right to continue in its service.

Love of the land is not inherited. One can be born on the land and bred to its ways, yet find it a bore. This love is not typical of all landowners. An estate well equipped and expertly managed may be owned by one who has little love of the land. His motives of ownership arise at different springs. Where the true experience is known, the land is usually managed and farmed to the best of an owner's ability. Passion for the land does not *ipso facto* lead to wise management and high farming although whenever it is experienced, the estate owner is eager to invest in the land his energies and his fortune, if need be for little or no monetary reward. The call of the land is a true vocation. In Britain today, there are landowners whose abilities, education, social background and wealth present to them a wide choice among life's activities. Love of the land keeps them at home, engrossed in the complexities of land management and agriculture, giving much thought and sparing no pains to understand the problems and pursue them where possible to successful conclusions.

Land management

Closely akin to love of the land is a cultured expertise in estate management. A landowner is wed to his land because land management is a chosen profession with him. This is not the same thing as love of the land. It springs of a different rationale. The estate owner is a professionally qualified land agent or surveyor. If he were not managing his own land, he would be managing the land of someone else. He is bound to the land by the many inducements to ownership, supported by the opportunity it affords of professional practice. Owners not professionally qualified but technically educated in estate management have a similar affinity with their estates.

Other estate owners who devote their days to the management of their lands and retain ownership for the purpose do not practice land management in preference to another professional career. Their heritage is their livelihood; the land their only calling. They have never thought to follow or prepare themselves for any other life. To sell the estate is to deprive them of the only living they know.

Collateral benefits

The National Coal Board owns extensive stretches of agricultural land, not for love of the land but for the sake of the mineral wealth that lies beneath the surface. Ownership of agricultural land is collateral to the main purpose of ownership. Similar principles govern the ownership of some privately owned agricultural estates. Principal reasons for ownership differ. Whatever the principal reason is, its purpose makes the ownership of agricultural land desirable, if not imperative. The agricultural interest need not be a tolerated means to an end. Usually the land is owned for its own sake, because it is agricultural, but the exploitation of other estate resources is so material to the solvency of the estate that without it ownership could not continue.

Among the estates studied with collateral benefits, the principal interests that sustain ownership are mineral wealth, timber

production and building development. In no instance is the ownership of the agricultural estate identical in principle with the ownership
of agricultural land by the National Coal Board. Always the agricultural land is held for its own sake. The nearest approach to the
National Coal Board principle is the ownership of estates with great
timber wealth, held mainly on account of their timber. Agricultural
land simply binds scattered woodlands together in a single unity of
ownership, management and administration. Without the agricultural land access to the woodlands would be difficult and it is
questionable if the estates satisfy the definition of an agricultural
estate. On the other estates agricultural land is unquestionably the
predominant feature of land use. The estates are agricultural, and
mineral workings or building development or timber production
while inducing the continued ownership of the estates are not
features of land use so prominent that they influence estate character.

Tax rebate

Mention is made elsewhere[1] of the rebate of income tax and surtax
which the Exchequer allows on capital invested in agricultural improvements. This concession, first granted in 1945, attracts capital
to agricultural land improvement and is an inducement to landownership.

Landowners in the main are anxious to improve their estates.
To do so from taxed income is, for most, extremely difficult if not
impossible. Tax rebate on capital expenditure is virtually a means
of relieving from tax the income spent on improvements. It makes
possible the improvement of agricultural land from an income that
would otherwise be taxed into impotency. This tax benefit has
heartened landowners. Some who would otherwise be in despair and
sorely tempted to give up the struggle are encouraged to hold on to
their estates. The benefit also makes the purchase of agricultural
land attractive to buyers who otherwise would not venture their
fortunes on its purchase.

Estate duty

A later chapter deals with estate duty, its incidence and impact, and
in particular the practical effects of the partial relief allowed on
agricultural land. What is there set out in detail need not be abridged
here. Here it is necessary to note that the benefits of partial relief
from estate duty afforded to agricultural land have induced the

[1]cf. p. 95 *ante*; and p. 129 *post*.

purchase of estates and prevented the sale of others. It is noticeable in Scotland where the alimentary life rent is inalienable, how the estate duty concession on agricultural land encourages trustees to retain agricultural land. But for the inhibition on sale the life renter would grant his life interest to another *inter vivos* and so lessen the risk of estate duty; whether that life interest were in land or shares would be a matter of indifference. Since no *inter vivos* transfer can be made, it is prudent to retain ownership of the estate duty favoured agricultural land.

Desire to escape or lessen the impact of estate duty induces owner-ship of agricultural land in other ways. An agricultural estate may be the gift of a wealthy man to a dependant or friend, and given with the intention of reducing the levy of estate duty on the donor's total fortune.[1] Sometimes the land is possessed by a private estate company and the gift is a transfer of shares. On one estate of valuable woodlands, the owner is retaining possession of certain agricultural and woodland portions so as to avoid payment of the estate duty for which the estate would be liable on the proceeds of sales of standing timber.

Stabilising investment

The purchase of agricultural land as a means of acquiring ownership of other more remunerative property is a policy of indirect invest-ment in agricultural land. It is not investment in agricultural land for its own sake. Some owners regard their agricultural land as a sound investment *per se*. Estate income will probably not be the attraction. These single-minded policies are inspired by stability of investment. We have seen[2] how a desire to spread the risk of investment can restrain the employment of capital in agricultural land. The reverse is true. Agricultural land is purchased or retained after inheritance, to keep a balance between land investment and other forms. Some investors are haunted by a half-formed notion that agricultural land is a hedge against inflation; whatever betides equities and money, the land endureth and agricultural land is the most stable form of property investment in an inflationary economy.

Spirit of a trust

A basic principle of real property law in Britain is freedom of aliena-tion. Landowners down the ages have battled for the right to tie up

---

[1] The gift is deemed to be a *donatio mortis causa* until five years after the transi-tion; and does not escape estate duty until that period has elapsed.

[2] cf. p. 90 *ante*.

the heritage and control its devolution upon their descendants. Provisions were usually aimed at the right of sale or alienation. So long as an owner can prevent the heritage being sold or given away, he will master its destiny. The struggles came to nought. Whoever has what in England is called the legal estate has an absolute right of disposal; and there is no land without a legal owner. In principle the same is true in Scotland, but there until the passage of the Entails (Scotland) Act 1914 it was possible to settle an estate on trustees by a trust which deprived them of all power of alienation.

The nearest an estate owner can come to controlling the devolution of a landed heritage is conveyance of the property to trustees who administer it according to the terms of the trust. But the law invests the trustees with power to sell the land and holds them to the limits of the trust only in respect of the proceeds of sale. Nevertheless, trustees who have been appointed by an estate owner to administer an ancestral landed estate in the interests of the family are usually disposed to honour the family succession to the land. Whatever freedom of sale they may have at law, the spirit of the trust holds their hands and confirms the continuity of the family title in the land.

Particular circumstances

Each of these inducements to landownership of agricultural estates is common to a number of the estates studied. Particular circumstances have influenced the estate owners to some extent. On some estates inducements exclusive to the circumstances of the owners are the main reasons for ownership. An owner of one estate, for example, is much influenced by arrangements he has made with the National Trust to whom he has given the ancestral mansion and grounds. These exceptional inducements defy classification. Their presence must not be overlooked or the picture of inducement will be too simply drawn.

Frequency of inducement

Although the inducements just described are a synopsis of the opinions of owners of large estates and do not include any evidence from smaller estates, it is worth while considering the frequency of their occurrence. Diagram III depicts this. The Diagram is based on the same principle as the diagrams showing the frequencies of restraints. The items arranged in the frequency histogram are inducements; the number does not correspond to the number of the estates because on some estates more than one inducement motivates landownership.

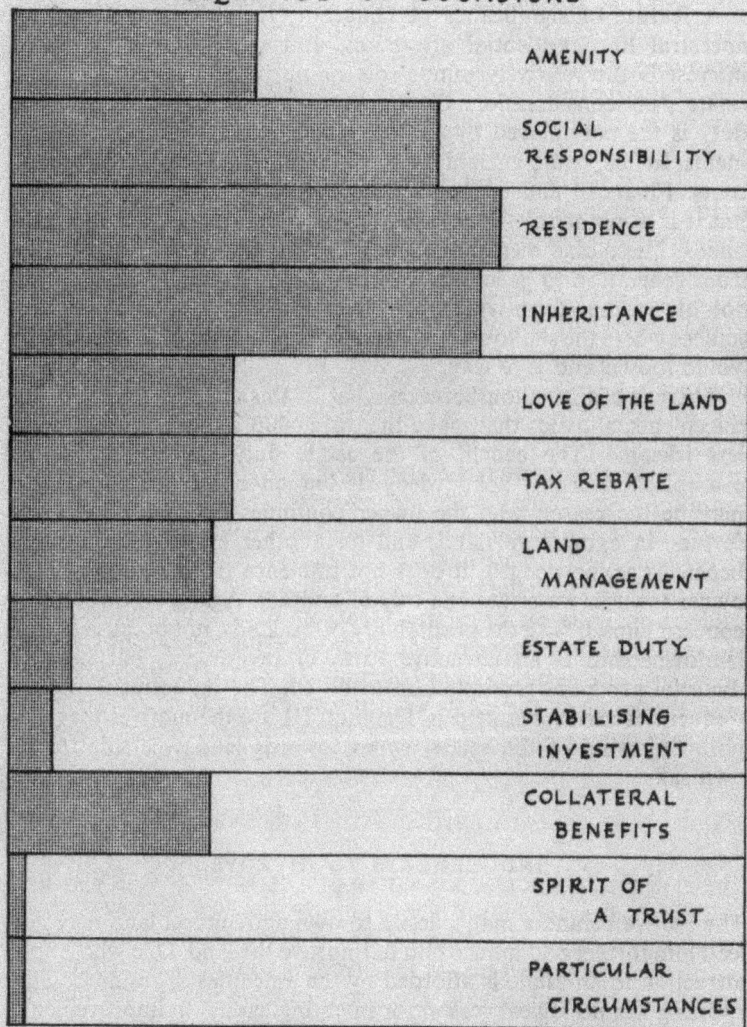

FREQUENCY OF OCCASIONS

AMENITY

SOCIAL RESPONSIBILITY

RESIDENCE

INHERITANCE

LOVE OF THE LAND

TAX REBATE

LAND MANAGEMENT

ESTATE DUTY

STABILISING INVESTMENT

COLLATERAL BENEFITS

SPIRIT OF A TRUST

PARTICULAR CIRCUMSTANCES

DIAGRAM III. INDUCEMENTS TO LAND OWNERSHIP

A feature of significance of Diagram III is the prominence of ancestral ties, residential attraction, and social status. Of equal interest is the relatively minor role of purposeful investment, and estate duty consideration. Contrasting with the influence of estate duty is the part played by the tax rebate on agricultural improvements. In fine, landownership of these larger estates has deep-running roots. Financial and economic considerations have a part to play but it is a minor role. Home and kindred and service are the great bonds. These bind men to the land. These lengthen the roots of title from generation to generation. In them is strength. These roots do not lift in the storm-wrack of depression and straitened circumstances where the shallow roots of economic and financial expediency would loosen and give way.

There is a distinction between what in this chapter are called inducements, and aids that make the ownership of agricultural estates less irksome. The benefit of the estate duty concessions is, for example, universally acknowledged; but on one estate the benefit may be the reason why the owner continues to leave part of his fortune in agricultural land; and on another estate, although the benefit is acknowledged, it does not influence the intentions of the owner towards his estate one way or another. Again, an owner may concern himself with the profitability of his lands, not because to him landownership is an attractive form of investment, but because financial prudence prompts him to do so. The inducements whose frequencies are represented in Diagram III are the motives that dispose the mind of the estate owner towards landownership for its own sake.

INDUCEMENTS TO IMPROVE

The motive behind a man's desire to own agricultural land may not lead him further and induce him to improve the land. One whose sole attraction to an estate is afforded by the amenities of residence and sporting has no logical reason for investing capital in improvements to enhance its productivity. A conscience alive to the past and its claim upon the present to sustain and continue an ancestral title to land, can be dead towards the claims of the land for new techniques of cultivation and new living standards in cottage and farmhouse. The inducements to landownership briefly described above are uncertain guides to the motives that prompt owners to improve their estates.

The owners of the thirty-seven estates who gave reasons why they continue to run their estates also commented upon their attitude to land improvement. Of the thirty-seven, four have made little or no attempt to improve the land. In these cases the owners are struggling with what capital they have to pay off recent levies of estate duty and have nothing to spare for improvements.

Sense of duty

Two inducements more than any other have prompted the owners who can afford to do so, to make improvements. One, which accounts for 21·8 % of the opinion, is a sense of duty to the land and the estate tenantry. This corresponds with the moral convictions that play so prominent a part in the minds of landowners and inspire them to continue in landownership. Post-war legislation makes pointed reference to what it calls the landowner's responsibility to manage the land in accordance with 'the rules of good estate management'.[1] Nowhere does it directly impose obligations upon landowners to honour these rules, although it empowers the Government to take compulsory action where the rules are broken. The sense of duty that moves the estate owners to improve their land is in nowise evoked by fear of Government compulsory action. Doubtless the new emphasis quickens the conscience. It would be wrong, however, to regard this very real sense of obligation as anything but autonomous. It is one with the call to social responsibility so deeply embedded in ownership of agricultural estates.

Whether this moral imperative would by itself be strong enough to induce the owners to improve their freeholds cannot be known because on all except one estate other considerations in addition to the owner's sense of duty encourage an improvement policy. For two-thirds of the moralists the supporting considerations are financial: tax rebate, Government grants or remunerative interest. The virtue of the moral inducement is not diminished thereby. One who wishes to do good is no less virtuous for want of power to carry through his intentions. The majority of estate owners who are moved by moral considerations say in effect: this thing must be done and will be done if it is financially possible to do it.

Tax rebate

The other inducement that stands out with the moral sense above all others is the attraction of tax rebate on capital expenditure. This influences 21 % of opinion. The incidence of these two inducements is not identical in other respects. Although equal in the number of occasions of influence the estates affected are not the same. On only 40 % of the estates whose owners are moved by a sense of duty to

[1] Agricultural Act 1947, Section 10.

the land is improvement policy stimulated by the attraction of tax rebate.

Although the attraction of the rebate is in the forefront of the inducements encouraging improvement, it is surprising that it is not far in advance of all other inducements. Estate character can lessen its attraction.[1] Another reason why it is not more widely appreciated is the mistaken idea that it takes back with one hand what it gives with the other. There is no benefit, so the argument runs, since the augmented income from improved land does not attract tax rebate. A landowner who receives 10 % interest on improvements is assessed to tax on this and the amount of tax so levied equals the yearly tax rebate on a tenth of the outlay. This is a specious argument. If the tax rebate were not allowed, the capital expenditure would be made virtually from taxed income and tax on the enhanced income from improvement would be additional. As it is, the estate owner is allowed income tax remission on a capital payment and, in the example just given, the tax rebate equals the tax levy on the additional income; looked at another way, the tax on the income is defrayed by the tax rebate and that additional income is virtually tax free.

Financial reward

Next in order of frequency among the inducements that encourage improvement expenditure, is the receipt of adequate financial reward on the capital invested. The inducement hardly touches owner-occupied estates. An estate owner farming his own land is assured of reaping the rewards of improvement. An owner of let land is dependent upon the attitude of the tenants. Let land in some measure is characteristic of all the large estates whose owners expressed opinion, and 15 % of this opinion has been persuaded to improve let land mainly on account of the readiness of tenants to pay what the owners consider to be remunerative interest on capital invested in improvements.

In the normal course of events, the estate owner bargains with his tenants for interest payment on specific improvements and agrees the matter with them prior to making the improvement. On some estates a consistent improvement policy is worked through and after completion rents are revised; the purpose of this is to avoid charging interest *per se* on the improvements, since by so doing the expenditure is denied acceptance in the maintenance claim. There is a certain risk in this procedure, because the estate owner cannot tell in advance what rewards the improvement investments are likely to

[1]cf. p. 95 *ante, et seq.*

reap. A variation of the theme, found among the large estates of the sample, is to bargain with each tenant for an increase in rent before agreeing to do the improvements, on the understanding that the rental increment is conditional upon the improvements being made.

Grant-aid

An improvement stimulus influencing 15 % of the opinion is afforded by Government grants. Direct grant does not compete with tax rebate. It is noticeable that among the estates whose improvement policies are stimulated by the offer of Government grants only one in six commented on the additional inducement of tax rebate. More landowners would take advantage of grant-aid if application for it were less complicated and uncertain. Complicated procedures certainly deter owners whose tax rebate means most to them.

Grants for water supplies and drainage were little spoken of and do not appear to be decisive inducements on the larger estates.Time and again reference was made to the benefit of the housing grants and hill land improvement grants. Housing grants are undoubtedly a telling influence in the improvement of agricultural dwellings and farmhouses. The grants are of two kinds. One is a yearly contribution to the cost of erecting new cottages[1]; the other is a lump sum grant towards the cost of improving existing cottages and dwelling houses.[2] The latter is the greater stimulus to improvement. Hill land improvement grants[3] have probably directly prompted more improvement than any other form of practical financial assistance. For many landowners with upland and mountain on their estates hill land improvement finance is a *sine qua non* to continued improvement.

Orderliness

Love of the land that lures men to landownership may drive them to improve the beloved possession. Desire does not always arise. Less than one in ten of the estates owned for love of the land are improved for the same love's sake; and even then it is not the same strong passion. Love of the land can be a bohemian love. An estate owner warmly attached to his land can be nonchalant towards its demands for improvement. The soul of ownership is not one with the soul of improvement. Attractions are different. Improvement means change, a giving of new for old, a planned purpose; sometimes it is deeply surgical. The sentiment that urges forward improvement and comes

---

[1]Housing Act 1952 *et alia.*   [2]Housing Act 1949.
[3]Hill Farming Act 1946.

nearest to love of the land is a craving for orderliness. Owners improve their estates because they cannot brook neglect and untidiness.

In every case where this opinion was expressed the desire for orderliness was accompanied by a sense of duty. Yet, the two are not the same. Sense of duty springs from a moral code; it is a precept from without. Desire for orderliness, to have an estate ordered and orderly, is subjective and not provoked by external stimulus. It is closer to the aesthetic than the moral. An estate owner reconditions an entire terrace of cottages, when only one or two have attracted grant-aid or have agreed to an increase in rent, because to recondition the odd one or two offends his sense of ordered treatment and makes of the property a patchwork. And so it is with the farms. His soul cannot rest until he has given equal treatment to all parts of his estate, so far as it is in his power to do so.

Partiality

When an owner is restrained from improving a particular portion of his estate, the principle of exclusion acts counterwise as an inducement to improve the other part. This is especially noticeable in Scotland. The rigid restriction of the Agricultural Holdings Act 1949 on the estate owner's freedom of management over let land makes him partially minded: he is induced to employ his resources to the improvement of land in hand and to neglect, avowedly, the let land. This attitude of mind is understandable and is provoked solely by the one-sidedness of the law in Scotland. Its contrast ennobles the far more frequent sense of duty and love of orderliness which move owners to improve all their land, whether let or in hand.

Estate duty

Capital invested in agricultural improvements attracts the 45 % estate duty concession. Here and there estates are found where this attraction has induced improvement. Instances are few in the sample; not more than $6\frac{1}{2}$ % of the opinion. This low ebb of inducement, or more likely of awareness of the benefit, corresponds with the low place in the scale of inducements to landownership taken by estate duty concession. Lack of interest is the more remarkable because capital transferred to agricultural improvements from investments liable to a full estate duty not only attracts the estate duty concession but also rebate of income tax and surtax. In the event of death these rebates are claimed by the next in title to the land. A high surtax payer who improves his estate and leaves it to one with sufficient income to reap the benefit of the tax rebates on the improvements made by the deceased can thereby place a large proportion of the transferred capital beyond the range of estate duty[1] and leave into the bargain an immaculate estate to his successor.

Compulsion

Throughout the opinion expressed, only one estate owner admitted to being influenced by the Government's power,[2] exercisable through the agricultural executive committees, of directing owners to make improvements. He like Brer Rabbit of childhood's memory lies low and does nothing, until he is spurred into action by an agricultural executive committee waving a big stick.

[1]The greater the amount of surtax the higher will the proportion be; a man paying 18s. in the £ stands to receive as tax rebate 90 % of the transferred capital —and this is placed beyond estate duty so far as the rebate is claimable by the successor in title.
[2]cf. Agriculture Act 1947, Section 14 (3).

CHAPTER NINE

Estate Duty and Tax Rebate

PRIVATE capital in Britain is subject to heavy inheritance taxation. Until 1947 inheritance taxation, or death duties, comprised estate duty, legacy duty and succession duty. In that year all death duties were rolled into one. Legacy duty and succession duty were abolished and estate duty became the sole form of inheritance taxation. Estate duty was first imposed in 1894. It caused a certain amount of consternation in the hearts of landowners, but the levy was comparatively light. Not until after the third decade of the present century did the rate of the levy assume formidable proportions.

Estate duty is a tax on capital and some attention must be paid to its incidence upon estate capital and external funds. Since 1925 agricultural land has enjoyed abated rates of estate duty. And the income tax and surtax rebate, introduced in 1945, on capital invested in agricultural improvements is a counterpoise to estate duty. These two mitigating factors must be taken into account.

The main sample is a fairly balanced representation of estate character traits.[1] Estates suffering estate duty are balanced in number against estates that have escaped. The range of evidence touching estate duty is thus limited. There is no reason why a special study of estate duty should be restricted to the estates in the main sample; and every reason why the evidence should be as far-reaching as possible. Consequently certain facts given in this chapter relate to many estates excluded from the main sample.

Simple facts have been gathered at random from 2,750 estates covering over $5\frac{1}{2}$ million acres; an area approximately equivalent to a tenth of Britain's agricultural land surface. The 2,750 estates are classified into two primary classes—those of old title and those of new title.[2] Estates of old and new title are classified further as those that had suffered estate duty and those that had remained free of it up to the date of the investigation. A third classification sets the estates in size classes.

[1]cf. Appendix, p. 199.   [2]cf. p. 27 *ante*.

Survival power

Among the 2,750 estates 901 boast old titles and 1,849 new. Table XII shows the proportions of old and new titles in the size-classes and in the whole sample.

TABLE XII

INCIDENCE OF ESTATE DUTY ON 2,750 ESTATES
OF OLD AND NEW TITLE COVERING
5,600,000 ACRES

Size Class	Percentage of Numbers in size class				Old titles as percentage of estates not suffering duty in each size-class	Estates not suffering duty as percentage of old titles in each size-class
	Estate duty suffered	Estate duty not suffered	Old title	New title		
Acres	%	%	%	%	%	%
100–499	18·7	81·3	9·4	90·6	3·7	37·4
500– 999	37·2	62·8	25·9	74·1	7·2	17·5
1,000–2,499	62·4	37·6	61·2	38·8	24·0	14·8
2,500–4,999	76·4	23·6	76·4	23·6	29·5	9·1
5,000–9,999	75·0	25·0	88·7	11·3	67·7	19·1
10,000 and over	78·3	21·7	82·6	17·4	45·0	14·5
Percentage of total	38·4	61·6	32·7	67·3	9·04	16·9

These percentages tell something of the survival power of agricultural estates under the threat and actual levy of estate duty. Every one of the estates with an old title means an unbroken inheritance longer, probably far, far longer, than the history of estate duty itself. And yet numerically the estates of old title account for 32·7 % of the total number of estates in the sample and for about 64 % of the total land area. The last figure is impressive. It reveals how age attracts acres. The ratio of old titles to new increases rapidly once the 1,000-acre class is entered, and gives evidence of survival power

among the large and old inheritances unsuspected by many. Different
causes may account for this. A market for the larger estates restricted
by want of purchasing funds or reluctance to sell would do so. A
more likely explanation is the partition for sale of large estates. The
bald percentages of the Table point either way. They cannot be
taken as evidence of estate duty causing the break-up of the estates.
Our suspicions are aroused; but until the origins of the smaller
estates are identified, no clear answer can be given. Perhaps these
origins will never be known. Perhaps the bits and pieces will prove
as tiresome as Humpty Dumpty and defy all attempts to put them
together again. And in any event, the percentages do not wholly
exclude new titles from the larger size-classes. Of 216 estates over
5,000 acres each, which absorb 60·6 % of the land area of the
survey, 14·3 % are in the new title class. Lower figures than these
will be necessary before we can speak of the passing into history of
the large country estate.

The percentages of Table XII show also the ratios of burdened
estates to free estates. Taken together, there is close similarity
between the ratio of the victims to the spared,[1] and the ratio of old
titles to new.[2] The similarity tempts us to associate the estates of new
title with the fortunate ones that have remained free, and vice versa.
Association of this kind is of course likely because the newer the title,
other things being equal, the less the chance of estate duty levy. In
point of fact, the extremely close correspondence is accidental. A not
insignificant proportion of the fortunate estates are estates of old
title. The average percentage is 9·04 % and the percentage is much
greater among the larger estates and is as high as 67·7 % in the size-
class 5,000–9,999 acres. High percentages among the larger estates
are due to the preponderance of old titles. A better focused picture
of the extent to which estates of old title have continued free of
estate duty is gained by the percentage of their own number that have
remained free. On average the figure is 16·9 %; with the exception
of the smallest estates, there is little divergence either way from this
average among the size classes.

Frequency of estate duty

The estates of old title, lines of unbroken inheritance since before
1900, provide evidence of the frequency of estate duty levy. Where
an estate remains in the same family for generations, the frequency
of the occasion of estate duty levy will depend upon the ages of the
successive owners and heirs and also upon the ability of the estate to
avoid the imposition of the levy. The number of years from one

[1] i.e. 38·4 % and 61·6 %.   [2] i.e. 32·7 % and 67·3 %.

occasion to the next cannot therefore be calculated actuarially from mean expectation of life tables. This interval between the levies we may call the cycle of frequency, and a rough calculation can be made of the number of years in the cycle from what we know about the estates of old title.

No estate owner of the 901 estates of old title claimed immortality in this life; death attended his footsteps continually. Ruling out the remote probability of a title suffering two deaths in one year, the number of chances of these estates becoming burdened by estate duty can be expressed as the number of estates multiplied by the number of years from 1900 to the time of survey. The product, divided by the number of occasions when estate duty was actually suffered, gives a figure for the cycle of frequency; the number of occasions is greater than the number of taxed estates because some estates have suffered more than once. Information from fifty-two estates of old title shows on average 1·28 levies per estate. Using this ratio, the period of the cycle of frequency works out[1] as fifty-one years.

The burden on each acre

The cycle is true only of the whole range of estates taking one year with another. It must not be regarded as a criterion of the specific case, for a particular estate may suffer estate duty levy at intervals of a few years. A frequency cycle of fifty-one years strongly suggests that a run of levies at short intervals is exceptional and likely to be followed by a lull. For the range of estates as a whole it indicates the length of interval and can be used as a factor in calculating the yearly burden per acre which estate duty has imposed on the land of the estates since 1900. Let it be assumed that a levy occurring over fifty-one years is redeemed by a sinking fund over that interval; the annual burden per acre is then the amount of sinking fund required to redeem the estate duty per acre.

The average levy of estate duty per acre has been calculated on the evidence of ninety-two estates of old and new title covering approximately 704,000 acres. This average figure is based on the acreage of each estate at the time of death if it was known. Where it was not known the size of the estate at the time of survey was taken. Allowance was made for the reduced rate of duty attracted by agricultural land unless it was known that an estate had failed[2] to attract this

[1] The formula used for the calculation is $55n/1·28m$,
    where $n =$ the total number of estates of old title
    and $m =$ the number of estates of old title suffering levy since 1900.
[2] An example of this was an estate which lost its entire agricultural concession amounting to £210,000 because at the time of death the estate was owned by an estate company and duty was charged on the shares.

benefit, in which event the full amount of duty suffered is included in the calculation; when there was uncertainty the estate was given the benefit of the allowance. On some estates the actual amount of reduction was not calculable because the year of death was unknown and in these cases the reduction was estimated to be 45 % of the normal rate of duty. On a number of the smaller estates the only information available was the amount of estate duty levied on the total fortune. Where this was so the calculation proceeded on an estimate of the proportion of the total levy probably contributed by the landed estate; the probability was based either on an estimate of the value of the landed estate at the time of death, or an estimate of the probable ratio existing at death between estate capital and external funds.

TABLE XIII

AVERAGE ESTATE DUTY LEVY PER ACRE
SINCE 1900 ON 92 ESTATES COVERING
704,370 ACRES

Size class (acres)	Old title	New title	All
	£	£	£
100–249	12·0	6·24	9·1
250–499	11·2	6·9	9·0
500–999	10·15	4·2	7·1
1,000–2,499	11·9	7·4	9·6
2,500–9,999	6·7	7·5	7·1
10,000+	2·8	3·9	3·3
Average of all classes	9·1	6·0	7·5

Table XIII shows the average estate duty levy per acre for estates of old title and new title arranged in size-classes. The figures do not represent the estate duty on the principal or total fortunes of the landowners but the estate duty on the landed estates as those total fortunes have influenced it. The average for all titles and sizes is an estate duty levy of £7 10s. per acre; if the larger estates are excluded the figure may be rounded off at £8 per acre.

There is significance in the consistently heavier average levies on the old title estates up to 2,500 acres. In this size range of estates the principal fortunes at time of death associated with the old title estates tended to be greater than the principal fortunes associated with the new title estates, and this suggests that at the time of death the old title estates were better supported than the new title estates by consociate capital. Owners of recently purchased large estates are as closely wedded to their land as the owners of all old title estates hence with them there is little or no difference in the proportion of landed wealth to other wealth. The smaller estates recently acquired are backed mainly by fortunes invested in farming stock and are the properties of owner-occupiers farming their own lands. Smaller estates of old title tend to be backed by fortunes invested otherwise than in farming; the remnants, probably, of wealthy inheritances which in the past supported greater estates. The heavier burden on the estates of old title is more remarkable when it is remembered that they had a greater chance than the estates of new title of benefit from the low estate duty rates of the past.

The consistently lower burden per acre on estates over 2,500 acres both of old and new title is important. Acre for acre, despite greater principal fortunes, the larger estates, and their agriculture with them, carry a lower burden on each acre. The cause has not been investigated. A probable explanation is the influence of size and tenure: spread of capital equipment, paucity of soil, preponderance of let land and a high proportion of woodland tend to reduce the value per acre of the larger estates and *pro rata* the estate duty.

The rounded average of £8 per acre estate duty is a reasonable basis for calculating the hypothetical sinking fund and the yearly burden per acre. Accumulating at 3 % compound interest over fifty-one years, the annual burden would be approximately 1s. 6d. per acre.

This figure is the result of past values, past fortunes and past rates of estate duty. Save in principle, it is no guide to the yearly burden imposed by the present threat of estate duty. Calculations based on the present value of the estates, present principal fortunes and current rates of estate duty have been made in respect of those estates where the fortunes are known.[1] The calculations suppose the present estates to be agricultural and wholly capable of attracting the 45 % estate duty concession. Allowance has been made for the probable frequency of levies by multiplying the estimated levy per acre by 1·1;[2] this presupposes subsequent levies of estate duty per acre being equal to current levies and has probably biased the figures towards a more liberal result than future events will justify.

Table XIV shows the average rate per acre for the size groups and for all estates. The averages follow the pattern for the figures for the past levies. Old title estates still carry the greater burden.

---

[1] i.e. those contributing to the evidence for consociate capital.
[2] The multiplier of 1·1 was computed from the formula: $f \times c/55$,
   where $f =$ the frequency factor 1·28
   and $c =$ years in cycle of occurrence (i.e. 51).

What is more apparent in these estimated figures is the tendency for medium-sized estates to attract the highest burden per acre. This is understandable when we consider how regular is the mode of the ratio of net consociate capital to estate capital.[1] On a medium-sized estate the value of an acre of land usually is not noticeably lower than the value of an acre on a smaller estate, but the rate of estate duty is higher because the total fortune is greater. For reasons previously given, the burden of duty per acre is lighter on the largest estates. Discounting somewhat this lighter burden, the overall average

TABLE XIV

ESTIMATED AVERAGE CURRENT ESTATE DUTY
PER ACRE ON 113 ESTATES COVERING
1,184,882 ACRES

Size class (acres)	Old title	New title	All
	£	£	£
100–249	11·7	13·9	12·8
250–499	31·7	16·9	24·3
500–999	16·8	16·1	16·5
1,000–2,499	15·4	14·3	14·8
2,500–9,999	13·3	18·2*	15·7
10,000+	9·1	5·4	7·2
Average of all classes	16·3	14·1	15·2

* interpolated

can be rounded off at £17 per acre. On the principle of a sinking fund to redeem the duty over a fifty-one-years interval, the yearly burden is 3s. per acre.

Estate duty and capital formation

Again we must remind ourselves that a yearly burden calculated in this way is no measure of the actual burden in a particular case. On a given estate the yearly burden depends on the actual interval between levies. The fifty-one-years cycle suggests that in the general course of events a levy will be made once every fifty-one years. It may fall at any time within that period; the younger the successor to the deceased,

[1] cf. p. 67 *ante*.

the greater the chance of a long period before the next subsequent levy. It would be wrong to suppose that heirs and other successors are more likely to be young than old; the grey steals the amber from the head while the heir waits for his inheritance. For practical purposes it would be wise to assume a half-way interval of twenty-five years—the accepted duration of a generation. Over a period of this length the yearly burden per acre becomes 9s. 2d.

This is not the end of the story. If we think of the sinking fund as a practical means of measuring the yearly burden of estate duty we must take into account income tax and surtax. Sinking funds will have to be found from taxed income. Presupposing a standard rate of income tax at 9s. in the £, the yearly burden leaps to 16s. 9d. per acre. Moreover the basic figure of 3s. per acre takes no account of the probability of a cash redemption fund lifting the total fortune of the deceased into a higher rate of estate duty. The 16s. 9d. per acre figure leans therefore to the conservative side.

A burden of 16s. 9d. on the acre must adversely influence the competence of an estate to form capital from estate income. On an incompetent estate the question does not arise. The average estate income of the wholly competent estates of Table II is 12s. 3d. per acre before anything is allowed for landlord's interest on estate capital. This bare working margin which has been sufficient to finance such capital formation as has taken place in the past ten years is wholly swallowed up by an estate duty burden of 16s. 9d. per acre. And on the partially competent estates whose average estate income is a mere 2s. per acre, the impact is annihilating.

Capital appreciation

The value of land can appreciate without appreciation of estate income and an estate may be able to offset estate duty against capital appreciation. Agricultural land has risen in value over the last twenty years, especially when in possession. This is exemplified by the history of twenty-eight of the estates that have suffered estate duty since 1935. From probate to the time of survey, the value of these estates rose by £1,649,270. During this period, the total estate duty levied on the estates was £647,615. Some of the rise in value may have resulted from improvement of land and equipment since probate. During the period £195,800 was spent on improvements. The value of the land would not have increased £1 for £1 of expenditure. But even if it had done so, the net increase in value is over twice the sum of the total estate duty. The increase means that a 44 % mortgage of the enhanced value of the land would meet the estate duty. Looked at another way: at the time of death 29 % of the land would have had to be sold to discharge the duty, but at the time of survey a 16% partition would do. However, this is not an entirely happy solution. Mortgage of inflation value tells a sorry tale in days of deflation. And sale of part of an estate, however small, is a death duty sale and at best a Pyrrhic victory. Continuous inflation cannot altogether halt the grindstone of estate duty imposition although it can retard its process of attrition.

There are avenues of greater hope. One is timber growth. On the estates where the timber values are known, the timber increased in value from probate to the date of survey by £583,310. At the last death, this timber became answerable for £68,753 estate duty leviable on sale. The increment in timber value after the payment of all estate duty on the timber exceeds by 30 % the estate duty on the land of these estates. These are aggregate figures. Conditions on particular estates differ widely. Nevertheless, they illustrate how timber growth is a practical way of providing a redemption fund to meet estate duty. The yearly increment is not subject to income tax, and at death timber is not aggregated with the deceased's other estate for the assessment of principal value and thus does not raise the rate of duty.

Significance of estate duty concession

Since 1947 the estate duty abatement on agricultural land has been 45 %. By transferring capital from other investments to agricultural estate a man may reduce almost by half his liability for estate duty on the capital transferred. The average fortune of landowners whose estates were used to estimate the burden of estate duty per acre would at present full rates of duty carry on average a 44 % levy. The market value of the estates is £16·6 million and if a like sum had been invested in stocks and shares the estate duty would amount to £11·3 million. Since the estates are mostly agricultural land the actual duty will be in the neighbourhood of £6·2 million—an alleviation of £5·1 million. Thus a substantial sum is preserved from estate duty.

We have seen how the capital levy of estate duty can be expressed as an annual burden by calculating the yearly sinking fund required to build up a capital fund commensurate with the levy. Turning this principle back to front, a reduction in the capital levy means a saving in income. A capital fund equal in amount to the £5·1 million saved could be provided by financing a sinking fund from income. A sinking fund over twenty-five years at 3 % compound interest would amount to £13,770 per year. This figure would have to be found from the incomes of the estate owners each year to meet estate duty at the full rate. Investment in agricultural land can thus be said to relieve income to this extent. And the relief can be regarded as the earnings of the agricultural investment; earnings that can be expressed as a percentage of the capital invested in agricultural land. For full measure, calculating the reward of the agricultural investment should ideally take into account income tax and surtax and the saving of additional estate duty which a cash fund would attract; the fact that a cash fund is itself taxable might add to the rate of duty on the land by increasing the principal value of the landowner's fortune and lifting it into a higher grade of estate duty. Income tax influences the calculation of reward because sinking contributions would have to be found from taxed income. The total reward gained by agricultural land investment would be the saving of the sinking fund contributions required to provide a sum commensurate with the estate duty relief, plus the saving of income tax and surtax on the gross income from which sinking fund contributions would be provided.

The magnitude of the percentage reward on capital investment which the saving of estate duty represents will depend upon the rate of duty leviable, the period of years over which the hypothetical sinking fund is presumed to accumulate, the rate of compound interest of the sinking fund and the rate in the £ of income tax or surtax payable by the landowner. The percentage is a function of these factors and can be written mathematically as

$$P = f\left[\frac{9}{100}\left(\frac{rs}{20-t}\right)\right];$$

where
$P =$ percentage earned on capital value;
$r =$ rate per cent of estate duty without agricultural concession;
$s =$ annual sinking fund in £s;
$t =$ shillings in the £ of income tax and surtax

Values of this function are given in Table XV.

The figures show how materially the estate duty concession beneficially affects the investment return from agricultural land and the advantage gained from this type of investment by investors liable for high surtax and high estate duty. Advantages gained would be greater than shown in the Table because the figures do not allow for the estate duty which a cash fund, set aside to meet the estate duty on the land, would itself attract.

Tax rebate: a counterpoise of estate duty

The rebate of income tax and surtax allowed since 1945 on agricultural land improvements can be looked upon as an Exchequer

9

TABLE XV

Estate duty rate (r) 60 %				Estate duty rate (r) 80 %			
Sinking fund				Sinking fund			
25 years		10 years		25 years		10 years	
Tax rate (t) =		Tax rate (t) =		Tax rate (t) =		Tax rate (t) =	
9s.	18s.	9s.	18s.	9s.	18s.	9s.	18s.
P=1·3	7·2	4·2	23·4	1·7	9·7	5·7	31·3

counterpoise to the levy of estate duty. By transferring capital from another investment to agricultural improvements a contribution is won from the Exchequer purse that would not otherwise be forthcoming. This is a repayment of tax revenue and can be set off against estate duty.

On fifty-two of the estates whose estate duty burdens furnish the facts of Table XIV, tax rebate has been claimed on agricultural improvements. Since 1945 the total of income tax and surtax reclaimed approximates to £182,970. The total estate duty levied on these estates since 1935 is £462,251. The tax rebates thus amount to 40 % of the estate duty levy. Precise reckoning would probably show a greater percentage. The tax rebate figure was calculated from the rate of income tax and surtax payable by the landowner at the time of survey. In most cases the declared rate was the rate of tax after reduction of the assessed income by the allowance of the maintenance claim and the improvement expenditure claim; it is possible that the rate of tax actually reclaimed was higher because the grossed-up income would be in a higher tax rating than the net income after repair and improvement allowances. Against this must be set the possibility of lower income in past years attracting lower rates of tax. The approximate figure suffices to illustrate the principle and the extent to which tax rebates can act as a counterpoise to estate duty. From what we know of the levels of investment on these estates, there is reason to suppose that on the majority of them there is another and similar ten-years improvement programme waiting fulfilment. If this were undertaken and tax rates remained steady, the total tax rebates would at the end of the period, together with those already won, equal 80 % of the past estate duty levy.

Immediately before money is actually invested in agricultural improvements it exists as consociate capital; this is true even of monetary funds saved from estate incomes. As consociate capital, it runs the risk of meeting the full weight of estate duty. Employed in agricultural improvements it attracts the 45 % estate duty allowance. Here is an additional tax concession gained by the money transferred to agricultural improvements. On forty-nine[1] of the estates just mentioned, the total improvement expenditure attracting tax rebate amounts to £264,000. If estate duty were levied on this improvement money before it was invested in agricultural improvements, the duty would total £113,100. After investment the levy at most would be £62,100, a saving of £51,000. This saving is 13·2 % of the past estate duty. At the end of a further and similar ten-years improvement programme the saving would be doubled, and 26·4 % of the past estate duty.

When capital as a monetary fund is spent on agricultural improvements or transferred from another investment for that purpose, it runs the risk of suffering an immediate drop in value. This cannot be precisely illustrated from the evidence of the fifty-two estates. Indeed little is understood of the relationship between cost of improvement and resulting capital value.[2] On one estate where £376,000 has been spent on the modernisation of cowhouse and dairy stock accommodation, it is estimated that the increment in market value was only £110,000. It is important to bear this risk in mind, lest the benefits gained by transferring capital to agricultural improvement be overestimated.

[1] i.e. forty-nine of the fifty-two estates: three are excepted because information of existing principal value is not available.
[2] cf. p. 193 *post*.

CHAPTER TEN

Physical and Primary Character Traits

THE picture of estate capital so far drawn gives a general impression. Each estate contributes a part and helps to shape the broad strokes and massed outlines in a way peculiar to itself. Some add, some take away: the average and the mode are the features of the picture. Attention has not been focused on estate character. With the exception of size, no attempt has been made to show how estate character influences the provision of estate capital. Size of estate obviously has a bearing upon it. This chapter and the next rearrange the evidence to show how far other traits in estate character influence revenue, income, external funds and other criteria of estate capital.

Physical character traits are paired with primary traits, and abstract traits with secondary. The reason for doing so is a practical one: should a statistical survey of estates and estate character ever be conducted in the interest of agricultural finance it would be easier to identify the physical and primary traits than the abstract and secondary.[1] The physical and primary traits are dealt with in this chapter, and the abstract and secondary in the next.

Size

Size in estates is so much more than the bare sum of acres. There is a correlation between size, income and investment. The greater the size the less the monetary demand per acre for investment. On estates over 10,000 acres in the sample, the average cost per acre of past improvements over the ten years from 1945 is 30s.[2] On the smallest estates below 250 acres, the figure is as high as £32. And for sizes in between cost moves in regular inverse ratio.[3] Outgoings from the

[1]cf. p. 192 *post.*

[2]This figure is arrived at after excluding the evidence of two estates where the expenditure was abnormally high. If included the average expenditure would be £5 6s. per acre; these exceptionally high expenditures have been allowed to influence the figure of past expenditure in Table X.

	acres	£ per acre
[3]i.e.	10,000–2,500	2
	2,500–1,000	7
	1,000– 500	15
	500– 250	19

132

extended and previous surveys show the same tendency. On the largest estates the average yearly outgoing is £1·13 per acre; on the medium-sized estates it rises to £1·28 per acre; and on the estates between 2,500 and 1,000 the figure is £1·47 per acre. Figures are not available for the estates of the central survey. Rental revenues display the same correlation. The revenues of the giants average £0·81 per acre. As size decreases revenue increases, thus: £1·54 (2,500–10,000 acres); £1·74 (1,000–2,500 acres); £2·2 (500–1,000 acres); £2·3 (250–500 acres); and £2·4 per acre on the smallest estates of all.

Yet all estates have not the same degree of competence. Revenue, outgoings and improvement expenditure moving in an opposite direction to the size of estate, move at different velocities. As acreage decreases, outgoings and expenditure rise faster than rental revenue. Tenanted estates under 1,000 acres tend at best to be partially competent, while larger properties, except very extensive estates, are inclined to be wholly competent. The competence of these larger estates is mainly due to low standards of expenditure and would not be so impressive if expenditure was nearer normal. This does not alter the fact that partial competence, more often than not, is caused by rent failing to keep pace with improvement and maintenance expenditure.[1] Although rents are higher per acre on the small estates than on the large estates, the percentage increase in rental revenue required to meet improvement loan redemption is four times greater on the smallest estates (100–250 acres) than on the most extensive properties; and as size increases the necessary proportionate rental increase diminishes.[2] Again, the yearly cost of improvements per acre on the smallest estates is twenty times the cost on the largest estates.[3] But the rental revenue per acre of the smallest estates is only three times that of the largest properties.[4]

Nevertheless, the smaller estate cannot be regarded as the most prone to incompetence. Rents do not keep pace with improvement expenditure, but compared with the largest estates of all, a small estate is more likely to have something to contribute from income to estate capital formation. The small estate gives the impression of struggling to form capital from an inadequate purse, but with greater chance of partial success.

Estates between 1,000 acres and 10,000 acres appear to be the most competent. Many are incompetent, but they have among their number the greatest percentage of wholly competent estates.

[1]cf. p. 54 *ante*. [2]cf. Table XI, p. 86 *ante*.

[3]On the smallest estates the figure is £3·2 per acre; and on the largest estates £0·15 per acre.

[4]On the smallest estates the figure is £2·4 per acre, and on the largest estates £0·8 per acre.

Compared with estates larger than 10,000 acres they are vigorous. A glance at the figures just given shows them on average with a positive estate income, while the largest estates have overspent their revenues. This is no cause for criticism of the largest estates. It merely endorses what has previously been said, that the seeming competence of the medium-sized tenanted estates is due to low expenditure standards and the rents on the largest estates have failed to comprehend normal outgoings.

There is a remarkable correlation between estate size, the magnitude of external funds and the level of investment. The small estates are more securely backed than the larger. The smaller estate tends to finance improvements from the profits of farming enterprise and the larger estate from timber. In item deficiency the larger estates are worse off than the smaller, but there is hardly any difference in percentage deficiency among the size-classes.

Estates of 500–1,000 acres lie across the divide between the smaller estate and the larger estate, and are particularly interesting in consequence. For instance, theirs is the most heavily mortgaged land. At the same time the general standard of equipment and land improvement is good. And yet, the cost of providing outstanding improvements, expressed as a percentage of estate capital, is the highest among the size-classes. These anomalies probably arise because the estates lie between the extensive properties that finance improvement from timber sales and land partition and the smaller estates whose farming enterprise contributes more liberally to total income. In size they have something of the pride of ownership that induces investment but they lack range and variety in estate resources. They are comparatively well supported by external funds, but have a greater percentage than the larger estates of their external fortune in farm stock. The lack of liquid consociate capital probably accounts for their reliance on loans. The cost of providing outstanding improvements is not abnormal, although when expressed as a percentage of estate capital value it is the highest of all. This incongruence suggests that the market value per acre of these estates is out of keeping with their demand for investment in fixed equipment; and hence what is normal expenditure leads to abnormal borrowing.

Estates between 250 and 500 acres have anomalous tendencies of an opposite kind. The rented among them are the most incompetent of all the smaller estates. Both in percentage deficiency and item deficiency their record is the poorest. Past provision is noticeably lower with them than with the smallest estates. And yet they are the least burdened with mortgages and boast the second highest ratio of consociate capital, and the highest ratio of adventitious capital of all the size-classes.

Altogether they give an impression of apathy and indifference. Size probably is responsible. They are essentially farms: too large to be merely residential and benefit from the improvements a residential owner will make for the sake of appearance; and too small to evoke pride of ownership or indeed any sense of landownership and its attendant responsibilities.

The more or less regular ratio between consociate capital and estate capital issues in a higher burden of estate duty per acre on the medium-sized estates.[1] An acre of land on a medium-sized estate bears a higher rate of duty than an acre on a smaller estate because the total fortune of the owner of the smaller estate attracts a lower rate of duty. Estate duty per acre tends to be heavier on the medium-sized estates than on the largest estates because on an extensive estate value per acre is usually lower than on a smaller estate.

Rate of capital provision tends to be slower on the larger estates than on the smaller. Size as such probably has little to do with this, although the more extensive the estate, the greater will be the total demand for investment and the sheer weight of this demand must influence the extent to which it can be satisfied. Tenure pattern rather than size is the greater influence upon the rate of investment. The comparatively slow rate on the larger estates is due to their being entirely tenanted estates.[2]

Size of estate has some bearing upon the motives that restrain investment in agricultural improvements. When the occasions of restraint were numbered, the restraint most frequently encountered was the attraction of better alternative investment, and the next most prominent was the rate of capital formation. Frequency of occurrence does not show how estate size influences motive. Restraints frequently met with on large estates and not on small are the more serious for agriculture.

Restraint can be related to acreage. Diagram IV shows the results. On the large estates better alternative investments do not yield their place as the most prominent form of restraint. But prominence is given to restraints of unwilling tenants, management restriction, estate duty threat, the tax rebate. These on the large estates are almost as serious checks to investment in agricultural improvements as the pull of better alternative investment. Tax rebate is the most serious. Capital is invested in agricultural land improvement until the owner's entire income is no longer sufficient to reap a full rebate. Almost of equal moment is the chagrin and frustration provoked by rigid security of tenure and other aspects of current land policy that curtail a landowner's control of his land and deprive him of a sense of responsibility. Threat of estate duty ranks next; it is a disturbing

[1] cf. Table XIV, p. 126 *ante*.   [2] cf. p. 150 *post*.

ACREAGE REPRESENTATION

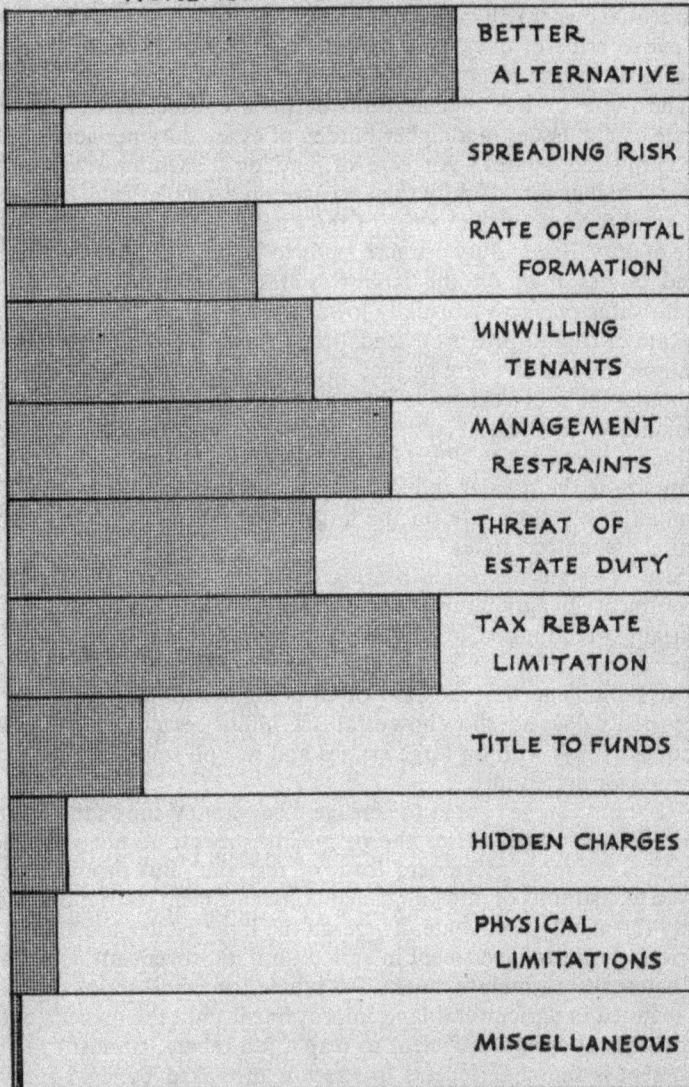

	BETTER ALTERNATIVE
	SPREADING RISK
	RATE OF CAPITAL FORMATION
	UNWILLING TENANTS
	MANAGEMENT RESTRAINTS
	THREAT OF ESTATE DUTY
	TAX REBATE LIMITATION
	TITLE TO FUNDS
	HIDDEN CHARGES
	PHYSICAL LIMITATIONS
	MISCELLANEOUS

DIAGRAM IV. RESTRAINTS ON INVESTMENT IN LAND IMPROVEMENT: ACREAGE REPRESENTATION factor on the larger estate and hence of serious consequence to agricultural finance.

Shape

Compact estates take many forms. Whether elongated, square, rounded or polygonal each lies within a ring-fence. The ring-fence is the hallmark of character. There are no degrees of compactness. Not

TABLE XVI

Competence class	Scattered estates	Compact estates
	% of numbers	% of numbers
100 %	20·8	21·3
50 %+	2·0	12·9
50 % –	18·7	4·7
Nil	50·0	42·3
Tenants' provision	8·5	10·6
No expenditure	—	8·2
	£	£
Revenue per acre	0·98	1·4
Outgoings per acre	0·93	1·25
Improvement expenditure per acre	0·15	0·21

so the scattered estate: its loose-jointed members can lie close together, or be flung apart. There are degrees of scatteredness. The point is not unimportant. An estate of many parcels closely clustered has the appearance and attributes of a compact estate, but one of scattered portions, radiated many miles from a centre, differs much from the compact type. Scattered estates should be graded according to their degree of disjunction. Time has not permitted this. A simple comparison of the compact and the scattered must suffice; but the probable influence of degrees of scatteredness must not be forgotten when weighing the evidence.

TABLE XVII

ESTATE CHARACTER TRAITS AND CO-EFFICIENTS OF SUPPORT FROM EXTERNAL FUNDS

EXTERNAL FUNDS	ESTATE CHARACTER TRAITS							
	Owner-occupied	Tenant-occupied	Compact	Scattered	Estate duty	No estate duty	Surtax	Income tax
CONSOCIATE CAPITAL: Gross total funds	1·78	1·66	2·0	1·14	1·13	2·2	3·61	1·51
Net total funds	1·27	1·58	1·57	1·25	1·12	1·73	0·81	1·11
Net liquid funds	0·53	0·63	0·7	0·44	0·38	0·88	0·87	0·32
ADVENTITIOUS CAPITAL: Total funds	1·78	3·29	3·09	2·61	2·07	3·61	3·84	2·34
THE AVERAGE PERCENTAGE OF ESTATE CAPITAL AND GROSS CONSOCIATE CAPITAL	0·96	0·92	0·95	0·82	0·85	1·05	1·0	0·81
No. of estates in maximum representation	86	99	112	73	82	103	99	86

Arranged in competence classes there is nothing to choose between the competence of scattered and compact estates. A fifth of the number of each type are competent, as Table XVI shows. What difference there is suggests less competence among the scattered estates. The percentage of incompetent estates is higher among the scattered estates than among the compact and points to a weakness in the income of the scattered estates due to relatively low revenue and high outgoings.

Further analysis supports this. Figures of revenue, outgoings and expenditure are given in Table XVI.[1] Rental revenue of the scattered estates is undoubtedly low. The low revenue cannot be explained on the ground of size. Care was taken to provide as far as possible proportionate representation of scattered estates in each size-class. The ideal has not been reached, but the result is near enough to ensure that the evidence for the scattered estates is not biased by an overweight of large estates. Outgoings on the scattered estates are 94 % of revenue compared with an 89 % toll on the compact estates.

Partially competent scattered estates lie mostly in the under-50 % competence class and only a small proportion is over 50 % competent. The reverse is true of the compact estates. From what we know of the causes of partial competence it looks as though improvement expenditure is relatively light on the compact estates. The gist of the evidence is weak but so far as it goes the scattered estate appears the weaker of the two because rents tend to be lower and maintenance and improvement relatively higher than on the compact estates.

Compact estates are more strongly supported than scattered estates by external funds. Table XVII compares the ratios. Degrees of support do not differ greatly. Nevertheless, the compact estates are consistently better covered by gross, net and liquid funds, and by adventitious capital. The advantage of the compact estates is further evident in the comparison of the figures for the ratio of average estate capital to average gross consociate funds. Scattered estates absorb a landowner's total fortune to a greater extent than compact estates do. This is in keeping with their character. Scattered parcels of land are usually more cumbersome to manage than estates in a ring-fence, and one who continues to hold them must be tenacious of his land title and disinclined to transfer capital from land to other purposes.

Shape has little influence upon the sources of consociate capital; see Table XVIII. Difference however occurs in the proportions of consociate capital in agricultural land and other land; the consociate capital of compact estates has the higher proportion.

[1]These are for the larger estates only.

TABLE XVIII

ESTATE CHARACTER TRAITS AND PERCENTAGE CONTRIBUTION
TO CONSOCIATE FUNDS

ESTATE CHARACTER TRAITS

SOURCES	Owner-occupied %	Tenant-occupied %	Compact %	Scattered %	Estate duty %	No estate duty %	Surtax %	Income tax %
Timber	2·1	12·7	7·47	8·1	14·1	2·4	5·63	10·5
Farm stock	46·0	13·2	27·5	31·3	25·8	31·4	25·92	32·9
Agricultural land	3·8	5·7	5·6	3·4	2·9	6·3	4·65	5·1
Other land	2·7	12·7	8·86	6·5	9·0	7·2	7·70	8·5
Stocks and shares	22·9	37·8	31·76	28·7	27·2	33·4	35·97	23·4
Monetary funds	5·4	4·8	4·91	5·3	6·3	4·1	4·37	5·9
Otherwise	17·1	13·1	13·9	16·7	14·7	15·2	15·76	13·7
Number of estates	86	99	114	71	82	103	103	82

Shape appears to influence the level of investment. Percentage deficiency is slightly greater on the compact estates (7·2 %) than on the scattered (6·7 %): see Table XIX. Item deficiency follows suit. Past expenditure[1] on the scattered estates averages £14 6s. per acre, and on the compact estates £22 12s. per acre; and the cost of providing what is wanted averages on the scattered estates £15 6s. and on the compact estates £14 2s. The difference between these latter figures is the reverse of the difference between the percentage and item deficiencies. The cost is more on the scattered estates with their lower deficiencies than on the compact estates where deficiencies are greater. This suggests that the missing items of equipment on the scattered estates are more costly than the missing items on the compact estates. Farmsteads on scattered estates are smaller and more numerous area for area than on compact estates. Want of a single item on a scattered estate would not be as proportionately great as the want of a similar item on a compact estate but it could well be more costly to provide.

Total investment, past provision and present need, is more costly on the compact estate than on the scattered estate. Higher item costs and lower aggregate costs indicate a lower standard of equipment on the scattered estates. Owners of the compact estates are keener investors in improvement. This is supported by a comparison of the response to the total demand for estate capital. Table XXII[2] gives figures for the estates in the main sample. The performance of the scattered estates lags far behind the achievement of the compact estates. Compact estates in the whole sample have provided 62·6 % of the capital demanded, against a 43 % supply achieved by the scattered estates.

A revealing sidelight showing how higher costs per item of equipment may well explain the paradox between physical deficiency and cost of provision on the scattered estates, shines upon the evidence from a further analysis of the motives restraining investment. Physical difficulty in providing fixed equipment and undertaking land improvement is one of the prominent features of restraint on scattered estates. And scattered estates more often than compact estates are restrained in their investment by fetters on the land titles, again illustrating a similarity of character with estate old title.

Structure

All estates in the main sample are agricultural estates but the agriculture varies from estate to estate. The larger estates often have no

---

[1]These figures relate only to the smaller estates for which figures of percentage deficiency are available.   [2]cf. p. 163 *post.*

TABLE XIX
ESTATE CHARACTER TRAITS AND PERCENTAGE DEFICIENCY AND ITEM DEFICIENCY
(Estates under 1,000 acres)

ESTATE CHARACTER TRAITS	CO-EFFICIENT OF DEFICIENCY									GENERAL PERCENTAGE DEFICIENCY
	Housing	Dairy stock accommodation	Yards and boxes	Barns and stores	Implements	Land improvement	Reclamation	Services	Average	
Owner-occupied	40	10	70	70	40	110	20	160	60	7·6
Tenanted	10	30	40	40	40	60	3	210	40	6·1
Compact	20	20	60	60	50	100	10	190	60	7·2
Scattered	40	20	50	60	30	70	10	160	50	6·7
Estate duty	20	20	50	70	70	100	10	240	70	6·6
No estate duty	30	20	60	50	40	80	10	140	50	7·3
Surtax	20	20	50	50	30	80	10	220	60	5·7
Income tax	20	30	60	70	60	90	20	140	60	8·5

dominant type of agriculture to give a distinctive agricultural character and structure. Hence estates over 1,000 acres are treated differently from the smaller estates. Structure distinction on the smaller estates is determined on the area principle. Structure takes its character from the dominant type of farming whether arable, pasture, intermediate, hill-farming, fruit and hops, or market gardening.

The larger estates are classified as agricultural; residential; and silvicultural and mixed. On every estate agricultural land is dominant acre for acre, although on the large upland estates what is styled agricultural land is as much given to sport as to agriculture. Residential estates are distinguished from the agricultural estates by the unit principle.[1] A residential estate carries a mansion house; and the term is used also of an estate that has a village or villages within its purlieus. A mansion house let to a tenant responsible for full maintenance of the fabric is disregarded and does not give a residential character to the estate. Silvicultural and mixed estates are distinguished by the values principle: the term is used of all estates whose standing timber is worth more than 25 % of the market value of the agricultural and residential portion of the estate. Some estates are given to other enterprises and where these occur the estates are included among the silvicultural and mixed estates.

Representation of the three structural types—agricultural, residential and silvicultural and mixed—is fairly well balanced numerically but the silvicultural estates incline to be the more extensive properties. Estates classified by structural type have been compared for competence. An outstanding feature of the comparison is the general low level of competence of the estates in the silvicultural and mixed group. Nearly two-thirds of their number are incompetent. Admittedly, the other third are mostly among the competent, but this figure of 29·1 % is low in comparison with the competence percentages of the agricultural and residential estates. At first glance, the competence of the residential estates appears superior to the competence of the agricultural estates, but the agricultural estates boast a monopoly of tenant-financed estates. This greatly strengthens them and when it is remembered that the competence of the wholly competent is largely a vain glory, there is little doubt that the agricultural estate is truly most competent. The presence of partially competent estates among the agricultural and the residential estates conveys an impression of incomes struggling to achieve something. In contrast, the silvicultural and mixed estates seem to have no inclination to strive. Incompetence is probably due to a preponderance of the most extensive estates. Further analysis is required to discover whether dominant silvicultural enterprise is the cause of

[1]cf. p. 24 *ante.*

incompetence or whether the incompetence is simply a consequence of size.

The number of hill-farming estates, estates given to market gardening or fruit growing is an insignificant sample. The smaller estates are therefore classified as arable, pasture and intermediate. Estates given to pasture farming are distinctly more competent than the others. The arable estates are the weakest. The pasture farming estates have a relatively high proportion of wholly competent estates among them. But their superiority does not rest solely on that questionable ground. Many of them have formed over 50 % of their recent investment from estate income; and they include in their number a goodly representation of the estates whose tenants have financed all improvement investment. Contrasting with this is a high percentage of incompetence and sheer non-investment on the arable estates. The element of non-investment is important because its unfavourable testimony marks the difference between the achievements of the arable and the intermediate types. The intermediate estates have a large proportion of incompetents among them but are not guilty of non-investment.

The superior competence of the pasture estates is not due to high rental revenue. The average rental of let land on the pasture estates[1] is 39s. 9d. per acre; on the intermediate estates it is 49s. 5d. per acre; and on the arable estates it is 45s. 3d. per acre. Nor is the competence of the pasture type due to low improvement expenditure or indifferent standards. Past expenditure on the pasture estates averages £20 12s. per acre compared with £21 10s. per acre on the intermediate estates and £13 15s. per acre on the arable estates. Estimated costs of outstanding improvements move in a reverse ratio: on the pasture estates they average £7 2s. per acre; on the intermediate estates £12 2s. and on the arable estates £17 10s. Clearly the pasture estates have achieved a high level of investment.

Figures for the relative investment levels of the three types of estate confirm this. With the pasture estate the general percentage deficiency is 5·5 %; with the intermediate type it is 7·7 %; and with the arable type it is 8·8 %. Item deficiency figures run parallel with these. The secret of the competence of the pasture types probably lies with outgoings.[2] Support for this deduction is provided by the item deficiency figures for the arable types; these show that the arable estates more frequently than the other types are deficient in services to farmhouses and cottages and they are more heavily burdened with the upkeep of cottages.

[1]Inclusive of those owner-occupied estates with let land.

[2]The large representation of wholly competent estates would probably reduce the average cost of maintenance.

Absolutely and relatively the arable estates have a poorer record than the pasture and intermediate types. Past expenditure and cost of outstanding improvements are in sum lower on the arable estates than elsewhere. And the arable estates have only met 48 % of the total demand for improvement compared with 68 % on the intermediate estates and 77 % on the pasture estates. Doubtless the absolute differences in cost are consequent upon the type of farming, but the low relative achievement of the arable estates points to lethargy and a low standard of equipment. Moreover, the arable estates are the least well supported by consociate capital; a ratio of 1·14 compared with 1·84 on the intermediate estates and 1·28 on the pasture estates. On the arable estates, 52 %[1] of the consociate capital is farm stock and on the pasture estates only 21 %[1] and on the intermediate estates 30 %[1] is immured in this way. Incompetence is associated with a poor supply of liquid funds.

Structure in the larger estates shows a decided correlation with the ratio of estate capital and external funds, especially so with the ratios of consociate capital. Residential estates have the least cover: the average consociate fund gives a £1 for £1 support. Silvicultural and mixed estates do better: a £1 of estate capital is covered by £1 3s. of consociate funds. The most liberal cover is given to the agricultural estates: £1 of estate capital covered by £1 4s. 7d. of consociate capital. The figures for consociate capital are gross. Support from net liquid funds presents a different picture: silvicultural and mixed estates drop to third place. Agricultural estates also receive the more generous support from adventitious funds, and residential estates are second best.

The residential estate appears as the main focus of an owner's fortune. The agricultural estate and the silvicultural type compete with other investments and enterprises to share the fortune. This impression is confirmed by the investment patterns of the consociate funds. Residential estates, occupied for their own sake, spread their consociate funds between timber (30 %), farm stock (15 %), sporting rights (14 %) and stocks and shares (29 %). Silvicultural and mixed estates display their dual character by an emphatic investment in timber (44 %) and a mid-way policy between the residential and the agricultural; besides the 44 % investment in timber, 12 % is in sporting rights, 7 % in farmstock and 29 % in stocks and shares. Agricultural estates are essentially the property of the investor in land; 60 % of the funds are in other land and 24 % in stocks and shares. Timber, farm stock and sporting rights barely have a place.

[1]These percentages have been adjusted to allow for the ratio between tenanted and owner-occupied estates in the sample.

10

Estate structure is also reflected in investment levels. Past investment on the agricultural estates has met 61 % of the total demand.
On the silvicultural and mixed estates the achievements average
49 %.[1] And on the residential estates the percentage sinks to 39 %.
The praiseworthy achievement of the agricultural estates is in keeping
with their investment character.

Holdings pattern

Few estates in the main sample satisfy the definition of a smallholdings estate.[2] All estates over 1,000 acres and 7 % of the smaller
estates fail to qualify. Such evidence as is available reveals an
exceptional competence in the smallholdings estate. Over 75 % of the
few smallholdings estates are either wholly competent or partially
competent. The corresponding figure for the largeholdings estates
is 37 %, if the contribution of tenant-financed estates is counted.
    An explanation of this extraordinary competence does not lie
with rental revenue. Rental revenue on the largeholdings estates
averages £2 3s. per acre; and on the smallholdings estates is £2 2s. 6d.
per acre. Nor is low expenditure nor low standards an explanation.
Past improvement expenditure on the smallholdings estates averages
£28 12s. per acre and on the other types £25 18s. per acre. Estimates
of future expenditure are £8 8s. per acre on the smallholdings estates
and £14 16s. on the largeholdings estates. These figures are paralleled
by the figures for investment level. On the smallholdings estates the
percentage deficiency is as low as 3·3 % and on the estates of larger
holdings it is 7·3 %. Item deficiency figures follow suit. It is the item
deficiency figures that hint at the probable heart of the competence.
The largeholdings estates have a markedly higher deficiency co-
efficient than the smallholdings estates for services to cottages. The
secret of the smallholdings estate may well be in a low maintenance
bill; the holdings are too small for cottages but the tenants are substantial enough to carry responsibility for moderate repairs to the
farmhouses. This hypothesis agrees with the general observations
on competence which stress the relatively low figure for outgoings.
Low outgoings, as explained in the course of the general comment,
may be a cause of genuine competence and not evidence of neglect
and low standards. If the observations just made on the figures for
the smallholdings estates are sound, then these estates provide a
good example of genuine competence through low outgoings.

---

[1]Excluding the anomaly mentioned in note p. 153, the figure becomes
44 %.
    [2]cf. p. 25 *ante*.

Tenure pattern

Although the owner of a large estate may farm an extensive acreage in hand, only very rarely is it sufficient to regard the estate as an owner-occupied estate. Owner-occupation of large estates is so rare that it was not possible to furnish the main sample with an adequate number of owner-occupied estates above 1,000 acres. Comparisons between the owner-occupied and tenant-occupied estates in the main sample have to make allowance therefore for an overweight of tenant-occupied estates among the larger estates.

Comparison of competence is not possible between owner-occupied and tenant-occupied estates. Competence depends upon estate income derived from rental revenue and owner-occupied estates by definition have no significant rental revenue. Rent is the yearly consideration paid for the use of the land and buildings by the farming community who hire land. Ideally it is a contribution from the annual earnings of the industry. Owner-occupiers make analogous contributions in the form of interest on capital invested in the ownership of land and buildings, as expenditure on the maintenance of buildings and fixed equipment and as yearly investments to a capital in improvements. It is reasonable therefore to compare the competence of tenant-occupied estates to form capital from estate income with the competence of owner-occupied estates to form capital from farming profits. Competence is thus compared in Table XX.

More has been achieved from farming profits than from rental income. The difference, though distinctive, is by no means striking. Of ninety-one owner-occupied estates only 13 % are wholly competent, compared with a percentage of 7·6 % among the tenant-occupied. When the tenanted estates whose tenants have contributed the entire improvement expenditure are taken into account, the percentage of competent estates among the tenanted properties jumps to 23 % and definitely outpaces the owner-occupied achievements. The owner-occupied have the best showing in the percentage of the numbers competent to form over 50 % of the estate capital. On the other hand, 33 % of their number are incompetent; a percentage not far below the incompetent 43 % of the tenant-occupied.

Gross consociate funds give stronger support to owner-occupied estates than to tenant-occupied as shown by the ratios of Table XVII. This is not true of net and liquid funds. Nor is it true of the adventitious funds. The average ratio of gross consociate fund to estate capital on the tenanted estates does not differ materially from the corresponding ratio on the owner-occupied estates. It is depressed by the influence of the low ratios characteristic of the largest

TABLE XX

COMPETENCE TO FORM CAPITAL FROM RENTAL INCOME COMPARED WITH COMPETENCE TO FORM CAPITAL FROM FARMING PROFITS

COMPETENCE CLASS	TENANT-OCCUPIED				OWNER-OCCUPIED			
	100–249 acres	250–499 acres	500–999 acres	Average	100–249 acres	250–499 acres	500–999 acres	Average
	% of class	% of class	% of class	% of class	% of class	% of class	% of class	% of class
100 %	18	—	4	7·6	13·2	20·0	6·5	13·2
50 %+	14	4	18	12·1	30·0	36·7	38·7	35·1
50 %–	5	14	14	10·6	3·3	10·0	16·1	9·9
Nil	31	59	42	43·9	43·6	20·0	35·5	33·0
Unknown	—	—	4	1·5	6·6	10·0	3·2	6·6
No Expenditure	9	14	4	9·1	3·3	3·3	—	2·2
Tenant sole contributor	23	9	14	15·2	—	—	—	—
Number of estates	22	22	22	—	30	30	31	—
Acreage	3,731	7,887	16,424		5,142	10,430	21,608	

estates. When comparison is limited to the estates under 1,000 acres, the relationship of the ratios alters. Support from gross funds behind the tenanted estates becomes stronger than the corresponding support behind the owner-occupied estates.

The superiority of the external funds supporting the tenanted estates is not apparent when the figures are compared for the ratio of the average sum of estate capital and the average consociate gross fortune. These figures tend to reflect the mode of the ratios of the individual fortunes. Between the owner-occupied and the tenanted estates there is almost parity, although the tenanted estates gain somewhat if the figures for the larger estates are excluded. Parity does not mean that acre for acre, the tenanted estates are as well-supported by external funds as the owner-occupied. Land values must be reckoned with. Let farms are notoriously less valuable than farms with vacant possession. At the time of the surveys this was more evident than it is today. A £1 for £1 support, therefore, is likely to mean more per acre for an owner-occupied estate than for a tenanted estate. Measured against the market value of the estate the external funds of the tenanted estates appear to be superior to the funds of the owner-occupied estates, but in absolute fortune the owner-occupied have the advantage.

This advantage of the owner-occupied estates will tend to offset the greater support behind the tenanted estates expressed by the ratios of Table XVII. But the equalising principle is only true of the total fortunes behind the estates. When the sources of consociate capital are discovered and compared, advantage undoubtedly rests with the tenanted estates as Table XVIII illustrates. Liquid funds are proportionately greater. Of the consociate capital behind the owner-occupied estates, 46 % is locked away in farm stock and only 28 % is available as stocks and shares and monetary funds. With the tenanted estates, 26 % is locked away in timber and farm stock and 42 % is available in stocks, shares and monetary funds.

The more liberal supply of liquid funds to the tenanted estates has not led to a higher level of investment. On the owner-occupied estates the average percentage deficiency is 7·6 %; and on the tenanted estates is 6·1 %: see Table XIX. The difference is not great and it does not follow that the tenanted estates have provided a more substantial investment in estate equipment and land improvement. Past improvement cost on the tenanted estates[1] averages £11 18s. per acre, and on the owner-occupied estates £25 2s. per acre. The estimated cost of outstanding improvements on the tenanted estates is £11 6s. per acre; and on the owner-occupied estates is £16 18s. per acre. Estimated expenditure on the owner-occupied

[1]On the smaller estates for which percentage deficiency figures are available.

estates is thus 49 % greater than the corresponding figure for the tenanted estates and yet the disparity in physical deficiency is only 20 %.

What is true of the provision of equipment in general is paralleled by the figures for item deficiency. On tenanted estates the most prominent lack is services to cottages and farmhouses; there are three tenanted estates for every two owner-occupied estates in need of these improvements. Tenanted estates on the other hand are well off for housing. Inadequate services is the most serious lack of the owner-occupied estates, although the tenanted estates have the greater absolute deficiency. And the owner-occupied estates are more conscious than the tenanted estates of a need for land improvement.

Comparison of supply and demand figures also shows the tenanted estate to disadvantage. Table XXII[1] gives the figures. The tenanted estates of the main sample have, on average, met only 50·1 % of the demand. On the owner-occupied estates the achievement is 64·5 %. The disparity is not influenced by estate size. Admittedly all the larger estates are tenanted, but the verdict of the figures for the smaller estates is no more favourable to the tenanted estate: an average of 53·1 % for the tenanted contrasts with a 64·5 % for the owner-occupied. Although the owner-occupied have achieved so much they are the least satisfied of the two types. Clearly their owners are aiming at higher standards. The figures of Table XXII confirm that the lower achievements of the larger estates shown in the figures of Table X are not due to the size of estate but to the influence of tenure pattern. The larger estates have a poorer record of achievement because they are all tenanted estates.

[1] p. 163.

CHAPTER ELEVEN

Abstract and Secondary Character Traits

THE previous chapter has told only half the story of estate character traits and the provision of estate capital. Abstract and secondary traits must be considered. Hence we turn now to duration, ownership personality and taxability.

Duration

Tradition and a sense of the historic are strengthened by the passage of time. Although the roots of tradition grow quickly, estates of old title are likely to be more sensible of traditions and history's antecedents than estates of new title. The past can dominate the present in landownership. It may inspire a present moral rectitude and in the mind of one for whom improvement of the land is a solemn duty provide a strong motive for investment irrespective of the competence of estate income. Age-honoured tenurial ties and set ideas of estate management are one with the character of estates of old title, and may materially and adversely affect estate income. Estates of old title it might be supposed would be more incompetent than estates of new title.

Comparison of the competence of old and new title estates does not entirely support this hypothesis. The percentage of wholly competent estates among those of old title is double that of the estates of new title. But if the percentage of tenant-financed estates among those of new title were added to the percentage of competent estates, the sum would almost equal the percentage of competent estates of old title. This is a justifiable addition. Estates whose capital is formed from tenants' improvements have a very real competence, indeed a competence more worthy than one occasioned by low standards of repair.[1] Paradoxically, the estates of old title have a decidedly higher percentage of incompetence than those of new title. But the new title estates have a black record of non-investment. The percentage of their non-investment corresponds closely with the difference between the higher percentage of incompetence in old title estates and the percentage of incompetence in new title estates.

[1]cf. p. 53 *ante.*

It more than counterbalances the greater incompetence of the old title estates. A high percentage of incompetence is far more worthy than a low percentage of incompetence and a high percentage of non-investment.

Old title estates are not less competent than estates of new title, nor are they superior. The balances are even. But the behaviour of the old title estates is conventional. They form capital, when they form it at all, from estate income. The new title estates, less orthodox, break away from the conventional and encourage tenants' investment. The achievement would be more spectacular if the majority of the tenant-financed estates were not those with special tenurial arrangements, close family and other affinities binding landlord and tenant.[1] A low percentage of incompetence among the estates of new title is somewhat illusory because what is gained thereby is lost by the percentage of non-investment.

Estates of old title on average are more highly regarded than new title estates by their owners, for a greater proportion of an owner's fortune is invested in estate capital. Estates of old title are supported by smaller external funds than estates of new title. On the old title estates a £1 of estate capital is backed by £1 8s. 7d. consociate capital and £1 0s. 5d. adventitious capital; on new title estates the supporting funds are £1 15s. 7d. and £3 8s. 5d. respectively. A majority of large estates among those of old title would account in some measure for the weaker supporting funds. Comparison of the consociate funds supporting estates below 1,000 acres does not show a similar disparity. Indeed, the evidence indicates that old title estates in the size range 250–1000 acres tend to be somewhat better supported than the new title estates by consociate capital, and hence they tend to suffer a higher estate duty burden than new title estates[2] do. With the larger estates consociate capital gives weaker support to the old title estates than to the new title estates, because the value per acre tends to be higher on the old title estates. Elimination of the larger estates makes no difference to the ratio of adventitious capital.

There is a predisposition among owners of old title estates to let their land. Admittedly old title estates are inclined to be large and hence to be tenanted. But old titles among the lesser estates are inclined to be tenanted estates. Analysis of their sources of consociate capital endorses this.[3] Consociate capital of old title estates is contributed mainly from stocks and shares and other land, to the extent of 40 % and 22 % respectively; these figures contrast with

[1]cf. pp. 171-172 *post.*   [2]cf. pp. 124-126.

[3]Evidence for estates from 100 acres–2,500 acres in the central survey is analysed because for these estates there is evidence of the sources of finance for past improvements.

29 % and 12 %, the corresponding percentages for new title estates. Consociate capital behind new title estates is 37 % in farm stock. Past improvements on old title estates have been financed from rent, other income and stocks and shares in the percentages 17 %, 28 % and 16 % respectively. To past improvements on new title estates these sources contributed 11 %, 58 % and 11 % respectively; the bulk of the 58 % other income is farming profits. Timber sales, sales of land, loans and realisation of other forms of investment on old title estates contributed more liberally to the finance of past improvements than on new title estates. A picture emerges of these smaller estates of old title committed to agricultural tenancies, yet bravely realising a comparatively limited consociate capital to finance estate improvements.

Duration has little influence on the investment pattern of consociate funds supporting the larger estates. Farm stock is below 10 %. Both old and new titles have about 30 % invested in timber. Differences occur in the percentages contributed by other land, by stocks and shares and by sporting rights. Old title estates spread their resources: 22 % in other land, 24 % in stocks and shares and 15 % in sporting rights. New title estates concentrate investment in stocks and shares, 34 %, and leave 17 % in other land and 5 % in sporting rights.

Old title estates of the smaller size-classes have a general percentage deficiency of 6·1 % compared with a 7·2 % deficiency among the new title estates. Past improvement on old title estates has only met 55 % of the total demand but on new title estates has made a 66 % provision; and old title estates have a higher item deficiency. Moreover, improvement expenditure per acre both in the past and as estimated for present needs is relatively low. The sum of this evidence suggests that the demand for improvements on the old title estates is not so much a demand for new accommodation as for the improvement of existing accommodation, often costly and difficult to do. This is borne out to some extent by a high item deficiency in services to farmhouses and cottages on the old title estates. What is known of investment levels on the larger estates corresponds with these facts. Old title estates have provided for 34 %[1] of the total demand for investment but new title estates have managed 50 %, and yet the cost per acre of providing for the estimated need on the old title estates averages £3 8s. compared with a corresponding figure of £5 8s. on the new title estates.

Forces restraining the investment of consociate funds in agricultural improvement differ in emphasis between old and new title estates. Legal restrictions clogging the title of ownership are apt to

[1]Exclusive of an exceptional anomaly; cf. p. 146 ante.

be a greater hindrance on old title estates than on new title estates. Owners of the old title estates appear more cautious than the owners of the new title estates and spread their risks more widely. But the need to conserve capital is a more influential inhibition on the new title estates than it is on the old.

Ownership personality

Representation of ownership personality in the sample is entirely fortuitous. Of the tenanted estates 66 % belongs to real persons, either individually or as joint tenants; joint tenancies could not be classified apart from simple proprietorships, since there were insufficient joint tenancies to justify classification. Trustees own 24 % of the tenanted estates; the trusts vary greatly, but studies of distinctive trust forms were not possible. Although joint tenancies at law are a form of trust, they have not been included among the conventional trustee proprietorships and are included among the estates of real persons. The remaining 10 % of the rented estates is owned by private companies, mainly estate companies. Incorporate bodies other than limited liability companies were not represented in the main sample; two estates only are owned by public joint stock companies.

Comparison of competence would be more satisfying if numbers were better balanced. The figures portray correlation between competence and what may be termed the personal element in ownership. Of the three types of ownership personality, ownership by a real person is the most personal. Ownership by trustees comes half-way between this and ownership by a limited company, which is the most impersonal form. The less there is of a personal element the greater the competence. If estates with tenant-financed capital are included among the competent, 36 % of the estates owned by companies are competent. The corresponding percentages for trustee-owned estates and estates owned by persons are 26 % and 27 % respectively. All estates owned by companies have made some effort at investment, and these estates boast the lowest percentage of incompetence. Trustee-owned estates show an achievement superior to the estates of persons by a relatively high percentage of partially competent estates, especially the percentage of estates forming over 50 % of capital from estate income.

Allowing for a poor representation of company-owned estates, the evidence indicates that the estates of real persons compared with trustee and company estates have weaker estate incomes. Better representation of company-owned estates might alter the picture. As it is, it leaves an impression of greater business efficiency among estates owned by private companies, of a tighter grip on out-goings, and of a comparative reluctance on the part of the personal owners to face the problem of rental revision.

Ownership personality exerts a potent influence upon the ratios of estate capital and external funds, especially upon the ratio of adventitious capital. Estates held by trustees more than estates owned by private companies and real persons are generously supported by adventitious funds. A trust often associates two or more fortunes: the fortune in trust to which the estate belongs and the fortunes of the beneficiaries. Fortune belonging to a beneficiary on whose behalf an estate is held in trust can be a useful source of adventitious capital, especially if the beneficiary is a tenant for life under a settlement. Estate capital of the trustee-owned estates in the sample has on average a fourfold cover from adventitious funds. Estate capital owned by real persons is twice covered by adventitious funds. And the adventitious funds supporting company-owned estates give an almost £ for £ support. Consociate capital does not provide a similar pattern. Estates of real persons are the most strongly supported, and company-owned estates the least. The evidence is not as definite as the evidence for adventitious capital and certain extreme anomalies have been excluded from the figures. Both company-owned and trustee-owned estates are the subjects of transferred fortunes; he who alienates the estate may also pass with it part of a fortune which in the transaction becomes the consociate capital of the estate. It is understandable that consociate funds should be greater with the estates of real persons than with those owned by companies and bodies of trustees.

Consociate funds reflect through their investment patterns, no less strikingly than by their relationship to estate capital, differences in the ownership personality of the estates they support. Trustees among the smaller estates surveyors avoid business enterprise and invest consociate funds mainly in other land (29 %) and stocks and shares (39 %) and barely at all in farm stock (6·9 %). In stark contrast is the company-owned estate with the major part of consociate funds invested in farm stock (38 %) and other business projects (31 %) and with comparatively light investments in stocks and shares (8·4 %). Funds owned by real persons display the farming interest of the company-owned estates and have 33 % in farm stock; and the security sense of the trustee-owned estates, by a further 33 % in stocks and shares. Contributions to the finance of past improvements are in keeping. Trustee-owned estates have relied mainly on sales of land (29 %) and sales of stocks and shares (23 %). Company-owned estates have drawn major percentages from rents (17 %), other income (60 %) and loans (12 %). And on the estates of real persons the main contributions have been rent (14 %), other income (53 %) and the sale of stocks and shares (12 %).

Ownership personality of the larger estates influences the investment pattern of their consociate funds along parallel lines. Investment in timber, however, takes the place occupied by farm stock on the smaller estates. Correspondence is not exact since the trustee-owned large estate shows a greater interest in timber investment (28 %) than its smaller prototype shows in farm stock. But like its smaller counterpart, the larger trustee-owned estate has a high percentage of its funds in other land (34 %) and a goodly portion in stocks and shares (28 %). Emphasis on business investment is again evident in the consociate funds of the company-owned estates; 56 % is in timber, 14 % in other business enterprise and only 15 % in stocks and shares. Ownership by real persons discloses the personal touch in the investment policy by relatively high percentages in farm stock (11 %) and sporting rights (14 %) and the bulk of the remaining investment divided between timber (24 %) and stocks and shares (37 %).

The smaller estates owned by real persons have, in contrast to trustee and company estates, attained a higher level of investment. General percentage deficiency on personal estates is 6·9 %; on company estates 7·2 %; and on the trustee estates 8·7 %. Trustee estates make poor showing from all angles. Past improvements on them have only met 48 % of the total demand. On the personal estates the achievement is 65 %; and on company estates is 60 %. Item deficiency figures follow suit. Expenditure on the trustee estates is half what it is on the company estates and two-thirds of the expenditure on the personal estates.

The larger estates are in contrast with the smaller. Trustee estates take the van; and the estates owned by real persons are in the rear. The trustee estates have provided 58 % of the total demand for investment; company estates 40 %; and the personal estates 30 %. Moreover, the low standard of investment so patent with the smaller trustee-owned estates is not indicated by the evidence for the larger estates.

Restraints differ in emphasis with ownership personality. Tax rebate plays a dominant role in the experience of company estates. Estates owned by private companies more than others are prone to suffer from shortened incomes restricting the advantages of tax rebate on agricultural improvements. Prominent among the restraints troubling trustees are the threat of estate duty and fettered land titles prohibiting or restricting the employment of capital funds in land improvement. Trustees, however, are not so inclined to husband their capital to provide an income for financing improvements.

Taxability

When taxability was described earlier a simple distinction was made between taxable estates and estates exempt from taxation. Estates exempt for one reason or another were designated 'Charity Estates'. These are considered in a special chapter set aside for the purpose. Other estates differ in taxability. Differences determine estate character and we must here consider how far this character variation affects the provision of estate capital.

Estate Duty

The special study[1] of the incidence of estate duty for the purpose of analysis distinguishes between estates that have suffered the impost and estates that have escaped it. All the estates are potential victims and many of the favoured have suffered duty under previous owners. The abstract character of an estate links together land and title. An estate is classed as not suffering estate duty if during the period of the present title the land has escaped the impost. New titles are better advantaged than estates of longer duration; but among the favoured are properties whose owners have held them since the first days of estate duty in 1894; and others, passed as gifts from living hand to living hand, have escaped the ill consequence of a death. Land of an incorporate company does not attract estate duty, for the company cannot die although estate duty is borne by the shares of a deceased shareholder. When a majority shareholder in an estate company dies, the effect of estate duty on the shares differs little from the effect of a direct levy on the land;[2] estates that have borne estate duty in this way are included among the sufferers. Incidence and payment are not the same thing. Estate duty imposed on estate capital can be met from consociate capital. Classification follows the incidence and not the source of payment. Estates classified as suffering estate duty have at some time been the subject of a levy, irrespective of the manner of its payment.

Estate duty as a levy on capital is not likely to influence the formation of estate capital from income, although much depends upon the manner of measurement. If the competence of income to meet past yearly investment were the measure, imposition of estate duty would not influence the degree of competence. But if competence were measured as the power of estate income to contribute both to past investment and present needs, a drain of capital as estate duty may have left an entail of neglect and impoverishment and this would reflect upon the competence of the income. There would be no point

[1] cf. Chapter IX.   [2] cf. p. 94 *ante.*

in measuring competence by this second method if there was reason to believe that past investment on all estates was uniform, and hence the relative power of estate incomes to meet it was a genuine measurement of competence. Unfortunately we cannot have this confidence.[1] It is necessary, therefore, to attempt a comparison of the competence of the favoured and the suffering estates by measuring the competence of their estate incomes to meet the joint demand of past investment and present needs. Estate incomes are only known for the estates of the previous and extended surveys. Comparison on this basis and limited to these estates is made in Table XXII. Between the figures for the sufferers and the favoured there is a striking similarity. The impost of estate duty does not appear to have influenced adversely the competence of the estate incomes.

Clearer distinction marks the support of external funds. The sufferers are less well supported. Table XVII gives the ratios between estate capital and external funds. Both in consociate and adventitious funds the sufferers are poorer than the favoured; a disparity true also of net and liquid funds. There is greater difference between adventitious funds than between consociate funds. For every £1 of estate capital the sufferers are backed by £1 3s. of consociate capital (gross) and by £2 1s. 3d. of adventitious capital; the favoured estates are backed by £2 4s. consociate capital and £3 12s. adventitious capital. Blame for the shorter funds behind the sufferers must not be laid entirely at the feet of estate duty. More estates of old title are among the sufferers and estates of old title are less well-endowed, £ for £ of estate capital, by consociate and adventitious funds.[2] Estate duty, however, cannot be wholly exonerated: differences between the average support co-efficients of old and new title estates are less than the differences in these ratios between the sufferers and the favoured. Some other reducing agent has been at work, and it is reasonable to suspect estate duty.

Advantage lies also with the favoured estates in a higher percentage of liquid assets among their consociate capital. Table XVII shows the liquid funds of the favoured estates giving more than double the support given to the sufferers by their liquid funds. And what is more, this double strength has already borne greater mortgage burdens than the burdens deducted from the gross funds of the sufferers to give a net figure. Obviously the percentage of total fortune invested in liquid assets is greater with the favoured. Comparison of the investment patterns provided by Table XVIII shows to what extent. The favoured estates have a liquid consociate investment of 37·5 % and the sufferers one of 33·5 %. Timber accounts for the difference. The consociate funds of the sufferers have 14 %

invested in timber against a 2·4 % of the consociate funds of the favoured. Timber attracts estate duty concession and the sufferers have probably learnt a lesson from the past.

Low consociate capital means less support for agricultural estate investment. Estate duty can be more than a personal grievance. Reduced external funds are likely to lead eventually to lower levels of investment. Although comparison of competence shows no difference in the power of estate income to form capital, an analysis of the figures for investment levels indicates a tendency among the sufferers to have a standard of equipment lower than the standards of the favoured estates. Old title estates being greater in number among the sufferers may be a partial cause. Percentage deficiency of the sufferers is 6·6 % and on the favoured estates is 7·3 %. At first glance therefore the sufferers appear the better provisioned. Item deficiency reverses the evidence, especially deficiency in services to farmhouses and cottages: see Table XIX.

Cost of making outstanding improvements on the land of the sufferers is estimated as £13 10s.; and on the favoured estates is £15 6s. Expenditure in the past on the land of the sufferers has been £17 2s. per acre and on the estates of the favoured £21 12s. per acre. Achievements in supply and demand are remarkably alike: the sufferers have supplied 52·9 % of the total demand, and the favoured 52·8 %: see Table XXII.

In sum, the evidence points to an investment per acre on those estates where estate duty has been suffered lower than the investment per acre on the favoured estates. The high item deficiency suggests relatively petty wants and the whole pattern is noticeably similar to the deficiency pattern of old title estates.[1] Indeed the preponderance of old title estates probably more than the direct impact of estate duty influences the adverse evidence for the sufferers. Conversely, a majority of sufferers among the old title estates could account for the similarity of evidence.[2]

Further, restraints cramping investment on the lands of the sufferers are similar in many respects to the restraints on old title estates. And, what is also logical, the sufferers more so than the favoured are sensitive to threats of estate duty.

Income tax and surtax

Income tax is a tax on income. All incomes are assessed to tax, whether incomes of people, incorporate bodies or other fictitious persons. Surtax is discriminating. It is first cousin to income tax but is a tax on the higher levels of the income of real persons. Surtax is

[1]cf. pp. 153, 154 *ante*.   [2]cf. Table XII.

not levied *per se* on the income of an institution, company or fictitious person. The Revenue authorities, however, can deem undistributed income of a company to be the income of its members,[1] and only in this oblique fashion and to this extent can a company be said to bear surtax.

Surtax is graduated according to the amount of the income and is additional to income tax. At the time of the surveys the combined weight of income tax and surtax would subject incomes above £15,000 a year to a tax of 19s. 6d. in the £; the rate diminished regularly to 11s. 6d. in the £ on incomes between £2,000 and £2,500 a year. On a large estate with a five-figure rent-roll, increase in rental revenue is of little moment, unless it is spent on repairs or improvements and the expenditure is set against the assessment of estate income to income tax and surtax. On an agricultural estate maintenance and improvement expenditure can be set off against income not derived from the estate. Wealthy owners of agricultural estates may therefore be tempted to disregard the rental revenues of their estates so long as total income is sufficient for all repairs and improvement expenditure to be deducted. Such a policy would impair the competence of estate incomes.

Table XXI compares the competence of estates whose owners are subject to surtax with the competence of estates whose income is charged to income tax only.

The surtaxed estates are less competent than the others; the percentage of competent numbers is lower, and the percentage of incompetent numbers is higher. But the degree of difference, especially the difference in competence, is very slight. Although the surtax estates outnumber the income tax estates, they are fairly evenly distributed among the size-classes and size of estate is not likely to influence these percentages. However great the temptation to neglect estate revenue and boost estate expenditure may have been, it was successfully resisted.

A surtax payer is obviously possessed of greater income than a man liable for income tax only, but it does not follow that the surtax payer has the larger fortune. A man with a high salary and relatively small capital would pay surtax. And an estate company as we have seen is never liable for surtax but might well own extensive consociate funds. Nevertheless, a surtax payer is more likely than an income tax payer to have a deeper purse. But it does not follow that the estate he owns would have greater support from consociate capital: he may invest a larger percentage than the income tax payer of his fortune in his land. Table XVII shows that at large the surtax estates sport a higher ratio than the income tax estates of external

[1]Income Tax Act 1952, Section 245.

funds to estate capital. On the surtax estates the ratio between estate capital and consociate capital gives a cover of £3 12s. for every £1 of estate capital; on income tax estates the cover is £1 10s. For adventitious capital the respective figures are £3 16s. 9d. and £2 6s. 9d. In all funds the surtax estates are the stronger, an advantage also borne out by a comparison of the figures for the ratio of the average estate capital to the average gross consociate fund.

TABLE XXI

TAXABILITY AND COMPETENCE TO FORM ESTATE CAPITAL

COMPETENCE CLASS	* Estate duty suffered	* No estate duty	Surtax	Income tax
	% of numbers	% of numbers	% of numbers	% of numbers
100 %	39·2	38·5	20·0	22·4
50 % +	3·6	7·6	9·4	8·6
50 % −	7·2	3·9	9·3	10·4
Nil	50·0	50·0	48·0	41·3
Tenants' provision	—	—	9·3	10·4
No expenditure	—	—	4·0	6·9
Number of estates	67	66	75	58

* Competence is measured as the power of estate income to meet both past and present needs; and the evidence limited to the estates of the previous and the extended surveys.

Nowhere is the advantage of the surtax estates more pronounced than in the percentage of liquid consociate funds. Liquid funds behind the surtax estates give support almost three times as great as the support given by liquid funds to the income tax estates. The key is given in Table XVIII. Only 29 % of the consociate funds of income tax estates are in stocks, equities and monetary funds; the

11

corresponding percentage with the surtax estates is 40 %. Income-taxed fortunes are more heavily invested in farm stock. This is not surprising. What is curious, is 10·5 % of these fortunes lodged in timber, a percentage almost double the timber investment behind the surtax estates. Ownership personality is a probable explanation: certain of the large, timber-bearing estates do not belong to the surtax group, despite the size of their gross incomes, because they are owned by companies and trusts not subject to surtax.

Investment levels also differ. Surtax estates have an average percentage deficiency of 5·7 %; for income tax estates the figure is 8·5 %: see Table XIX. Surtax estates clearly have the higher level of investment. Surtax estates, low in percentage deficiency, have nevertheless as many needy among their numbers as the income tax estates. Item deficiencies are equal. Parity in item deficiency does not betoken a lower standard of provision on the surtax estates. Past improvements on these estates average £22 6s. per acre, compared with £16 6s. per acre[1] on the income tax estates. Moreover, the cost of making good the 8·5 % deficiency on the income tax estates is £17 10s. per acre; and the cost of making good the 5·7 % deficiency on the surtax estates is £12 4s. per acre.

Lower deficiency on the surtax estates is the direct outcome of generous investment in the past that has made the present task correspondingly lighter. Equality in item deficiency is only true of the average figures. For every item save one, deficiency on the surtax estates is less than on the income tax estates. Services to cottages and farmhouses is the exceptional item: see Table XIX. Deficiency on the surtax estates for this item is 50 % higher than on the income tax estates. Now tax rebate for agricultural improvements is claimable on one-third only of expenditure on farmhouses. It is reasonable to postulate that expenditure on the surtax estates has been concentrated on the provision and improvement of items other than farmhouse improvements. The word 'farmhouse' in the Statute[2] that prescribes the limitation is loosely construed by the law courts. In common parlance farmhouse means a house occupied by a farmer; but the law courts liberalise the meaning to connote a farmhouse occupied by a farmer's employees.[3] A stricter construction would go some way to relieving the restraint which the present legal construction puts upon investment in the improvement of farmhouses.

Supply and demand figures given in Table XXII, support the above evidence. Surtax estates on average have provided a 54·9 % of the total demand, and the income tax estates a 50·9 %. The figures for the smallest and largest size-class are of some moment. In both, the

[1] These figures are for the smaller estates only.
[2] Income Tax Act, 1952, Section 314 (2) (a).
[3] cf. *Lindsay* v. *C.I.R.* (1953), 34 T.C. 289.

TABLE XXII

ESTATE CHARACTER TRAITS AND PERCENTAGE OF TOTAL REQUIREMENT
PROVIDED BY PAST IMPROVEMENTS

SIZE CLASS (acres)	ESTATE CHARACTER TRAITS								
	Size %	Owner-occupied %	Tenant-occupied %	Compact %	Scattered %	Estate duty %	No estate duty %	Surtax %	Income tax %
100–249	70·1	63·4	66·7	68·1	47·1	63·4	64·2	71·9	46·7
250–499	59·0	61·5	52·2	81·6	55·8	61·6	57·6	59·8	58·3
500–999	60·8	68·8	40·5	65·6	51·2	48·8	65·1	55·2	65·4
1,000–2,499	51·2	—	51·2	69·2	42·8	78·1	40·2	50·5	71·6
2,500–9,999	42·5	—	42·5	45·0	38·6	41·7	43·7	44·0	41·1
*10,000+	47·7	—	47·7	46·5	22·7	23·8	46·3	48·2	22·8
Average all size classes	55·2	64·5	50·1	62·6	43·0	52·9	52·8	54·9	50·9

* Excluding one exceptional anomaly.

surtax estates achieve something far more spectacular than the achievement of the income tax estates. Owners of the largest estates are likely to have incomes attracting surtax at a high rate. Surtax estates among the smallest estates probably have the highest proportion of consociate income to estate income[1] and a greater total income per acre with a correspondingly wider capacity for tax rebate.

When restraints on investment are compared one feature above all others distinguishes the surtax estates from the income tax estates: tax rebate. Investment is limited on the surtax estates far more than on the income tax estates by the capacity of income to attract tax rebate; incomes obviously are not straitened, but the excessive tax burdens they carry render tax rebate on agricultural improvements of greater moment to the recipient.

[1]cf. Table V, p. 65 *ante.*

CHAPTER TWELVE

Tenant Opinion

A different viewpoint

WHEN land is let the landowner is out of touch with the practical requirements of every day. He does not use the buildings and other fixed equipment and test at first hand the effectiveness of land drainage and reclamation. Equipment is in the tenant's hands. The tenant experiences the practical and effectual consequences of land improvement. A landowner judges the needs of the land for fixed equipment, and hence the investment level, from a viewpoint peculiar to himself. His notion of what is required can differ from the tenant's ideas not because he is indifferent, or allows his judgement to be swayed by the attraction of alternative investment, but because he is influenced by his estate in the land. For him equipment is an investment in estate capital. Should he own the fee simple in the land, his judgement is coloured by his perpetual inheritance. Instinctively, he thinks of the long future and not of the immediate present. What may be warranted today, with the land let to the present tenant and farming policy pointed by present preferences, may be of no consequence to-morrow. Time alters both tenancy and farming policy.

The tenant sees things from a different viewpoint. He is the producer, the man of the moment, and of present circumstances. He thinks of farmsteads and fencing, roads and reclamation, as he thinks of his implements. They are means of production, geared to a present economy and set to an immediate purpose, and by these criteria must their adequacy and effectiveness be judged. Nevertheless, an intelligent tenant informed by experience is in some respects better qualified to give a sound opinion of the capacities of the land than a landlord who has never farmed it. A tenant's perspicacity may well be the shrewder insight into the long-term needs of the land. At all events, sound judgement requires the one opinion to be weighed with the other.

Comparison of opinions

The influence of a different emphasis and change of viewpoint upon the measurement of the investment level of estate capital is demonstrated in Tables XXIII and XXIV. Percentage deficiency and item

TABLE XXIII

PERCENTAGE DEFICIENCY OPINION OF LANDLORD AND TENANT COMPARED

(82 estates of central survey)

SIZE OF ESTATE (acres)	IN GENERAL		ACCORDING TO GRADED CONSEQUENCE							
			FIRST		SECOND		THIRD		FOURTH	
	Landlord	Tenant	Landlord	Tenant	Landlord	Tenant	Landlord	Tenant	Landlord	Tenant
100–249	5·60	7·87	3·81	7·05	9·53	9·72	4·69	7·50	4·22	7·27
250–499	8·31	8·83	6·61	7·87	10·70	9·96	11·00	11·00	0·00	5·67
500–999	6·31	7·97	7·04	6·66	4·89	9·50	7·39	8·04	1·89	1·95
1,000–2,500	7·91	10·28	7·64	9·54	7·73	11·37	7·00	8·00	4·50	6·00
Average all size classes	7·03	8·74	6·27	7·78	8·21	10·14	7·52	8·63	2·65	5·22

deficiency from the viewpoint of the landlords are compared with the opinions of tenants. The tenant's observations on each farm are averaged for the estate.

Opinions do not differ radically. Average percentage deficiency in general equipment, as the tenants see it, is 8·74 %: as the landowners see it, it is 7·03 %. In two instances the landowner's estimate of need is greater than the tenant's estimate. Here and there opinions agree. As a rule the tenant has a sense of greater need than the landowner. Over the general level, divergence of opinion is greatest with the smallest and the larger estates. Landowners and tenants of estates between 250–499 acres almost agree; both viewpoints accept a requirement consonant with a comparatively low standard of equipment. Within the classes of consequence divergence varies. It widens as the function of the equipment becomes of less consequence to farming operations. This tendency is more marked among the larger size-classes; landlords are more ready to agree with their tenants over vital matters than over items of secondary and lesser importance. With the smallest estates (100–249 acres) the opposite pertains and the greatest divergence of opinion is over items of prime importance.

The landowner's long-sighted vision probably accounts for this change of emphasis. On the smallest estates the size of a typical holding would be smaller than on the larger estates. Items of prime consequence to present farming economy would on these estates mean a greater concentration of capital investment per acre. It is easier to over-capitalise smallholdings than large; outlay of capital on items of prime importance to the present economy but ill-suited to adaptation, is a grave risk on small estates. A landowner is inclined to think of the farmstead of a small farm as a general purpose affair. A tenant farming the place, and acutely aware of good prospects for milk, would deplore the lack of adequate milking facilities; but a landlord would be more inclined to take notice of a shortage of loose-boxes or other general purpose buildings. On the smallest estates the landlord's opinion diverges least from the tenant's over the supply of equipment of secondary consequence to the farming economy. Landlords of the smallest estates tend to be remote from the farming world.

Sympathy of opinion with the farming tenants comes more easily to landlords who are farmers and understand the farming world of their tenants. Hence the larger estate with land in hand does not present so intractable a problem of reconciliation of viewpoints. Marginal investment, for one thing, is less easily overstepped. There is greater scope for long-term specialisation, and a landowner sees the farms of his estate in categories of primary function: dairy holdings; corn and stock; stock rearing; and so on. By these primary functions he judges the capital needs of the holdings and of the estate. His opinion consequently is not so apt to differ from the opinions of his tenants. Matters of a general order, less specialised needs recognisable more readily by one who is farming the land, are the cause of incompatible opinions. On the larger estates, divergence of opinion is wider over items of third and fourth consequence than over primary needs.

Item deficiency figures when compared endorse and further illuminate these divergences. Co-efficients of deficiency for land improvement and reclamation and for items of equipment grouped as previously, calculated from the opinions of landowners and tenants, are arranged for comparison in Table XXIV. In the broad view, tenant opinion does not flagrantly contradict the estimates of the landowners. Over lack of services to cottages and farmhouses, the most frequently occurring of all deficiencies, views are identical, although there is some divergence of opinion concerning the supply of cottages and farmhouses. Landowners of estates in the 500–999 acres size-class have an acuter sense of need than their tenants have for dairy stock accommodation. Again, the landowners of the estates of 250–499 acres more frequently than their tenants expressed a need for barns and storehouses. The average co-efficient of landowner's opinion is 57; and of the tenants' opinion is 81.

Grouping of equipment and land improvements for measuring item deficiency does not dovetail exactly with the classes of consequence arranged for comparing percentage deficiencies. Cottages, for example, would be regarded as items of primary importance to an estate where agriculture is wholly dependent upon domestic labour; but they would be regarded as of secondary or even of third-rate consequence on an estate whose agriculture needs a comparatively small labour force and whose lands are situated close against a town where labour is readily available. Housing and services as grouped for item deficiency may on one estate be of primary consequence and on another of secondary consequence.

Nevertheless, there is a rough principle of correspondence between the grouping and the arrangement. Dairy stock accommodation, and yards and boxes, so essential to dairy farming and stock husbandry, tend to be of primary consequence in all cases. Likewise, accommodation for implements, tractor sheds, fuel stores and so on, and land improvement, water supplies to fields, drainage, fencing, ditching, roads are important for efficient farming but not, as a general rule, of prime consequence: the farmer can get on haltingly without them. Bearing the approximate correspondence in mind, it should be noted that the greatest divergence of opinion between landowners and tenants over item deficiency supports the observations

TABLE XXIV

COMPARISON OF CO-EFFICIENTS FROM VIEWPOINT OF
LANDLORD AND TENANT

(82 tenanted estates of central survey)

CO-EFFICIENTS OF ITEM DEFICIENCY

SIZE OF ESTATE (acres)	Housing		Dairy Stock Accommodation		Yards and Boxes		Barns and Stores		Implement Accommodation		Land improvement		Reclamation		Services	
	L'ld	T	L'ld	T	L'ld	T	L'ld	T	L'ld	T	L'ld	T	L'ld	T	L'ld	T
100–249	4	0	22	37	29	69	22	22	29	46	37	46	0	4	83	83
250–499	9	53	35	64	43	64	76	64	27	53	53	187	4	15	228	228
500–999	18	30	62	44	30	116	30	52	52	160	85	136	8	13	225	225
1,000–2,500*	33	33	33	45	128	167	128	167	33	100	77	100	14	14	167	167
Average all size classes	16	29	38	47	57	104	64	76	35	89	63	117	6	11	175	175

* Weighted to allow for comparative shortage of numbers in sample.

made when comparing percentage deficiencies. With the smallest estates, 100–249 acres, divergence of opinion between landowners and tenants averages 27 for all dairy stock accommodation, cattle yards and boxes, and 6 for all other types of equipment and land improvement. With the other estates, 250–2,500 acres, the greatest disagreement occurs over the provision of land improvement and implement and machinery accommodation; the average divergence between the co-efficients is 68 for these items compared with an average divergence of 16 for all other types of equipment and improvement.

On the other hand, the close agreement between landowners and tenants over percentage deficiency on estates in the 250–499 acres size-class does not find a counterpart when comparing opinions on item deficiency. More frequent deficiencies are seen by the tenants than by the landlords, and yet when each totals the sum the answers agree. It follows that while the landowners are less willing than tenants to admit deficiencies, when they do so they take a more serious view than the tenants of the extent of deficiency.

Tenants' resources and investment level

Although there is no serious cleavage of opinion between landowners and tenants, the sum of the evidence shows the demand for equipment and land improvement as the tenants see it to be somewhat greater than the demand as the landowners see it. Is it not possible for the tenants to help themselves? Uncertainty of compensation for improvements made to the landlord's reversion, and of the effectualness of their rights to safeguard capital invested in this way are doubtless deterrents checking the employment of tenants' resources.[1] Doubts like these can be dealt with by exposition of the law and alteration of its precepts if necessary; inadequate knowledge and an indifferent law do not make the use of tenants' resources impossible. But tenants cannot help themselves if their resources are straitened and no margin remains for investment in land improvement.

Measurement can be made of the potentiality of a tenant's resources to effect improvements by setting the sum of them against the cost of what needs to be done, and judging the extent to which it would be practical to employ the capital resources in the provision of improvements.

On certain farms[2] of the tenanted estates in the central survey information was obtained of the tenants' capital resources. These

---

[1] cf. pp. 52-59 ante.   [2] Ninety farms and fifty-six estates.

average £69 16s. per acre. Of this sum £49 14s. is in farming stock, crops and stores. Liquid assets, available as cash or stocks and shares average £20 1s. per acre. Averages have been taken out for the funds arranged in size-classes from 100–1,000 acres: there is very little difference in the averages for the size-classes; as might be expected the figures move in inverse ratio with farm size but movement is slight. Outstanding improvements from the landlords' point of view average £12 16s. per acre; and from the tenants' point of view £15 12s. per acre. Once again the large farms have the lower figures and the variation between size-classes is not significant.

On the wider demands of tenant opinion the outlay required to undertake all improvements is on average 21 % of a tenant's gross resources; but of liquid assets it is 75 %. It would be unreasonable to expect tenants to finance improvement fully from liquid assets and leave themselves a bare 25 % margin of spendable resources. Even so a third of the demand could be met by an expenditure of a quarter of the tenants' resources. Of greater practical significance is the ratio of the improvement expenditure to gross resources. The figures for gross resources have allowed for existing bank overdrafts. It would appear therefore that a 20 % loan secured against a tenant's farming capital would defray the necessary expenditure on improvements. Facilities for credit were not investigated. But on the face of the facts there seems to be a case for improvement of credit facilities. Certainly, so far as this evidence goes, it cannot be said that the tenant's resources are too straitened for them to undertake investment in improvements.

Affinity of landlord and tenant

On every tenanted estate of the main sample legal tenancies create *bona fide* landlord and tenant relationships. Here and there, tenancies are claimed and supported by little or no evidence. Usually there is family affinity or other close relationship binding landlord and tenant. These have been disregarded. Proper tenancies, however, occur where affinity between landlord and tenant is equally close. Often landlord and tenant are of the same family, and of near kin: father lets to son, or brother to brother. Or the landlord and tenant, legally distinct and self-subsisting, may *de facto* be the same person. An instance of this is a landowner who creates a private company to farm the land, becomes chairman and controlling shareholder of the company and lets his freehold to the company; or, again, a landowner may be the partner in a farming partnership to which he has let his land. Family and near-kin relationships are quite common especially among the smaller estates. On 42 % of the tenanted estates contributing evidence to Table XXIII, the tenants have a close affinity, family or otherwise, with the landlords.

These affined tenancies are of some moment. Identity of persons in the tenancies blurs the essential distinctions of interest in the land between landlord and tenant. Opinions of the need for capital investment in improvements are biased either towards the land-owner's or the tenant's viewpoint. Opinions tend to merge. While the general average divergence of opinion between landlord and tenant over percentage deficiency is 1·76 %, of estates with affined tenancies the divergence is only 0·77 %. The general figures are undoubtedly coloured by this affined opinion; but for this opinion the divergence would be greater.

Certain attributes of contractual tenures are illustrated in a novel way by these affined tenancies. Identity of person or close-knit family bond overcomes the conflict of competing interests. Uncertainty of compensation which cautions the mind of the typical tenant and restrains the investment of tenant's capital in durable improvements to the land loses its inhibiting power; what is lost by Mr. Hyde the tenant is gained by Dr. Jekyll the landlord. Of the tenanted estates[1] whose tenants have wholly financed all improvement, 91 % have affined tenancies. Furthermore, of the estates with affined tenancies, 63 % have improvements wholly or partially financed by the tenants. The corresponding percentage for the other tenanted estates is 41 %.

Estates with affined tenancies are mostly found among the smaller classes. The relatively liberal supply of adventitious capital pertaining to the smaller estates[2] is due in part to the influence of the affined tenancies. What is tenant's capital in the normal event is consociate capital to the owner-occupier, but to an estate whose owner in another guise is tenant of his own land, the farming capital is likely to be adventitious capital. Husband and wife are sometimes found owning an estate jointly in partnership and letting the land to the husband as a farming tenant. Farming capital owned by the tenant husband is not consociate with the estate in the land. The partnership owns the estate and only capital held by similar joint title is consociate with the estate. Nevertheless, the farming capital owned personally by the husband is available to the partnership through the joint interest with the wife, and hence is adventitious to the estate in land owned by the partnership. Similar relationships occur among the affined tenancies and inflate the degree of cover afforded by adventitious capital to the smaller estates.

[1]cf. p. 59 *ante*.   [2]cf. Table V.

CHAPTER THIRTEEN

Charity Estates

Exemption and immunity

ESTATES owned by charities differ in character from other estates because their income is exempt from income tax, and they are immune to the levy of surtax and estate duty.

Charity estates are immune from estate duty because the charitable bodies who own them are immortal and hence not subject to inheritance taxation. They are immune from surtax because the tax is personal and inapplicable to charity trusts and similar *persona ficta*. Exemption from income tax is another matter. Exemption unlike immunity, is not of nature. It is statutory and specifically bestowed. Lands owned and occupied by charities are exempt from income tax.[1] Charities also enjoy exemption from income tax on rents from land let by them; but only so far as the income from the rents is applied to charitable purposes.[2] Whether a body or institution is a charity and whether income is being applied to charitable purpose are questions of law. It is impracticable to litigate over every borderline case; Inland Revenue practice establishes general working rules. Much depends upon the constitution of the charity. Trusts whose constitution binds the trustees to use the trust funds for what are at law charitable purposes are treated by the Revenue differently from charities whose funds may, at the discretion of the trustees, be used both for charitable and non-charitable purposes.

Difference of treatment is an important matter for agricultural estates owned by a charity, since it touches the employment of estate income in the formation of estate capital. On the face of the Statute granting the qualified exemption, it is by no means clear that rental income invested in agricultural improvements is regarded as income applied to charitable purposes. The Revenue appears to look upon it in this way when the charity is single-eyed and can legally use its funds only to charitable ends. They make exception when the charity is authorised by its constitution to pursue activities both charitable and otherwise. Then, only income actually spent to charitable ends earns income tax remission. Whether invested in agricultural

[1]Finance Act 1921, Section 30 (1) (a).
[2]Income Tax Act 1918, Section 37 (1) (a).

improvement or not, all estate income of charities who have no power to employ their funds otherwise than for charitable purposes is tax free. But all the estate income invested in agricultural improvements of a charity with power to employ its funds in both charitable and non-charitable uses is taxable. There is no proportionate exemption of total income according to the ratio of charitable and non-charitable employment. This inconsistency is likely to restrain the investment of estate income in land improvements; income so employed attracts tax which would be avoided if the income were used to charitable ends. Admittedly improvement expenditure qualifies for tax rebate, but full tax relief means ten years waiting and in the meantime the balance of improvement money has to be found from taxed income.

Ownership of agricultural land is invariably an enterprise secondary to the main purpose of a charity: no charity exists to promote the ownership of agricultural estates, or to afford opportunities for carrying the responsibilities and enjoying the amenities of ownership. Rest homes and similar charities housed in country mansions occupy the mansion for the purpose of the charity, but have no cause to own broad acres; gardens and even parkland may be germane to the charitable purpose but not the ownership of sweeping farm lands and woods. An agricultural estate is never other than a capital asset to a charity. It may provide rich or lean income, but originally and always it is no more than a collateral and financial support to the main purpose of the charity. Although this is its essential function, decisions other than financial and reasons other than utilitarian may constrain a charity to retain its landed estates. Ancient charities are often moved by historic sentiment to prolong a centuries-old landed title. However, the emphasis of ownership is financial. And this should be borne in mind when considering estate capital in charity estates.

Competence to form estate capital

A number of charity estates have been made the subject of a special survey. All are not single-eyed and above suspicion. One at least is free to employ its resources on activities unacceptable to the Revenue as charitable purposes, and hence its income is not wholly exempt from income tax. Time has not permitted more than twenty-one charity estates to be surveyed. The majority are large estates over 10,000 acres but the smaller acreages are represented. Together they total 373,000 acres.

No attempt has been made to classify these charity estates in size-classes; the few below 1,000 acres have been excluded. As a group the charity estates may reasonably be compared with the non-charity estates of the main sample over 1,000 acres. Details cannot be compared. Only a small percentage of the charity estates could give any indication of outstanding improvements, and *a fortiori* would venture an estimate of the cost of providing them. It is not possible therefore to make a comparison of this feature. Estate income from the charity estates has been computed from the revenue and out-goings in the year 1954. Time did not permit a five years' average to be obtained. The year 1954 was selected as the year in which income and expenditure figures would be nearest the mean of the figures for the five-yearly periods used as a basis of measurement of estate income in the main sample.

TABLE XXV

COMPETENCE OF CHARITY ESTATES TO FORM
ESTATE CAPITAL FROM ESTATE INCOME

COMPETENCE CLASS	PERCENTAGE OF NUMBERS IN GROUP	
	Past improvements and interest at 5 %	*Past improvements and interest at 5 % on estate capital*
	% of numbers	% of numbers
100 %	84·2	5·4
50 %+	15·8	47·3
50 % −	—	47·3
Nil	—	—

Comparison of the powers of capital formation from estate income reveals the charity estates far in advance of the main sample estates. Table XXV shows the percentage of the numbers of charity estates competent and partially competent to form estate capital, pay 5 % interest on the capital formed and upon the estate capital *in toto*. No less than 84·2 % of the charity estates are wholly competent to form capital commensurate with investment over the past ten years and pay interest at 5 % on the capital formed. There is no incompetence nor partial competence less than 50 %; and 15·8 % are competent to form over half of the capital. A small percentage is competent even to earn 5 % on total estate capital, form new capital and pay interest thereon. Even with this burden to carry, 47·3 % of the charity estates are over 50 % competent and a like percentage under 50 % competent. These figures compared with the evidence in Table III show the charity estates to have outstandingly stronger estate incomes than the non-charity estates.

The cause of the comparative vitality of the charity estate incomes is patent in the rentals, outgoings and improvement expenditure. Table XXVI shows these figures against comparable figures for the non-charity estates over 1,000 acres. On the charity estates rental revenue averages £2·15 per acre and total outgoings £0·82 per acre; for the non-charity estates the respective figures are £1·29 and £1·26. Average expenditure on past improvements is more nearly equal: for the charity estates the figure is £0·46 and for the non-charity estates

TABLE XXVI

COMPARISON OF RENTAL REVENUE, OUTGOINGS, AND IMPROVEMENT EXPENDITURE ON CHARITY AND NON-CHARITY ESTATES OVER 1,000 ACRES

Item	Charity estates (£ per acre)	Non-charity estates (£ per acre)
Annual Rental Revenue	2·15	1·29
Annual Outgoings	0·82	1·26
Annual Improvement Expenditure	0·46	0·35*

* Inclusive of two estates where the expenditure has been exceedingly heavy.

£0·35. The strength of the charity estate incomes lies in a rental revenue 66 % higher than the rental revenue of the non-charity estates; and in yearly outgoings 34 % lower than the outgoings on the non-charity estates. Outgoings on the charity estates are 38 % of revenue, and the yearly improvement expenditure 21 % of revenue; and on the non-charity estates outgoings are 97 % of revenue and the yearly improvement expenditure 27 % of revenue.

The fundamental difference in the taxability of the two types of estate probably goes some way but not as far as might be supposed to account for the disparity between outgoings. Tax-free charity estates have no cause to establish maintenance claims. The maintenance claim is essential on the non-charity estate to adjust assessed income to actual income. The higher the maintenance claim the lower the taxed proportion of the income. Owners are permitted to include certain items of capital improvements in the maintenance claim and these are reflected in the yearly maintenance costs. Maintenance of the non-charity estate includes, therefore, an element of improvement cost which appears as improvement expenditure on the charity estates.

The pull of the maintenance claim has a counterpart on most of the charity estates. For one reason or another improvement expenditure finds its way into the figures for annual outgoings. Improvement expenditure in the form of annual repayments of capital loans from Government controlled assets is put into current expenditure. On the estates of one large landowning charity estate capital invested in improvements which fails to attract at least 5 % interest as increased rents from the tenants is included among the current repairs expenditure. However improvement expenditure is charged, the effect upon competence is as broad as it is long. A lower maintenance figure means a higher improvement expenditure, and either way effects equally the competence of the estate income to pay for the improvement.

If outgoings are added to improvement expenditure and the sums compared, the influence of the element of improvement expenditure in maintenance costs is eliminated. Even so, the combined outlay on the charity estates is but 76 % of the combined outlays on the non-charity estates. Lower outgoings on the charity estates are due in a small measure to management costs inextricably interwoven with the general expenditure of the charity. Nevertheless, the figures hint at a lower standard of upkeep on the charity estates. Many of the charity estates have no idea of the total cost of improvements required to be made on them at the present time. This strengthens the evidence, for it gives an impression of indifference towards maintenanace and improvement. On the other hand, the charity estates appear to have dealt vigorously with rent revision. Charity trustees are impersonal landlords, and the greater competence of the charity estates parallels the advantage that company-owned and trustee-owned estates display in comparison with estates owned by real persons.[1]

In line with the higher level of competence among the charity estates is a strong tendency to acquire interest payment from tenants for improvements made by the landlord. One[2] only of the charity estates fails to charge interest. More than half of them demand at least 8 %; on average the percentage is 7 %. Both the modal and the average figures exceed the comparable figures for the non-charity estates.[3]

[1]cf. p. 154 *ante.*   [3]cf. p. 55 *ante.*
[2]This is the estate whose income is not *prima facie* exempt from income tax.

12

A majority of the charity owners prefer to finance improvements and charge interest to the tenant, than allow the tenant himself to do improvement. Indeed, on over a half of the number of charity estates tenants are deliberately discouraged from making improvements. The estates which practise this restraint are not invariably those where the higher interest rates are charged. Behind the policy is a desire to keep investment in improvements under the direct control of the landlord, and to avoid cumulative indefinite compensation liabilities. Fear of unknown and unknowable compensation claims probably underlies the fact that only one charity estate is prepared to allow the Agricultural Holdings Act 1948 to take its course. All other estates, where tenants are encouraged or, at all events, not discouraged from making improvements, require a definite understanding about the amount of compensation. The majority enter into a sharing agreement with the tenant: the landlord finds a proportion of the cost of the improvement on the understanding that the tenant foregoes his claim for compensation; others require some form of amortization of the cost, thus enabling the landlord at any time to judge the approximate compensation liabilities.

Improvements financed by the landlord are almost a universal preference among the charity estates. The only exception to this otherwise common attribute is provided by the one estate whose income bears initial taxation because in the opinion of the Revenue the activities of the charity who own it are not consistently charitable uses. On this estate, a compact fertile block of 1,280 acres divided into six holdings each let to the same tenant, the tenant is encouraged to be both the prime mover and financer of improvements. His response is impressive. No interest is charged on improvements the landlord makes. For the majority of improvements full compensation rights are afforded the tenant in accordance with the Agricultural Holdings Act 1948. Where, on a rare occasion, the landlord has borne the cost of materials used in making an improvement, the tenant has agreed to accept the landlords' contribution in satisfaction of his compensation right. The tenant has improved the layout of the fields and made similar land improvements for which he asks no formal compensation. Rents, on the other hand, have remained constant.

Consociate capital

Competent estates among the non-charity estates are attended by liberal external funds. The charity estates, with their high degree of competence, are no exception to this principle. Behind the charity estates over 1,000 acres are consociate funds which on an average provide a fourfold cover of the estate capital. This average ratio is greatly influenced by two charities with exceedingly large fortunes. Excluding these prominent anomalies, the average ratio of gross total external funds to estate capital is 2·4. For the non-charity estates over 1,000 acres the corresponding co-efficient of support is 1·02. Another remarkable feature of the charity estates is an almost complete absence of mortgages and similar charges. Such burdens as there are, are so light that the average ratio of net consociate funds to estate capital equals the average ratio of gross consociate funds; for the non-charity estates the average ratio of net consociate funds is 0·94. The same superiority is seen in the average ratio of liquid funds to estate capital. Excluding the glaring anomalies previously mentioned,

TABLE XXVII

INVESTMENT DISTRIBUTION OF CONSOCIATE FUNDS ON CHARITY AND NON-CHARITY ESTATES OVER 1,000 ACRES

Estates	Timber %	Other land %	Stocks and shares %	Farm stock %	Other- wise %	Fund % of total fortune (average)
Charity	1·1	31·1	64·9	0·0	2·9	64·3
Non-charity	28·0	20·0	34·0	7·0	11·0	38·0

the average co-efficient for liquid funds is 1·4; the counterpart among the non-charity estates is 0·39. Gross funds supporting the charity estates give almost double the cover given by the gross funds of the non-charity estates; and the liquid funds of the charity estates give three times the cover of the liquid funds of the non-charity estates. Estate capital, on average, is 35·7 % of the total charity fortune. With the non-charity estates the average proportion of estate capital to total fortune is almost an exact reciprocal of the charity estates figure: 62 %. Capital locked away in historic and traditional colleges and places essential to the very character and nature of the charity is not included among the consociate funds.

The generous proportions of liquid capital in the consociate funds of the charity estates reflects a high percentage of investment in Government stocks and equities. Table XXVII compares the investment patterns of the consociate funds of the two types of estate.

Charity policy is concentrated upon investment in stocks and shares and in other land; what remains is of little consequence. Consociate funds of the non-charity estates are wider distributed. Difference in estate character is manifest in the investment pattern. With charity estates there is not the evidence of an intimate touch as there is with so many of the other types of estate. Charities avoid, if possible, the responsibility of land in hand, either farmed or given to silviculture. Land in hand calls for expert management of agricultural and silvicultural enterprise, a closer, more intimate contact with the land than the charity is prepared to cultivate. Hence, the consociate funds of the non-charity estates display a much higher percentage of investment in timber and farm stock. Again, these funds have a comparatively higher proportion of miscellaneous investments: the main constituent is life insurance—an effective, personal form of investment. Furthermore, the special treatment which timber receives at the hand of the Exchequer when subject to estate duty is lost upon the charity estates, and this no doubt accounts in part for the apparent indifference of the charities to investment in timber. What is held in timber investment by the non-charity funds appears from Table XXVII to be put into stocks and shares by the investors of the charity funds. For agriculture this is an advantage as capital in timber, especially immature timber, is more difficult to realise and transfer to land improvement than investments in stocks and shares.

Restraints and inducements

Against the superior cover which charity estates enjoy from consociate funds must be set certain restraints upon use. Some are peculiar to charities and others, met with elsewhere, are restraining influences to which charity ownership is prone. Many charities were founded for particular purposes and the trustees or governing bodies are obliged by the principles of the foundations to use the income for specific uses. Only when this obligation has been discharged are they free to employ the income elsewhere, in particular in the improvement of their agricultural lands. Use of capital is even more restrained. Special funds are ear-marked for definite purposes and cannot be used to improve the land. In many cases the administrators of a charity have to seek the acceptance of a Government Department or quasi-Government institution to a proposed policy of capital investment. Departmental control in some instances is limited to the landed estates of the charity, and monetary funds derived from the sale of such property. Overriding sanction of this nature can be detrimental to agricultural land: some charities hesitate to employ external funds in land improvement because by so doing the capital first as land improvement and later as money, comes under the sanction of an external authority. Other charities in a like case are not hesitant, for their experience of the superior sanction is a light, even benign, touch. It is not always so. Trustees have been required by a higher controlling authority to repay from estate income capital loans made to finance improvement. This puts an amortisation burden on the estate income, and trustees responsible for finding a minimum income from their funds may well hesitate before seeking authority to make capital improvements.

Spreading risk is one among the common restraints that weighs much with charity owners. Agricultural land investment has an allotted portion with industrials, Government stock and urban property. Beyond these set bounds investment will not go, however needy the land may be for want of capital investment. Better alternative investment is another restraint met with. Capital is not being invested in agricultural land and improvements because earning power is low, there is grave risk of immediate capital depreciation and uncertainty about the future of farming. Of these two restraints, the former, spreading the risk, is undoubtedly the more influential among the charity estates surveyed.

A balanced investment policy, on the other hand, is for the majority of the charities the main reason why they continue to hold and even buy agricultural estates. Investment-conscious trustees look upon the land, despite its low revenue, as an enduring asset, in which portions of the trust funds should rest as a reserve, while the remainder perform financial gymnastics to develop strength or precipitate a downfall as fate shall decide. And there is the hope with some that the agricultural land reserve, quickened to new life by rent revision, will in the future reward patience with payment. Much land is held from a high sense of historical obligation, insistent of tradition. With some of the charities, land titles run unbroken through centuries to the days of a medieval royal donor or other historic benefactor. Schools and colleges own agricultural land for amenity and the protection of school sites from encroaching development.

Many charities have invested funds in land improvement in an attempt to reverse a decline in the capital value of the land and improve its appearance. Sometimes the awakening has followed years of neglect. With at least two charities pressure by agricultural executive committees has initiated improvement programmes. Statutory protection of trust funds, wedding them to trust securities is responsible for agricultural land investments remaining in the ownership of certain charities; barred from investment in equities to which their financial inclinations lean, the charity trustees prefer agricultural land to gilt-edge stocks.

CHAPTER FOURTEEN

The Road Ahead

THROUGH the prosaic statistics of the previous pages a three-armed signpost points the road ahead. Of first importance is the single idea of the estate in land as a centre of capital formation and supply. Second, are common and particular trends in the circumstances of present-day agricultural estates that influence the provision of capital to agriculture. And third are the avenues to further investigation, hinted at in the hypotheses of the present findings and instant in what is superficial and half-digested of the statistics.

Estate in land: a fundamental and universal idea

The problem of capital for agriculture cannot be correctly comprehended unless the land and its fixed equipment are seen as estate capital and distinguished as such from other capital invested in agricultural enterprise. Provision of estate capital is the prerogative of landownership. It lies beyond agriculture proper. This is true whatever the system of landownership. The estate in land is not exclusive to the English landlord and tenant system; landownership is ubiquitous and elemental. Agriculture the world over lies in an estate of some kind and uses estate capital. Collective farms even in a highly socialised State are no exception; the proprietary interest, invested by the State in each individual collective is an estate in land, and exists as something apart, over against the State that creates it. The self-interest of the estate acts within the limits of its landright and determines what land and buildings shall be made available to its agriculture.

Estate capital is a concept not easily grasped by agriculturalists in Britain whose thought and upbringing associate the word " estate " with the extensive tenanted estates of the traditional landownership system. An owner who commands the landright over far-flung acres has indeed an estate in land, but in no higher degree than the farmer who owns and cultivates a few acres of his own. Owner-occupiers, it should be remembered, no less than the owners of tenanted land are deterred from investing consociate capital in agricultural land improvements by the restraint of more attractive alternative investments. A farmer who owns his farm when confronted by an alternative of this kind may think of it as a choice between putting his money into farming or using it elsewhere. In fact he is making a choice between investment in estate capital and other investment. If the agricultural expenditure were the purchase of livestock and not investment in land improvement, his decision might be different. To commit money to land improvement is to sink it in land proprietorship. Its fate as a capital investment is not determined solely by the profitability of the agricultural industry but by the dictates of the land market. Investment in agricultural land improvement is not therefore primarily an investment in agriculture. It belongs elsewhere. It is investment in estate capital. A farmer may prefer an alternative investment not because the earning power of capital put into agricultural land improvement is less than the earning power of the alternative, but because he fears a drop in the value of the capital sunk in land. If so, he is making his decision primarily as an estate owner and not as a farmer.

Distinction clarifies if we imagine two farms owner-occupied in circumstances in which the investment of capital in agricultural land improvement will be equally remunerative on either. One farmer keeps his money in alternative investments because of the risk of capital depreciation. The other farmer employs his capital to make agricultural improvements. He does so because of the taxability of his estate. Capital invested in his land reduces his net liability for surtax, and the reduction counterbalances the risk of capital depreciation attendant upon investment in land improvement. The surtax rebate is not peculiar to agricultural land, but is peculiar to landownership. Investment in agricultural land improvement is thus induced by a benefit provided to landownership, not to agriculture. Because the farmer is a landowner and the land law allows him to invest money in the improvement of the land, he can claim a tax privilege. His right is an estate right, not a farming right.

Much thought is given today to planning and constructing farmsteads to economise in agricultural labour. Capital is needed to finance the new layouts. So often the problem is approached as if it were solely an agricultural one. Increased profitability through labour economy is co-ordinated with the costs of provision, and if the higher profits remunerate satisfactorily the capital invested it is supposed that the virtues of the investment are demonstrated beyond question. No thought is given to the implications of the venture from the viewpoint of landownership. The new farmstead must stand on someone's land, and he it is presumably who will pay the piper. The countenance of the land market may be contrary and obliterate all economic advantage gained from labour economy. Furthermore tenurial restriction may deny the landowner a just reward, be the farming outcome never so successful. Farm buildings, together with all other fixed equipment and land improvement, are estate capital and not farming capital. Agriculture lies in an estate cradle. Its economic efficiency depends as much upon the cradle as upon its own dispositions.

COMMON TRENDS

Attractions of landownership essential to the finance of agriculture

Estate income as a general rule is too weak to pay a 5 % dividend on estate capital, and finance new investment. The degree of competence depends upon the rate of capital formation where there is a positive income. For many estates there is no estate income whatsoever. Reduction in the rate of formation cannot lift their impotency into competence. If we imagine the period of capital formation raised from ten to thirty years it does not greatly relieve the dolorous picture. The dark shadows of the negative estate incomes remain.

The future provision of estate capital must follow one or more of four courses. First, estate income must be substantially increased. Rental revision is of paramount urgency; maintenance economies are fundamental; and charging and keeping strict account of interest payments on improvements provided by landlords can contribute much. Improvement of estate income would not be so pressing if tenants were encouraged to finance their own improvements, and this provides a second course. That more can be done in this way is demonstrated by the achievements of the affined tenancies.[1] Revision of the present compensation law and the methodology used by valuers to compute compensation claims would be practical steps promoting encouragement.

Tenant farmers, it may be argued, cannot afford substantial increases in rent nor the finance of their own improvements. Agriculture by this argument is admitted impotent to form estate capital from its own industry. As a third course steps must be taken therefore to preserve the consociate and adventitious funds behind agricultural estates and guard the subtle virtues and attractions of landownership that induce men to dispense their fortunes for the good of the land. Income and surtax rebate on agricultural improvements and the 45 % estate duty concession are obviously essential. Yet something far more radical is necessary. An estate duty burden of £17 per acre[2] with a complementary and much greater capital burden

---

[1]cf. p. 171 *ante*.   [2]cf. p. 126 *ante*.

on the consociate and adventitious capital behind an estate will relentlessly deprive agriculture of its present main source of estate capital repletion. There is no cogency in the argument that high inheritance taxation will divide the large estate into small owner-occupied proprietorships on which agriculture will continue. This process deprives the agricultural estate of the consociate capital outside the industry; new title estates have a high percentage of their consociate funds locked away in farm stock.[1] Estate duty is forcing agriculture's eggs into one basket: a basket that, if tenants cannot afford higher rents, is patently too weak for its purpose. Fortunes outside agriculture invested in agricultural landownership are essential at present and must be sustained and expanded in the interest of agriculture.

A fourth course is the provision of estate capital by the State. Is it not logical to distribute the revenue from inheritance taxation as Government grants in aid of capital formation? The idea is logical only up to a point. Ultimately such a process must stop, if the land is to be preserved from a fragmentation quite unsuited to modern agriculture. Once stopped, from whence comes the money to continue the grants? Estate capital formation on agricultural land would be subsidised at the expense of a Revenue unsupported by estate duty levies. State revenue would carry the burden of capital provision now so largely carried by private landownership.

These four courses are not alternatives, each exclusive of the other. The private large estate plays an essential part in the finance of agriculture and if it is suppressed the industry will lose a means of capital provision most costly to replace. But it is not the only road to salvation. The smaller owner-occupied estate can obviously achieve much. Its superior powers of capital formation show clearly that rental levels especially of the smaller tenanted estates are out of step with the true strength of agricultural incomes, and the investment requirements of the land. All four courses should be woven into a single-aimed policy. The impulse of each one of these courses caught up together in a single policy would confirm the strength of each.

Restrained investment in land improvement

Personal and private fortunes are ranged behind agricultural estates of all sizes. There is a tendency for landowners to divide their fortunes equally between agricultural estates and other investment. Care must be taken lest we present as a universal and constant relationship what is no more than a general tendency. Many extremes and deviations lie either side of this rough mean, not least the deflexions consequent upon variations in estate character. Nevertheless, as a

[1] cf. p. 153 *ante*.

rude rule, a £1 of estate capital in agricultural land is backed by £1 of consociate capital and frequently by other external funds adventitious to the estate title.

The division in some cases is almost inevitable; in others it is the result of predetermined policy; or it may be merely fortuitious. Seldom is a whole fortune committed to landownership. It is probably well that in some measure this should be so. But the general pool of consociate capital is a reservoir of supply whose resources might be more readily disposed in agricultural land improvement if landowning was more remunerative and less restricted. The five most far-reaching restraints on further investment in agricultural land improvement, as evinced by the surveys, are:

(1) The attraction of better alternative investments.

(2) The need to preserve external capital to provide income for financing the yearly demand of the estate for improvement expenditure.

(3) Restriction of management over the land, by too rigorous a policy of tenurial security.

(4) Lack of income to reap the benefit of tax concession.

(5) Threat of estate duty.

Surtax and income tax rebate are undoubtedly inducements to improvement investment, but if the combined income from the estate and external funds is so limited that yearly improvement expenditure exceeds the income, full rebate is lost. Landowners are tempted to restrict expenditure by the capacity of their income. Estate duty abatement is also a decisive inducement to improvement investment, but the threat of estate duty acts as a restraint and capital funds are deflected from estate improvement to create an external shield protecting the estate from an estate duty that threatens partition of the inheritance. A crude indication of what this can mean is provided by the estimates of potential estate duty per acre on some 113 estates:[1] a threat of £17 per acre levy on an estate whose owner has a total fortune liable to a 44 % levy[2] would require an external fund of £30 per acre to give full protection: a significant figure when set beside £14, the average estimate of the expenditure per acre needed to-day to meet the total demand for improvements and major repairs on the estates of the surveys.[3]

[1]cf. p. 126 *ante*.
[2]The average percentages for the fortunes behind the 113 estates.
[3]cf. p. 188 *post*.

Providing estate capital to agriculture is not so much a problem of discovering new sources of supply, as of finding ways and means to attract private fortunes, personal and institutional, into landowner-ship and land improvement. An illuminative side-light is thrown on this aspect of the problem by the disinclination of landowners to mortgage their land titles. On numerous estates the estate capital itself is an untapped source of credit. Landowners hesitate to raise loans because estate incomes are too weak to meet interest and capital repayment. Yet the degree of rental increment required to augment incomes sufficiently to meet the yearly commitment is not fundamentally disturbing.

PARTICULAR TRENDS

Virtue in the farmed freehold

Estate character obviously influences investment in estate capital. An outstanding example of this is the difference between the invest-ment levels and the standards of achievement of the owner-occupied estates and those of the tenanted estates. Owner-occupation tends to have a standard of equipment higher than the standard of the tenanted estates and tends more successfully than tenanted estates to meet the demand for capital. These achievements demonstrate the virtues of the farmed freehold. But the farmed freehold has not a self-contained strength. The capital formed is not entirely within the competence of equivalent estate income. At a time of capital stringency this can be a real weakness detracting from the other manifest virtues of the farmed freehold.

Virtue in the leasehold

What is accomplished on the owner-occupied estates, and by tenant-finance under affined tenancies, indicates a certain potency for capital formation in the agricultural industry. On the tenanted estates this power loses energy. The power should flow from the industry to estate incomes through rental revenues, but, in the majority of cases, low rents set up a resistance: the rent-mesh is too close for a full flow. Nevertheless, as just observed, the performance of the owner-occupied estates is not an absolute competence. Only 13 % of the number sur-veyed were competent to finance past investment from farm profits, and 33 % could make no contribution at all.

Incompetence is not due entirely to the rent-mesh. The mesh could be widened and should be widened to release the full creative power in agriculture. But the industry at present appears incompetent in itself. Power of full capital formation is not held back by the rent-mesh from estate incomes: the power does not exist. External capital is needed. A virtue of the tenanted estate is the high percentage of its consociate capital not invested in farm stock and other forms of agricultural goods. Leasehold tenure is a conduit through which capital from many sources flows to the benefit of agriculture.

The large estate the salvation of the leasehold

Since the post-war policy of a tight security of tenure, extensive acreages have been taken in hand by landowners and run as exceptionally large owner-occupied units. Even so, most large estates are tenanted. The smaller the estate the more likely it is to be owner-occupied. Preservation of the tenanted farm is one with the preservation of the larger estate. It is essential for the preservation of the large estate to distinguish between agriculture and landownership. Landownership if fostered for its own sake will preserve the system most suited to its peculiar attractions. The larger the estate the more distinct is landownership from agriculture and the better preserved are the attributes and attractions of landownership.

Whatever accusations of over-capitalisation may be fairly levelled at industry, it is difficult to pillory the agricultural landowner. From the conservative evidence of the surveys the typical farm is 8 %–10 % deficient of necessary buildings and services. To make good this lack at to-day's prices requires an outlay of £7–£16 per acre. And this figure makes no allowance for major reparation work to dilapidated buildings; it is concerned only with the provision of what is additional. If to the improvement figure were added £2 10s. per acre[1] for the cost of rectifying major repairs, the total demand for capital investment would, on an estate basis, average £14 per acre.

On the smaller estates the investment of consociate capital in the improvement of the land is restrained mostly by more attractive investment elsewhere and by the conservation of external capital to supply supporting income. These restraints can only be removed by enhancing the competence of agriculture itself to form estate capital and pay fair interest on estate capital investment. Restraints on the investment of external funds in the improvement of land on the large estates have a different emphasis. Tenurial difficulties, management restrictions, legal clogs on the land title[2] and the threat of estate duty

[1]This figure is based on figures of outstanding major repairs used to calculate the value of the Capital Works Fund in the memorandum *Reserve Fund and Maintenance Funds* (p. 14), Department of Estate Management, Cambridge University, 1954.
[2]These take a peculiar form on Charity estates.

are prominent restraints. They differ from the inhibitions of the smaller estates, and their removal does not require a greater exertion in agriculture itself. These restrictions are peculiar to landownership.

The demand for capital and the plight of credit are cogent reasons for taking steps to reduce restraints. Amendment of landlord and tenant legislation and the law governing settlements and other trusts could remove the cause of three of these major restraints. Estate duty is a universal bondage. The duty tends to fall with exceptional weight on estates mid-way between 1,000 and 10,000 acres because on smaller estates the absolute burden is lighter and on larger estates the relative burden is lighter. Estate duty relief should be extended to a proportion of all consociate capital and in a way that would help to redress this unequal incidence.

Nadir of landownership: 250–500 acres

The smallest estates of all, 100–250 acres, are more residential than agricultural. Between these and the larger owner-occupied units are estates whose size makes a clear distinction between landownership and agriculture difficult and which aptly illustrate how too close an identity of agriculture and landowning can mean a poor sense of the responsibilities of landownership.

The 250–500 acres of this intermediate size-class is a typical farming acreage of the larger farms of Britain. It is reasonable to imagine the farmers more acutely aware of their farming than of the responsibilites and attractions peculiar to landownership. They own land primarily as a means of farming. Landowning for landownership's sake does not move them. By the ratio of consociate capital to estate capital they are better off than their larger neighbours. They appear also to be freer of the mortgagee. And yet the level of their investment in estate capital is the poorest among the smaller size-classes. The greater proportion of what has been achieved has been financed from farming income. Indeed among the owner-occupiers these estates have the highest competence percentage. Tenanted estates, on the contrary, in this size-class are the least competent.

The struggle to achieve capital formation from income and the relatively lower standard of investment give the impression that external capital is deliberately withheld from investment in improvements. In general, estates of this size are too large to attract the fortune of the wealthy seeking a small place in the country and prepared to see it kept up. What is spent on the land must be to practical farming purpose.

And yet we cannot suppose that the trouble lies no deeper than this. Consociate capital is probably not so freely invested on these smaller estates because, despite its ratio to estate capital, it is inadequate. Although the 250–500 acre estates have equal or higher ratios of consociate capital to estate capital than the larger estates, it does not follow that they are equally or more substantially backed. Erection of a cottage costing £2,000 is a more daring financial venture on an estate worth £8,000 with a consociate capital of like amount, than on an estate worth £20,000 with a consociate capital of £20,000. Behind the smallest estate of all are greater proportionate external funds which lift them out of the rut which confounds the 250–500 acre class. These latter lie too completely in the agricultural world to be comfortable. This observation is only valid for the estate in land. As a farm unit 250–500 acres may be ideal. If so, it is best for agriculture that the farms of this size should be tenanted farms on a large estate.

Difficulties of personal ownership

The smaller estates owned by companies and trustees have a lower investment level than the estates owned by real persons. Among the larger estates the reverse obtains. The reason for this is almost certainly found in the tenure pattern. All the larger estates are tenanted and the personally-owned tenanted estate is less competent than the tenanted estate owned by trustees or a company. Low rents and high outgoings are the cause and there is reason to think that the low rents reflect a reluctance, not suffered by private companies and trustees, to press for rental revision.

Ownership by private companies, especially estate companies, tends to reduce the potential benefit of tax rebate to agricultural land and the proportion of consociate capital to estate capital. Ownership by trustees has similar defects, not to the same degree. But trustees are often hampered in the employment of trust capital. Moreover estate duty often falls with exceptional severity on a trust estate, because the trust impose restrictions on capital alienation and gifts. Trustees who own the larger estates in the sample have an outstandingly impressive record and their evidence presses a case for removing the defects in trust law, and encouraging trustee ownership. In particular, ways and means should be found to attract and employ the fortunes of beneficiaries, the adventitious capital behind trust-held estates, in the improvement of agricultural freeholds in trust.

Rents and outgoings

Low competence among arable estates appears to arise from maladjustment between rental revenue and outgoings, and points to the failure of rents to reflect the degree of concentration of capital investment.

Further evidence of a similar defect is given by Table XI. A greater concentration of investment per acre on the smaller estates is not matched by a commensurate rise in rental revenue. Rents are related to the positive, productive potentialities of the soil and its fixed equipment, as if rent were simply a payment for the use of land and its equipment. Maybe this is an outcome of confounding agriculture and landownership. Rent is thought of as a debit: nothing more. But rent is the blood-stream of estate income, and if the body is to be kept healthy the stream must take the measure of estate obligations and be strong enough to meet them.

Services to cottage and farmhouse, and land improvement

Item deficiency shows what in the opinion of landowners and tenants are the wants most frequently met with, and because the most frequent, the most likely to be a common concern of agriculturalists. Great efforts are being made to improve dairy stock accommodation, cattle yards, stores and piggeries, grain-drying and grass-drying. But it is not in these that the evidence of the surveys shows the most frequent deficiency. On every hand, the gaping need is services to cottage and farmhouse—water, drains and lighting. And next in prominence is land improvements—water supplies, drainage, roads. Help has been generously given by the Government for years towards the cost of water supplies and land drainage. Recently announced[1] grants in aid of maintenance and improvement of fixed equipment will probably extend to farm road improvement. In any event, farm roads are among the first-ranking needs in the minds of many who own and till the land.

Something has been done and is being done to encourage the improvement of cottages and farmhouses. Housing grants are canalised through local government. Some local authorities honour the intentions of Parliament and offer the grants fairly and without discrimination; others are disinclined to do so. The grants at best are meagre. Application is complicated and the grant when offered is frequently hedged about by conditions detrimental to the interests of landownership. Weight of opinion among the landowners contributing to this survey was critical of the present housing grants. Landowners are particularly aware of the inadequacies of the housing grants because improvement of farmhouses does not attract full tax rebate and they are forced back on the housing grants.

[1] cf. Cmd. Paper 53, 1956.

QUESTIONS UNANSWERED

Nothing more is claimed for these surveys than a broad investigation into the manner of providing agriculture with estate capital and in particular the influence of estate character upon the process. More questions have been raised than answered. And these must be briefly set out in closing.

Estate character traits obviously influence the provision of estate capital. What this influence means for British agriculture at large will never be known until national statistics are compiled of our agricultural estates. Statistics[1] are available showing the division of land area between tenanted and owner-occupied land. We can tell the proportionate area of agricultural land subject to the characteristics of tenanted estates but we cannot go further and say how far estate size and other estate character traits exert an influence. A national survey of the full range of estate character is a formidable undertaking and would need to be revised frequently. It should be within the realm of practical possibility to compile statistics of the primary and physical estate character traits. Primary traits are relatively stable and the physical traits are more easily identified than the abstract ones.

Differences of estate character raise questions of origin and change. How is it that certain estates are what they are? How long will they retain their character? What causes change? The present surveys indicate the significance of estate size for estate capital. Agricultural wellbeing will require to know why some land is divided among small estates and other land belongs to extensive ownership. History of estate character is an absorbing and vital study hardly begun.

The correlation of estate size and estate income in inverse ratio demonstrated by the present surveys is not explained by them. Farms aggregated together in a single proprietorship apparently drop in rental value and reduce the burden of maintenance and improvement expenditure. Why is this? Patently it is not merely a matter of the degree of concentration in fixed equipment.

Of a different order are the legal problems. Anachronisms in real property law and the law of trusts affect adversely the investment of trust funds in estate capital. They need to be studied in depth and practical detail if solutions are to be found.

Credit presents other problems. Land as security for loans and banking is not only an economic question, it has social implications also. A particular aspect of the question of credit is the pledge of tenant's capital as security for loans to finance improvements.

[1] *National Farm Survey of England and Wales*, H.M.S.O., 1946 : and *Agricultural Statistics* (Yearly), Department of Agriculture for Scotland.

Running through the Tables and evidence from the surveys are details of maintenance and expenditure costs and other factors of estate income. Each factor needs specialised study, severally and in relation to others, so as to establish criteria by which to measure the economic efficiency of estates of different character. The fundamental question of the meaning of economic efficiency on agricultural estates is itself unanswerable at present. Does efficiency lie in income and its relationship to estate capital? What cognisance must be taken of capital appreciation? How is capital appreciation to be measured? One of the greatest enigmas of the present surveys is the riddle of capital value. Estate economy is wanting for definitions and a methodology of measurement, especially the measurement of the value of estate capital. A tentative beginning has been attempted in these chapters. What has been done needs the test of repeated application. A particular and pressing aspect of the problem of capital value is the relationship of costs and value. Why is the agricultural land market reluctant to give as increased capital value £ for £ of money invested in agricultural improvements? This is a problem of particular import for the owner-occupier of the small estate. Here he makes tangible acquaintance with the world of land-ownership.

These are a sample of the questions surrounding the problem of estate capital in agricultural land. They are mentioned not as an exhaustive review but as examples of the many aspects of a problem little understood and because this presentation of the problem touches many of them. Full consideration is outside what has been attempted here.

Other questions are provoked by the sheer inconclusiveness of what has been written. Certain features of the evidence need the refinement of deeper statistical investigation. Other lines of the enquiry are roads without termini and await completion: inducements, for example, that motivate landownership have been identified only on the largest estates. And a work of reconciliation is necessary to integrate more closely the observations of the surveys.

These questions are mainly set within the four corners of British domestic agriculture and behind them range the implications of estate capital for agriculture at large. Wherever man has settled he has created proprietorships in the land. The estate in land is part of the weave of civilised living, and investment in estate capital an inevitable commonplace. These pages are but a particular study of a general theme in need of development by comparative studies the world over.

13

APPENDIX

The Surveys

DATA given in this book have been gathered from four distinct surveys of selected agricultural estates. Depth of detail varies. But simple facts common to each survey represent 2,750 estates covering 5½ million acres in Great Britain. The four surveys are the central survey, the previous survey, the extended survey and the survey of charity estates.

The central survey

The central survey is foundational; the previous survey is built into it, and the extended survey is built upon it. The aim is a self-contained survey of capital investment in agricultural estates, its level, its source of finance and the influences that motivate it. Available funds imposed limitations. A previous survey had provided parallel but not identical information from estates lying mainly in the acreage range 1,000–10,000 acres. The central survey therefore was focused upon smaller estates and limited its range to estates between 100 acres and 2,500 acres.

It would have been logical to study analytically a selection of agricultural estates presenting different levels of capital investment and to identify as far as possible the nature and origin of the influences governing investment levels. But this method is impracticable if selection of the estates is made at random. Random selection would require a wide range of estates classified according to the level of investment in each. Classification would require identifications; and identification would require preliminary investigation almost as penetrating as a full survey. So profound a preliminary enquiry over a worthwhile number of estates would have been impracticable, and impossible within the time allowed for the complete survey.

An alternative procedure was followed. Estates varying in character were selected at random and the influence of character variation upon the provision of capital investigated. Character traits had to be few, easily identifiable and, on a reasonable hypothesis, likely to exert some influence upon the provision and formation of estate capital. The original choice was:

Size (100–2,500 acres)
Shape
Tenure Pattern
Taxability
Duration
Holdings pattern.

To these were added the sources of external funds and the age of farmsteads. Duration in principle was as described in the text,[1] but an additional date distinguishing old from new was 1947, the year of the Agriculture Act, and not 1900, as it was intended to exclude from the survey all estates with titles subsequent to 1947. No national statistic of agricultural landownership, even in the crudest form, let alone refined to reflect the nicer points of estate character, was available to guide selection. Representation of the national distribution of different types of estate was out of the question. Random selection therefore aimed at equal representation of different combinations of estate character traits.

The dearth of landownership statistics makes it worth-while to record the distribution pattern revealed by a selection field of 1,430 estates. The selection field consists of those estates whose owners returned information about the character of their estates: an 11 % contribution from some 12,400 estate owners representing a large majority of all owners of agricultural estates.[2] The distribution of estates within the selection field is as set out in Table A.

The selected estates were visited and surveyed. Attention was focused on the level of investment in fixed equipment and land improvement. Each farm on each estate was taken in turn. Wants were recorded item by item, as both the landowner and tenant described them. Details were obtained of external funds supporting the estates. Enquiry was made concerning the restraints that check the investment of these resources in fixed equipment and land improvement. Note was also taken of recent capital formation, the manner of its financing and of the motives inducing it. Current values of gross estate capital were not readily obtained; many landowners had scanty knowledge of the value of their lands and recourse to local professional opinion and other sources was necessary. Details of mortgages, loans and other charges were noted. As each farm was surveyed the pattern of cropping and land use was recorded. And on many farms the tenant volunteered information about his personal fortune.

[1]cf. pp. 26–28 *ante*.
[2]The response was in fact a 18 % response: the selection field was reduced to 11 % after refusals, and late and unsuitable returns had been extracted.

TABLE A
PERCENTAGE REPRESENTATION OF ESTATE TYPES AMONG THE 1,437 ESTATES IN THE SELECTION FIELD OF THE CENTRAL SURVEY

ESTATE SIZE:		100–249 acres				250–499 acres				500–999 acres				1,000–2,500 acres			
		Owner-occupied		Tenanted		Owner-occupied		Tenanted		Owner-occupied		Tenanted		Owner-occupied		Tenanted	
		S	C	S	C	S	C	S	C	S	C	S	C	S	C	S	C
INCOME TAX	Small-holdings			0·21	0·28			0·21				0·42	0·07				
	Large-holdings	2·57	21·64	1·04	5·36	2·02	13·92	1·25	3·48	1·04	5·43	0·84	2·44	0·49	0·76	0·21	0·84
SURTAX	Small-holdings			0·07	0·28			0·28	0·07		0·14	0·07	0·07			0·07	
	Large-holdings	0·76	5·29	0·49	1·60	1·46	6·54	0·14	3·13	0·97	5·84	1·25	3·83	0·42	1·04	0·70	1·04

S = scattered,   C = compact.

Note: The suffering of Estate Duty as a feature of estate character is not included here as distribution, in the selection fields of all the surveys, of estates that have suffered and those that have escaped duty is shown in the percentages of Table XII.

The extended survey

Work had begun on the central survey when an offer of additional funds made possible an extension. Extension in range was preferred to extension in depth. Arrangements for the central survey were not altered. The enquiry was extended by making a special study of the problem of capital provision as the largest estates experience it.

Agricultural estates over 10,000[1] acres are comparatively few in number and a representative selection of different types was thought to be unnecessary. Landowners of the majority of the exceptionally extensive estates were invited to contribute to the survey. Altogether seventy-three were invited, and 69 % agreed to help. The survey attempted no more than broad outlines. It was not possible in the time available to make farm surveys as was done in the central survey. In some respects the information obtained was more satisfactory. The financial policy of each estate was kept more firmly in focus. The broadly sketched pictures show rental revenue, outgoings, improvement expenditure from each estate as an entirety, and the place of farming and other estate enterprises in the investment programme. Enquiry was more discursive and yielded deeper insights into the rationale of landowning and investment in agriculture and land improvement. Otherwise the extended survey kept in step with the central survey.

The previous survey

Immediately prior to the present enquiry research studies had been made of the incidence and consequences of estate duty on agricultural estates. The studies were focused against a background of capital investment. Estate duty is a capital levy and attention was paid to the effect of the levy upon estate capital, in especial upon contributions to recent investment. Particular note was taken of the counterpoise provided by tax rebate on agricultural improvements. Competence of estate income to form capital and recuperate capital loss from estate duty was also germane to the studies. Much of the information therefore was similar to what was required of the present enquiry; indeed, in some measure, the present investigation was inspired by and issued from the estate duty research. The earlier work had concentrated on estates between 1,000 acres and 10,000 acres,[2] hence it seemed reasonable to regard this previous survey as a stop-gap between the smaller estates of the central survey and the larger estates of the extended survey.

[1] A few estates in the extended survey were less than 10,000 acres in size.
[2] A few of the estates in this previous survey were over 10,000 acres.

Selection of estates for the previous survey had proceeded along lines similar to the selection procedure adopted for the central survey. Preliminary information was asked of 1,370 estate owners in order to classify the estates according to character. Of this number 70 % contributed information. Each character class was determined by a combination of estate character traits. Estates were selected at random to make up a representative sample. The character traits were not the same as those used in the classification for estates of the central survey. Size-classes obviously were different. Other character traits were duration, and the incidence of estate duty. The size-classes and other traits combined to form sixteen character types and three estates of each character type were selected, contributing a representative sample of sixty-four estates; some proved unsuitable for survey and substitutes were selected.

The charity estate survey

Agricultural estates belonging to charities and other tax-exempt bodies, like the most extensive properties, are few in number. Moreover, they tend towards conformity of character: owner-occupation is rare and few of them are less than 1,000 acres in extent. It was not necessary to select at random representatives of character types, or even representatives of the charity-type itself. Numbers were too limited. The procedure followed the procedure of the extended survey. Owners were invited to participate in the enquiry, and the estates of those accepting were surveyed. Of ninety-two estate owners approached 60 % were willing to help. Time did not permit the survey of all; as the majority were over 1,000 acres preference was given to these as being more representative than the smaller estates of the charity estate as a type. All the estates surveyed are tenant-occupied and owned impersonally by trusts or institutions. Distribution among size-classes over 1,000 acres is fairly even. No attempt was made to classify the estates. Their homogeneous taxability, common tenure pattern, invariable lack of personal ownership and extensive acreages leave little room for character distinctions and tend to set them in a common mould.

The particular surveys also followed in principle the extended survey. Ownership and investment policies in broad outline were sought. An exact parallel with the extended survey was not possible. Special point had to be made of the investment powers of the charity estate owners, especially the extent of liberty to use consociate charity funds for the development of the estate. Time was short, and it was not possible to investigate revenue and outgoings over a series of years, as was done with the estates of the extended survey.

The main sample

As explained earlier it was not possible for the sample of estates selected for survey to be representative of any statistical universe. What was important was a balanced representation of different estate characters. The influence of character traits can only be discovered by comparisons; large estates must be compared with small, compact with scattered, and so on. Unless the sample has equal representation of the different estate character traits true comparison may not be possible, for a dominant character trait might introduce a bias. Large estates might be compared with small estates and certain results be observed, but if the large estates were predominantly owned by surtax payers and the small estates carried income tax at the standard rate, it would not be possible to say whether the observed results were due to differences in size or to differences in taxability. Only as the large estates are represented by surtax and income tax estates in the same proportions as occur among the small estates is the element of bias removed.

A sample had to be constructed to give as far as possible equal proportionate representation of character traits in each character class. To this end, selection was made from the estates of the central, previous and extended surveys. A fairly balanced sample was achieved. The sample is referred to as the Main Sample and the pattern of its construction is set out in Table B.

To achieve the degree of balance many particular estate surveys had to be discarded, especially among those of the central survey. The number of estate character traits represented in the sample also had to be curtailed: size, shape, taxability and tenure pattern had to suffice.

Selecting the sample revealed interesting associations of character traits. One or more traits would tend to associate exclusively with other traits. These affinities made it difficult to balance the sample, but they also throw light upon estate character and the distribution of estate types. Prominent among these associations was tenure pattern and size: estates over 1,000 acres are rarely owner-occupied, and it was not possible to find sufficient numbers of owner-occupied estates over 1,000 acres to contribute a balanced representation. Estate duty and size are also associated. Only among the medium-ranged estates was it possible exactly to balance the representation of estate duty sufferers and estates that had escaped. As size decreases the number of the favoured outpace the sufferers; and vice versa. Surtax and income tax present another example. Surtax estates are easier to find than those subject to income tax only; among the owner-occupied estates and estates over 2,500 acres, private companies and

TABLE B

STRUCTURE OF THE MAIN SAMPLE OF 224 ESTATES COVERING 1,510,500 ACRES

ESTATE SIZE:	100–249 acres		250–499 acres		500–999 acres		1,000–2,499 acres	2,500–9,999 acres	10,000+ acres	TOTALS
	Owner-occupied	Tenanted	Owner-occupied	Tenanted	Owner-occupied	Tenanted	Tenanted	Tenanted	Tenanted	
	Nos.	Nos.	Nos.	Nos.	Nos.	Nos.	Nos.	Nos.	Nos.	
COMPACT	19	14	17	14	20	15	15	18	13	145
SCATTERED	11	8	13	8	11	7	7	5	9	79
ESTATE DUTY	12	9	12	10	15	11	12	12	13	106
NON-DUTY	18	13	18	12	16	11	10	11	9	118
SURTAX	16	11	17	13	17	13	13	12	11	123
STANDARD TAX	14	11	13	9	14	9	9	11	11	101

trusts increase the number of income tax estates and a balanced representation is more easily achieved. With the smaller tenanted estates, especially those over 250 acres, representatives of income tax estates fall noticeably short of the numbers of surtax estates. And compact estates are more easily come by than scattered properties.

Other samples

The Main Sample is used in the illustrations and Tables of the text whenever possible. On occasion it is not possible or appropriate to use its evidence and special samples are employed. A special sample may be a particular sector of the Main Sample: evidence of the competence of estates to form estate capital from estate income, for example, can only be contributed by tenanted estates, and the 133 tenanted estates of the Main Sample comprise the special sample for this purpose. In some Tables a full employment of the Main Sample is not possible because certain estates have no information to offer; a clear example of this limited contribution is provided by the evidence for consociate and adventitious capital. When dealing with restraints and inducements the testimonies of a few larger estates not included in the Main Sample were added, because some of the larger estates in the Main Sample had given no information. If a special sample is unbalanced weighting devices are used to rectify the effect of disequilibrium. Lack of balance is likely when arranging evidence of the influence of estate character traits not represented in the Main Sample. When old title and new title estates are compared, for example, the evidence may have to be adjusted because old title estates tend to be larger than new title estates and the contribution from the old title estates would be tainted by the dominant influence of the larger estates. For the study of estate duty presented in Chapter IX, estates whether within or without the Main Sample with experience of the estate duty levy were included in a special sample.

N.B.—Members of the staff of the Department of Estate Management and others responsible for the field work of the surveys and the collation of material were:

Jack Burgon, M.A., A.R.I.C.S., Q.A.L.A.S.; D. R. Denman, M.A., PH.D., F.R.I.C.S.; Neil Elliott, M.A., A.R.I.C.S., Q.A.L.A.S.; T. R. F. Fenwick, B.A., Q.A.L.A.S.; Philip Harris, M.A., A.R.I.C.S.; John Lee, B.SC.; Mark Lister, B.A.; Brian Llewellyn, B.A.; H. A. R. Long, B.A., A.R.I.C.S., Q.A.L.A.S.; C. W. N. Miles, M.A., F.R.I.C.S., F.L.A.S., M. H. Maydew, Q.A.L.A.S.; Alan Ostler, B.A., B.C.L.; L. C. C. Pengelly-Phillips, N.D.A.; R. A. Rathbone, M.A., A.R.I.B.A.; Miss Hevina Roberts, B.SC.; Robin Stallard, B.A.; Miss Vivienne Stewart, M.A.

INDEX

AGRICULTURE ACT 1947
fixed equipment definition 15
power of direction 119
power of ejection 92

ALLOTMENTS ACT 1922
definition of allotment 23

ALTERNATIVE INVESTMENTS
restraint on improvement 89,
100, 135, 181, 182, 186

AMENITY
induces landownership 108

ANNUITIES
restraint on improvement 97

APPRECIATION OF CAPITAL
apart from income 127, 128
measurement 193

ARABLE ESTATES
competence 144, 190
external funds 145
improvement expenditure 144,
145
level of investment 144
rental revenue 144, 190

ARBITRATION
influence on estate income 100,
101, 104

AREA RATIOS (DETERMINE)
estate structure 23, 24, 143
holdings pattern 25
tenure pattern 26

BANK RATE
rise in 86

BARNS AND STORES
deficiency 80, 168

BOUNDARY
adjustment 91, 92

CAPITAL
agent of production 13
businessman's viewpoint, 14,
43
circulating 14

fixed 14, 15
in estate in land 14, 15
national 13
ownership of 13, 14
private 13
production capital 43
provision 15
related to land 14

CAPITAL FORMATION
estate in land, the ground of
182
in agriculture 15, 185, 187, 188

CAPITAL INVESTMENT
demand for, on estates 188
economic theory 43
viewpoint of estate owner 49

CAPITAL WORKS FUND
long period support 61

CENTRAL SURVEY
contribution of estate income
to improvements 47
description 194, 195
evidence of investment level 51
figures of outgoings not available for 133
physical measurement of investment level 76, 77

CHARITY ESTATES
consociate capital 178, 179, 180
formation of estate capital 173-
177
freedom from mortgage 179
improvement expenditure 176
indifferent to farming and
silviculture 180
influenced by historic sense
174, 181
outgoings 176, 177
rental revenue 176
restraints and inducements
174, 180, 181
survey of 198
tax-privileged 31, 32, 173

14

TENANT FOR LIFE (*cont.*)—
holding contractual tenancy 97
persons with powers of 30
powers 20, 30
trustee 30

TENANTED ESTATES
affined tenancies 172
competence 47, 48, 49, 50, 54, 189
finance for improvements, on 74
level of investment 51
ownership personality, and 154
redemption loans on improvement 87
size of estate, and 188
tenure pattern, and 26

TENANTS
compensation for improvements 57, 58, 178
contribution to estate capital 47, 57, 58, 59, 143, 144, 151, 152, 154, 172, 178, 184
fixtures 62
interest on improvements 55, 56, 57
resources 170, 171, 192
restrained by landlord 178
unwilling 91, 135

TENURE
estate character trait 28, 29
fee simple absolute 28
in Scotland 29
incidence of estate duty, and 125
rate of capital formation, and 135
security 88, 91, 92, 100, 135, 186, 188
term of years absolute 28

TENURE PATTERN
competence, and 147, 189
duration of estate, and 152
estate character trait 19, 25, 26
external funds, and 147, 148
level of investment, and 83, 149, 150

TIMBER
as consociate capital 70, 145, 149, 156, 159, 162, 171
as estate capital 62
estate enterprise 40, 89, 93
finance for improvements 72, 74, 134, 153
growth and capital appreciation 128
hauling equipment not estate capital 62
inducement to landownership 110
place in entire estate 36, 38

TITHE REDEMPTION ANNUITY
an outgoing 42

TITLE
restraint on improvement 97, 141, 153, 156, 180, 188

TRUSTEES
adventitious and consociate capital of 63, 96, 155, 156, 190
classes of 30
competence of estates owned by 154, 177, 190
estate owners 17, 20, 21, 27, 93, 94, 112, 154, 177, 190
give form to ownership personality 29, 154
honour spirit of trust 112
improvements of beneficiary, and 96
joint tenants 30, 154

For Product Safety Concerns and Information please contact our EU
representative GPSR@taylorandfrancis.com
Taylor & Francis Verlag GmbH, Kaufingerstraße 24, 80331 München, Germany